FAMILY HISTORY FOR THE CLUELESS

FAMILY HISTORY FOR THE CLUELESS

George D. Durrant and LaRene Gaunt

Jimmy Parker, Retired Manager of the Family History Library
Julie M. Durrant, Enthusiastic Beginner

BOOKCRAFT

SALT LAKE CITY, UTAH

FamilySearch™ is a trademark of Intellectual Reserve, Inc.

Visit us at www.deseretbook.com

Library of Congress Catalog Card Number: 99-76068

ISBN 1-57008-658-3

Printed in the United States of America   72076
Publishers Printing, Salt Lake City, Utah

10   9   8   7   6   5

To our families
both past and present

Contents at a Glance

Contents

Part 4: Ten Tens

Part 5: Appendixes

Acknowledgments

Thanks to everyone at Bookcraft, especially: Cory Maxwell, for his gentle leadership; Jana Erickson, for her decisive action and clear thinking; Janna DeVore, for her involvement with the first draft of this book; Lisa Mangum, for her expert editing of the final manuscript; and Aaron Taylor, for his lively cartoons and drawings.

Thanks to the David C. Gaunt family for the use of family photos, letters, and maps.

Thanks to David, LaRene, and Dennis Gaunt for all other photography in this book.

About the Authors

The authors of this book are a varied lot and span the spectrum of family history experience. Each adds his or her own voice to the project.

George Durrant's voice is one of inspiration and motivation. He is a longtime observer of a living family history, and he senses the importance of the past in relationship to the present and future.

The homespun author of numerous books relating to family life, George, along with Noel Barton, wrote the book *Fun and Names or How to Dig Your Family Roots without Really Prying.* He served for several years as the Director of Priesthood Genealogy for The Church of Jesus Christ of Latter-day Saints. He taught family history classes at Brigham Young University.

His stories provide a warm and accessible example to beginners and experts alike. Readers take confidence from him as he gently leads them into new areas of family history experiences.

He and his wife, Marilyn, are the parents of eight children and grandparents of thirty.

LaRene Gaunt's voice is one of organization, methodology, and practical details. She spent many years as a homemaker, but when her children started school, she moved into the world of professional publishing as a writer.

She is an accredited genealogist for the American Midwest. Author of six books, LaRene also created a family history board game for Latter-day Saints called "Forever Families." Currently an associate editor at the *Ensign* magazine, she has authored and edited many articles over the past ten years.

Her talents in family history, organization, and writing gave her the leadership role in writing and putting this book together. Weaving George's stories with her writing of the methodology, she produced chapters rich in both motivation and information.

She and her husband, David, are the parents of six children, three of whom are living.

Jimmy Parker's voice is one of expertise and credibility. Seasoned at both life and family history, he has extensive experience in raising a family and researching one.

Recently retired after thirty-five years at the Family History Library in Salt Lake City, Jimmy oversaw accreditation, training, and special projects. His ability to understand and remember important facts and history, coupled with his vast experience in genealogy, has made him an outstanding researcher and teacher.

His review of the finished manuscript with an eye for accuracy in genealogical content and methodology provides credibility for the entire book.

He and his wife, Sherry, are the parents of fourteen children, eleven of whom are living.

Julie Mink Durrant's voice is that of the enthusiastic beginner. She is a young stay-at-home mother, who only recently began her family history research. She serves as an example to all beginners.

She has a great passion for life, including family history. Remembering with clarity the intimidation she felt on her first visit to the Family History Library, this book has been kept simple so it would not discourage beginners.

She and her husband, Devin, have six children.

Foreword

This book is different from other how-to family history books—this is a how-to book with heart.

In addition to all the methodology, facts, and lists of reference materials, this book carries with it the warm and humorous experiences of George Durrant. The joyous spirit of family history flows through George's stories as he willingly shares the tender moments of his genealogical journey.

George and the other authors of this book—LaRene Gaunt, Jimmy Parker, and Julie Durrant—have not shied away from their Latter-day Saint belief that they have a responsibility to identify their ancestors and then perform sacred ordinances in their behalf in the temple. This conviction is the reason why so many Latter-day Saints search out their ancestors and why The Church of Jesus Christ of Latter-day Saints invests so many of its resources into family history work.

Salt Lake Temple

Out of this religious doctrine has grown one of the finest family history libraries in the world and one of the largest collections of genealogical data available. More than 3,400 branch libraries, called Family History Centers, are available throughout the world to help Latter-day Saints as well as people of all faiths identify their ancestors.

Commitment to these religious beliefs has also led the Church to use the Internet to make resources available to Latter-day Saints and all others who seek their ancestors.

FamilySearch™ at **www.familysearch.org** is only one of many resources that is available on the Internet.

As a result of this spiritual dimension to family history work, Latter-day Saints rely on more than academic research to seek their ancestors. Prayer is as important a component of family history as reading a microfilm. Many testify that when worldly resources have dried up on certain surname lines, spiritual promptings, inspiration, or dreams have led them to the needed records. Latter-day Saints are not alone in this experience.

The spiritual dimension of family history is evident in the pages of this book. Hopefully, you as a reader will feel it and recognize that coming to know and love your ancestors is more than a hobby; it has eternal rewards.

Yes, within this book you will find solid, academic methodology, facts, and bibliographies, but in addition, you will find the warm, spiritual joy that is so much a part of family history work. Truly, this is a how-to family history book with heart. Enjoy!

George Durrant
LaRene Gaunt
Jimmy Parker
Julie Durrant

Introduction

How This Book Is Organized

You should read this section. Once you understand how this book is organized, you can use it as your personal family history tool. You can read it from cover to cover or, since each chapter is self-contained, you can read only what you need at any given time.

Parts

This book has five parts. The first three parts work together to help you do family history. The last two parts are for reference.

Part one helps you get organized. Here are suggestions for making time and space in your life for this compelling pastime. Since family history is filled with detailed facts, you'll learn how to use forms, files, and your computer to help you keep track of everything.

Part two teaches you how to gather information about your ancestors. After collecting what you can from your family and from compiled sources, you'll learn the research cycle and be off on a great adventure. Learning to use the Family History Center and FamilySearch™ will be your first stop. Then you'll move on to government sources like census records, vital records, and military records. Suggestions follow on how to find heirlooms and information on a visit to your ancestral hometown with stops at the cemetery, church, local library, and old home. If all this seems like too much, the last chapter in this part tells you how to hire a professional genealogist.

Part three focuses on ways you can give the family history you have gathered back to your family. You will learn how to compile a family history, write your own personal history, and plan a family reunion. The last chapter in this part teaches you how to use TempleReady and prepare the names of your ancestors for their temple ordinances.

Part four contains ten lists of ten. Each list identifies an important group of reference materials, such as CDs you can use at home, Web sites, reference books, possible expenses, and the location of genealogy conferences.

Part five contains valuable appendixes. You will find a relationship chart and the addresses of libraries, historical societies, and Latter-day Saint temples. You'll also find tips on how to preserve old photographs, how to document your sources, and how to use the Internet to help you with your family history.

Next is an extensive glossary, which includes abbreviations and acronyms.

And last but not least, you will find examples of forms you can photocopy and use in your research: Pedigree Chart, Family Group Record, Research Calendar, Correspondence Log, Census Chronology Chart, and census forms for 1790 through 1920.

Chapters

Each chapter starts with a summary of the important points in the chapter. Then comes a homespun story from the life of George Durrant, told as only he can tell it. Filled with humor and warmth, these stories of George's experiences with genealogy are designed to help family history beginners feel comfortable and confident.

Following George's story is the genealogy methodology—the how-to. Here you'll find background, important facts, and how-to steps on a particular topic.

At the end of each chapter, you will find two headings. "Want to Know More?" is a bibliography of books, pamphlets, addresses, or Web sites where you can find more information on the topic of the chapter. "Try This" suggests simple "homework" assignments to help you apply your newfound knowledge and practice your family history skills.

Icons

Throughout each chapter, you will find icons that will help identify important parts of the text.

Vocabulary ⑦: Definitions of genealogy terms. Check glossary.

Caution ◉: Watch out for these pitfalls.

How-to ◉: Step-by-step procedures.

Cross-Reference/See Also ◉: References to related topics.

Point to Remember ★: Especially important points to remember.

Hint ◉: Information to help your research.

Who's George?

★ **IN THIS CHAPTER**
✔ You'll get to know George Durrant and his family
✔ You'll see why George loves family history so much
✔ You'll get started with your own family history

George's Story:
Gearge Dernt from American Fark, Utah

I was born in a town in Utah called American Fork. But in my childhood days we pronounced the "O" as "ah" and the "R" as it is pronounced in Noah's ark. So according to my folks, my birthplace was American Fark.

My father was Willard Albert Durrant, and my mother was Marinda Elizabeth Mayne. Of course, she added the name Durrant when she married Dad. In those days the locals pronounced the name Durrant as Dernt.

I was given the name George Donald Durrant or Dernt. And my first name, under the rules pointed out earlier, was pronounced Gearge. I was born on 20 October 1931, in American Fork, Utah County, Utah.

One day, when I was young, one of our family members went away to college and came home and said, "Hey! We are not Dernts, we are Du-rants." Well, we liked the sound of that. Then a teacher came into our school and taught us that our town was not American Fark but American Fork. Later still, I learned that my name was not Gearge, but George.

So who am I? I am George Donald Durrant born to Willard Albert Durrant and Marinda Elizabeth Mayne on 20 October 1931, in American Fork, Utah County, Utah. Nobody else in the whole world has that same combination of identification markers. These markers make me absolutely unique—almost as unique as my DNA.

You are unique, too. There is no one else now or ever, here or anywhere, who is the same as you are. Uniqueness is what makes family history so fascinating. Every one of your ancestors was different, so every one of their life stories is different, too. You'll find something unique to learn and love about each of your ancestors.

Genealogist of the Heart

One of the things you are about to learn about me is that I am a genealogist of the heart rather than the head. Research isn't really my thing. I just don't have the aptitude for it. I copy the dates down wrong because my mind wanders when I try to do exacting things. Even so, I can still do research because I know where to get help. So even though I'd rather be painting with watercolors than looking through records, I do it because I love my ancestors and their uniqueness. I love to find out about their joys, their sorrows, their work, and their dreams. I'll bet you'll feel the same way about your ancestors once you get to know them.

Who's Your Ancestor?

I once drove clear across the great state of Indiana. As I began the journey I was determined that once and for all I would find out just what a *Hoosier* really was. I asked every person whom I met at the rest stops, the gas stations, and the restaurants the same question: "What in the heck is a *Hoosier*?"

The answers varied from "I don't know. I never thought that much about it" to "I think it is some kind of a bird." But the most common answer was, "When our ancestors came to this area, the first question they would ask a stranger was, 'Whose yer father?'"

Whether that's the source of the word *Hoosier* or not, I don't know and neither do the people of Indiana. But to me it is the first and foremost family history question: "Hoosier father?" "Hoosier mother?" "Hoosier grandfather and grandmother?" and so on, one "Hoosier?" at a time.

Why I Want My Own Ancestors

Half serious and half lighthearted, I offer the following: My great-grandfather was John Durrant. I never knew him because he died a few years before I was born. So why should I care about him? Well, if he had been somebody else instead of who he was, then his appearance would have been 100 percent different than it was. That would have meant that his son, my grandfather, would have looked one-half different than he looked. And my father would have looked one-fourth different than he looked. And I would have looked one-eighth different than I do. That, my friend, would have been a real tragedy because, you see, if I looked one-eighth different than I do, then when my wife, Marilyn, saw me she would not have been so impressed with my "handsomeness," and she would have continued her search for the perfect-looking fellow. Or if she still had married me, each of my children would have looked and been one-sixteenth different than they are. I'm glad Marilyn married me because she sure has made me happy. And I like my children just the way they are. I don't want them to be one-sixteenth different.

So my point is, I am uniquely me because my ancestors were uniquely themselves. Part of what they were is part of what I am. I'm grateful for that.

You, Uniquely Identified

So now it's time to get to know you.

1. What is your full name—middle name(s) and all? Write those names here: _____ _____ _____.
(Now, if you lose this book, people will know whom to return it to.)

2. Next, write the full names of your father and mother: _____ _____ _____ and

_____ _____ _____.

3. Now, write your birth date, month, and year: ____ ____ ____.

4. And finally, write your birthplace, including town, county, and state: _____, _____, _____.

Now you are uniquely identified! Nobody else in the world could ever be you. Since you are, indeed, number one, put your name in the number one position on this pedigree chart. Then add your parents' names, first, middle, and last. Make sure you use your mother's maiden name instead of her married name.

2. My Father_____

1. Me_____

3. My Mother_____

See how easy that was? But now you ask, "Where do I go from here? I'm clueless." Well, that's why we wrote this book—*Family History for the Clueless*. It's just for you, and I'll be with you every step of the way sharing my family history experiences with you at the beginning of every chapter. So get going by reading the Introduction (if you haven't already read it) and see how this book is organized. Then come with me and "GET A CLUE!"

Want to Know More?

- Ask your mom or dad to tell you about their childhood.

- Ask your oldest living ancestor to tell you about the family.

- If someone in your family has a printed family history, read it.

Try This

- ❏ 1. Write down the birth dates and birthplaces and marriage date and marriage place of your parents. Include the death dates and death places, if your parents have died.

- ❏ 2. Read the section titled "Introduction: How This Book Is Organized."

You are unique and so is each one of your ancestors.

PART ONE:
Getting Organized

When Alex Haley wrote his epic book *Roots,* he found out who he was by finding out about his ancestors. He felt connected to his past as he discovered each generation of ancestors. He came to know more about himself as he learned the ways his father gained strength from his parents, and how they gained strength from their parents, and they from theirs, and on back. Millions of us who read the book, or watched the television series nearly two decades ago, felt the power of family as we were immersed in this story of love that stretched beyond the known generations.

Most of us long to feel connected to the past, to know how we fit into this "family of man." You may feel that it's too hard for you to discover your own roots, but this book will help you.

In This Part

- You'll discover that it isn't really that hard to get started. You'll get suggestions on how to find time to do family history, how to make space to work, and how to keep your papers in order.

- You'll learn how to be consistent in writing down names, dates, and places on a pedigree chart and on a family group record.

- You'll learn how to use your computer to help you keep track of everything.

- And best of all, George's stories will help you feel comfortable as you try new things.

Making Time, Space, and Order

George's Story: Becoming a Decathlon Champion

When I was a young man, Robert Mathias was my sports hero. He won the decathlon in the 1948 Olympics and again in 1952. He ran the 100 meters in 10.9 seconds. The winner covered the distance in 10.4 seconds, a half-second faster than Mathias. In the 400 meters, Mathias's time of 50.2 was far short of the 45.0 time of the specialized runner. Mathias high jumped 6 feet 2.75 inches—some 6 inches less than the man who won the high jump competition for those who had entered just that one event. His javelin sailed 194 feet 3 inches, far short of the 242 feet throw of the man who spent his entire effort in that event.

Bob Mathias wasn't the best at any one event, but he did each event well enough that when all his scores were added together, his *overall* score made him the decathlon champion.

Life is much like a decathlon. We don't have to be the best at one thing at the expense of something else. If we approach life with a sense of balance, we can be champions. We don't have to do more than we have time, energy, or ability to do.

When it comes to family history, we need to have the same sense of balance. Even though it is a lifelong endeavor, we don't have to do it all the time. We have seasons in our lives to live it and seasons to look back and remember it. So live your life well. Your life today will become tomorrow's family history. So enjoy making family history, but as you are living it, take some time to record it on paper, film, or tape. Remember that journal writing, taking photos, and telling family stories as bedtime stories to your children are part of recording family history, too.

If Not You, Then Who?

Many of us feel like the woman who said, "Find my ancestors? I don't even have time to find myself!" But sometimes minor adjustments in our schedule can give us a little time to do something we really want to do. So take a look at the way you spend your time. Write down everything you do in a week and how much time it takes. Is there anything that is out of balance? Where can you reduce the time spent on certain activities and what can you skip or cut all together? Can you double up on some of your activities? For example, can you:

- Pass up watching television one night?

- Do family history on Sunday instead of reading the newspaper?

- Set up a Friday night date with your spouse, help each other do family history, then have a bowl of ice cream together?

- Take the family history class during Sunday School?

These are just a few simple examples. Each of our lives is different and we do not have control over all of our time. However, we do have control over some of it. Consistency—even if it is at a slow pace or over a long period of time—is the best way to ensure the addition of this wonderful activity to your life.

DOES WATCHING "ALL IN THE FAMILY" COUNT?

What Do I Need to Get Organized?

❑ 1. A desk or table and a chair.

❑ 2. A box or a filing cabinet and manila folders.

❑ 3. Pencils or pens.

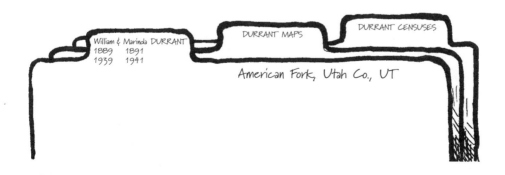

❑ 4. Paper, including pedigree charts and family group records.

❑ 5. A 3-ring binder for your pedigree charts and family group records.

❑ 6. If possible, a computer and family history software.

How Do I Get Started?

1. Set aside a space to work where you have room to spread out your papers and books. Your space may be as simple as a box you pull out so you can work on your kitchen table, or a card table in your bedroom, living room, or family room. You may be lucky enough to have your own home office. If you have a computer, you should have easy access to it.

2. Set aside a regular time to do family history. You may be able to find a whole day or half a day, but you may have to settle for a few hours on Sunday or on some other day of the week.

3. Get a box or filing cabinet and some manila folders for your family records. Start by labeling a folder with the name of your mother and father. For example, William and Marinda Mayne Durrant. Put their birth and death dates under their names. Include important locations associated with this family on the folder. Then make a folder for each set of grandparents and for all four sets of great-grandparents.

Later you will continue to add folders for additional families to this first set of folders. As you gather maps, census records, family stories, and other "clues" for existing families, you can add folders to hold these documents. Remember to keep your filing system clearly labeled so others can find what they are looking for.

4. If you have a computer, set up your family history software program and practice using it. Input (type in) all the names, dates, and places of your parents, grandparents, and great-grandparents. Remember, you can include stories and other interesting information in the notes section of your family history software program.

5. Be sure to learn how to document the sources for your information and include that also.

Want to Know More?

- Talk with family members. They may have suggestions on ways activities in your life could be delegated to others or cut altogether.

- Visit with someone you know who is very organized. See if they have suggestions that could work for you.

- Get to know your ward family history consultant and the volunteers at your local Family History Center.

- Read *A Member's Guide to Temple and Family History Work.* You can get a free copy of this booklet from your local Family History Center.

Try This

❏ 1. Set aside a place and a regular time to do family history.

❏ 2. Get seven folders and label them for your parents, grandparents, and great-grandparents.

❏ 3. Begin gathering family certificates, letters, and so on, from around your own home and file them in the appropriate folders.

CHAPTER 2

Keeping Track of Names, Dates, and Places

> ★ **IN THIS CHAPTER**
> ✔ How to fill out a pedigree chart
> ✔ How to fill out a family group record
> ✔ How to document your information
> ✔ How to organize your pedigree charts and family group records

George's Story: Sarah and Mark

Nearly twenty years ago, The Church of Jesus Christ of Latter-day Saints asked its members to send them copies of their pedigree charts showing their first four generations of ancestors. Members were also asked to include fifteen family group records—one for every couple on the pedigree chart. (Incidentally, these records became the basis for Ancestral File.) My wife, Marilyn, and I sent in our four-generation records, including our own family group record with the names of our six children.

Recently, while I was at my local Family History Center, I decided to look at the microfilm copy of the original records we had sent in many years ago. I excitedly examined them. There was our family: Marilyn and I as parents and Matthew, Kathryn, Devin, Marinda, Dwight, and Warren as our children. I felt a pang of sorrow in my heart because our last two children, Sarah and Mark, were not listed. I wanted to take my ballpoint pen and write their names on the microfilm, but, of course, I couldn't.

As I walked out of the Family History Center, I wondered what our life would have been like without Sarah and Mark. The thought wrenched my heart. Not to have tall, dark-eyed, dark-haired, beautiful-inside-and-out Sarah! Just thinking of her gladdened my heart. And the thought of not having Mark was unbearable. He had been our last child and at home long after all of our other children had gone their own ways.

Marilyn and I had treasured him. Life without those two, or without any of our eight children, would have been empty and incomplete for us.

I tell you this story to remind you of two things: (1) pedigree charts and family group records help us keep track of our ancestors as individuals and as families and (2) these forms need to be as accurate as we can make them. So let's see how pedigree charts and family group records can help us.

The Two Main Forms

(?)   A **pedigree chart** keeps track of your direct ancestors, also known as your bloodline or ancestral line. A pedigree chart lists only one name from each generation and links that name to his or her parents. Then the name of the father is linked to his parents and the name of the mother is linked to her parents. This pattern repeats for every generation.

> *Your goal is to complete a family group record for each couple listed on your pedigree chart.*

(?)   A **family group record** keeps track of the family unit of each of the couples listed on a pedigree chart. This form lists the names of all family members with the dates and places of their births, marriages, and deaths. The dates the temple ordinances were performed for them can also be listed.

Family Group Sheets?

In the "olden days" some folks referred to family group records as family group sheets. George humorously says he remembers hearing of a beginning family historian who went into the bedding department of a large Salt Lake City department store and asked where he could get family group sheets. The salesman said that they had single bedsheets, regular, queen, and king bedsheets but not family group sheets.

WE'VE GOT KING, QUEEN, AND TWIN. ...BUT NO "FAMILY GROUP SHEETS."

LINENS

Your goal is to complete a family group record for each couple listed on your pedigree chart.

As important as these two forms are, they are not your completed family history. They are only the bones upon which you add stories, photographs, and historical background to create the full story of your ancestors.

Keep It Consistent

Follow the same format when recording names, dates, and places.

Names: List first name,	middle name or initial,	and surname.
John Mary	D. Elizabeth	DOE JONES
• *Don't include titles, such as Mr., Mrs., or Dr., in the same space as the first name.*		• *Put the surname in all capital letters so readers can distinguish it from the rest of the name.* • *Always use the woman's maiden name.*
Dates: List day,	month,	and year.
22	April or Apr.	1943
• *List the day first to separate these numbers from the year.*	• *Write out the month in full or use a three-letter abbreviation.*	• *Include all four digits of the year.*
Places: List town or township,	county,	and state.
Dunkirk, Knox Township,	Jay County or Jay Co.,	IN or Indiana
	• *Use a map to find the name of the county.*	• *Use the two-letter post office abbreviation or write out the full name of the state.*

Be Accurate

1. Photocopy the information, if possible.
2. Print the information slowly.

3. Write down the information in full, exactly as it appears on the original.
4. Proofread (reread) what you have written. Double check it against the original records.
5. Make a note of discrepancies, but leave both versions in place until you have resolved the differences.

Documentation

 Document the source of every name, date, place, and relationship.

Appendix
C

1. List the information in the following order: author, title of printed material, place of publication: publisher (year), page numbers. Include the call number and the place where research is being done.

2. List the type of source: book, microfilm, microfiche, letter, family Bible, family member, and so on. If your source is in the possession of another person, include his or her name, address, and telephone number.

Ch. 5

3. When you write a letter or send an e-mail, keep a record of your correspondence on a correspondence log.

Ch. 4

4. When you do research, keep a record of your work on a research log.

Filling Out a Pedigree Chart

Your name goes on line #1. Your father's name goes on line #2 (top) and your mother's maiden name goes on line #3 (bottom). (See Figure 1.) The father's names always have even numbers, and the mother's names always have odd numbers. Of course, you include the dates and places of birth, marriage, and death for each name. Many pedigree charts also allow space to include a record of temple ordinances performed for each individual, including sealing to parents and sealing to spouse.

Each pedigree chart has a space in the upper right-hand corner for a number. Pedigree charts are kept in numerical order. Each time you extend an ancestral line from chart #1 to a new chart, simply put the number of the new pedigree chart on the small line provided on the far right edge of chart #1. The last name on chart #1 becomes the first name on the new pedigree chart. Wait until a surname actually needs to be extended beyond chart #1 before you assign it a number. (See Figure 2.)

Figure 1

Pedigree Chart

CHART NO. ___1___

(No. 1 on this chart is the same as no._____ on chart no._____.)

16 Hannaniah GAUNT II
B: 2 Jan 1707 *beps* cont.__2__
D: 6 Dec 1792

17 Ann RIDGWAY
B: 10 Oct 1710 *beps* cont.__3__
D: 6 Feb 1794

8 Joseph GAUNT
B: 31 Jul 1741 *beps*
P: Burlington Co, New Jersey
M: 5 Feb 1762
P: Evesham, Burlington Co, New Jersey
D: 30 Dec 1806
P:

18 John BORTON III
B: 4 May 1696 *beps* cont.__4__
D: 13 Apr 1759

19 Elizabeth LORD
B: 22 May 1711 *beps* cont.__5__
D:

4 Jacob GAUNT
B: 11 Jan 1765 *bep*
P: Burlington Co, New Jersey
M:
P:
D: 4 Dec 1824
P: Butler Twp., Columbiana Co, Ohio

9 Elizabeth BORTON
B: 1 Jan 1740 *beps*
P: Evesham, Burlington Co, New Jersey
D:
P:

20 John HOLME
B: 1708 *beps* cont.__6__
D:

21
B: cont._____
D:

2 Joseph GAUNT
B: 2 Aug 1799 *beps*
P: New Jersey
M: 30 Dec 1819
P: Columbiana Co, Ohio
D: 8 Nov 1875
P: Knox Twp, Jay Co, Indiana

10 John HOLME
B: 1728 *beps*
P: Salem Co, New Jersey
M: 1780
P: Salem, Salem Co, New Jersey
D: 11 Oct 1798
P: Creek Twp, Salem Co, New Jersey

22
B: cont._____
D:

5 Hannah HOLME
B: *bep*
P: New Jersey
D: 29 Aug 1875
P:

11
B: *bes*
P:
D:
P:

23
B: cont._____
D:

1 Jacob GAUNT
B: 1827 *beps*
P: Columbiana Co, OH
M: 23 Jun 1853
P: Wells County, Indiana
D: 6 Oct 1908
P: Dunkirk, Jay Co, Indiana

24 Matthias SWEM or Sr.
B: Aug 1707 cont.__7__
D: 16 Feb 1793

25 Sarah VAN ROOME
B: *bep* cont.__8__
D:

12 Matthias SWEM or Jr.
B: 1739
P: Kingston, Middlesex Co, New Jersey
M:
P: Possibly Burlington Co, New Jersey
D: 29 Nov 1818
P: Burlington Co, New Jersey

26
B: cont._____
D:

6 Isaiah SWEM or SWAIM
B: 1761
P: Burlington Co, New Jersey
M:
P:
D: 7 Dec 1816
P: Springfield, Columbiana Co, Ohio

13 Rachel HANKINS
B: *be*
P: Kingston, Middlesex Co, New Jersey
D: 17 Apr 1811
P: Burlington Co, New Jersey

27
B: cont._____
D:

3 Phebe Emily SWEM
B: 15 Apr 1803 *beps*
P: Bordentown, Burlington Co, New Jersey
D: 13 Mar 1870
P: Knox Twp, Jay Co, Indiana

28
B: cont._____
D:

14
B:
P:
M:
P:
D:
P:

29
B: cont._____
D:

7 Akady DE EMRY
B:
P: France, French Huguenot
D:
P: Alive 1816

30
B: cont._____
D:

15
B:
P:
D:
P:

31
B: cont._____
D:

Prepared by: John Doe

Date: 20 Aug 1999

Figure 2

Hannaniah Gaunt II

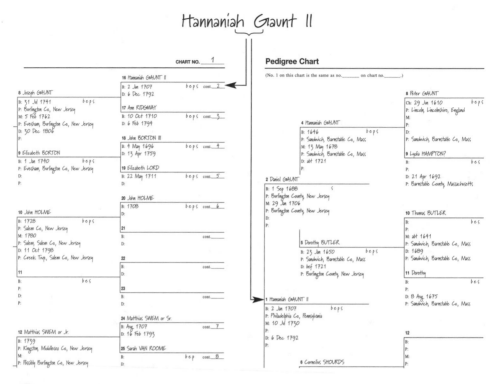

A blank pedigree chart is located in the back of this book in the
Forms section called Forms.

Filling Out a Family Group Record

A family group record contains the biographical information of one
couple and their children. If either the husband or wife has been married
more than once, a new family group record must be created for each
marriage.

Fill in as much information as possible for each person listed on the
family group record using suggested format on page 15 for names,
dates, and places. (See Figure 3.) Be sure to be consistent, accurate, and
to document the source of each name, date, place, and relationship.

A blank family group record is located in the back of this book in the
Forms section called Forms.

Figure 3

Family Group Record

HUSBAND: Joseph GAUNT		OCCUPATION:	SOURCES:
BD	2 Aug 1799	BP	New Jersey	
MD	30 Dec 1819	MP	Columbiana County, Ohio	
DD	8 Nov 1875	DP	Knox Twp., Jay Co., Indiana	Jay Co., IN Death Rcds.
BRD		BRP	Winters Cemetery, Hwy 1 & 26, Knox Twp., Jay Co., Indiana	

FATHER: Jacob GAUNT (b 11 Jan 1765) — MOTHER: Hannah HOLME

OTHER MARRIAGES:

RELIGION:		MILITARY:		SS	12 May 1972	SLAKE
B	1 Sep 1972 SGEOR	E	4 Nov 1972 SGEOR	SP	7 Dec 1972	OGDEN

WIFE: Phebe Emily SWEM			
BD	15 Apr 1803	BP	Bordentown, Burlington Co., New Jersey	Will of Isaiah Swem
DD	13 Mar 1870	DP	Knox Twp., Jay Co., Indiana	
BRD	Mar 1870	BRP	Winters Cemetery, Hwy 1 & 26, Knox Twp., Jay Co., Indiana	

FATHER: Isaiah SWEM (b 1761) — MOTHER (MAIDEN NAME): Alcady DE EMRY

OTHER MARRIAGES:

B	30 Mar 1972 ARIZO	E	26 Apr 1972 ARIZO	SP	8 Nov 1972 ARIZO

SEX	CHILDREN—NAME		DAY—MONTH—YEAR		CITY—COUNTY—STATE	SOURCES
1 M	Redden N. GAUNT	BD	16 Apr 1821	BP	Columbiana County, Ohio	
		MD	24 Aug 1843	MP	Jay County, Indiana	Jay Co, IN Mar. Rcds.
	SPOUSE: Pauline E. SMOAT	DD	22 Dec 1864	DP	Murfreesboro, Rutherford Co., Tennessee	Military Rcds.
	SS	27 Mar 1973 ALBER	BRD		BRP	27 Mar 1973	
	B	18 Apr 1978 PROVO	E	22 Jun 1978 PROVO	SP	17 Aug 1978 PROVO	
2 F	Hannah Holme GAUNT	BD	10 Nov 1825	BP	Columbiana County, Ohio	
		MD	30 Sep 1843	MP	Jay County, Indiana	Jay Co, IN Mar. Rcds.
	SPOUSE: George CLAYCOMB	DD	29 Aug 1875	DP	Jay County, Indiana	
	SS	11 Aug 1972 SLAKE	BRD		BRP	11 Aug 1972	
	B	18 Apr 1978 PROVO	E	22 Jun 1978 PROVO	SP	17 Aug 1978 PROVO	
3 M	Jacob GAUNT	BD	1827	BP	Columbiana Co., OH	
		MD	23 Jun 1853	MP	Wells County, Indiana	
	SPOUSE: Melvina F. BENNETT	DD	6 Oct 1908	DP	Dunkirk, Jay Co., Indiana	
	SS	10 Aug 1972 ARIZO	BRD		BRP	10 Aug 1972	
	B	3 Jul 1971 ARIZO	E	16 Oct 1971 ARIZO	SP	11 Aug 1972 ARIZO	
4 F	Elizabeth Ann GAUNT	BD	13 Apr 1832	BP	Delaware County, Ohio	
		MD	19 Jun 1859	MP	Jay County, Indiana	Jay Co, IN Mar. Rcds.
	SPOUSE: Samuel ROWLAND	DD	11 May 1880	DP	Jay County, Indiana	
	SS	11 Aug 1972 SLAKE	BRD		BRP	11 Aug 1972	
	B	18 Apr 1978 PROVO	E	22 Jun 1978 PROVO	SP	17 Aug 1978 PROVO	
5		BD		BP		
		MD		MP		
	SPOUSE:	DD		DP		
	SS		BRD		BRP		
	B		E		SP		
6		BD		BP		
		MD		MP		
	SPOUSE:	DD		DP		
	SS		BRD		BRP		
	B		E		SP		

PREPARED BY: John Doe
ADDRESS: 1212 Main
Anytown, UTAH
TELEPHONE: (000) 555-1212

DATE: 20 Aug 1999
E-MAIL:

OTHER MARRIAGES OF CHILDREN:

BD=BIRTH DATE	MD=MARRIAGE DATE	DD=DEATH DATE	BRD=BURIAL DATE	B=BAPTIZED	SP=SEALED TO PARENTS
BP=BIRTH PLACE	MP=MARRIAGE PLACE	DP=DEATH PLACE	BRP=BURIAL PLACE	E=ENDOWED	SS=SEALED TO SPOUSE

Organizing Your Pedigree Charts and Family Group Records

Most pedigree charts and family group records are 8½" x 11" and fit nicely into a 3-ring binder. Some of the older forms are 8½" x 14" and will fit into a binder designed to hold legal-sized paper.

The most common way to organize these forms in a binder is to:

- First, arrange the pedigree charts in numerical order.

- Second, file the family group records in alphabetical order by surname. Use dividers for each letter of the alphabet. Within each surname, arrange the records in alphabetical order by first name. If you have more than one person with the same name, arrange them in chronological order with the oldest person first. (See Figure 4.)

Later, when you have too many family group records for one binder, you can follow the same pattern suggested above but use a series of binders—one binder for pedigree charts, then one binder for each individual surname.

Of course, there are other ways to organize these forms. If you choose another organizational pattern, remember to be logical and consistent so that others can find their way through your records.

Keeping Track of Ancestral Tracks

Along with filing your pedigree charts and family group records, you will need a plan for organizing your "other papers": vital record certificates, censuses, compiled family histories or biographies, and so on. The goal of a good filing system is to have quick access to each piece of paper through the use of logical divisions and clear labeling.

Logical Divisions

Organize your papers first by surname, second by location, third by topic in alphabetical order within each section. Keep your correspondence file separate. Don't let your file folders get so full that it is difficult to find things in them. It is better to have many folders with only a few papers in each folder than have a few folders bulging with papers.

Figure 4

Pedigree Charts

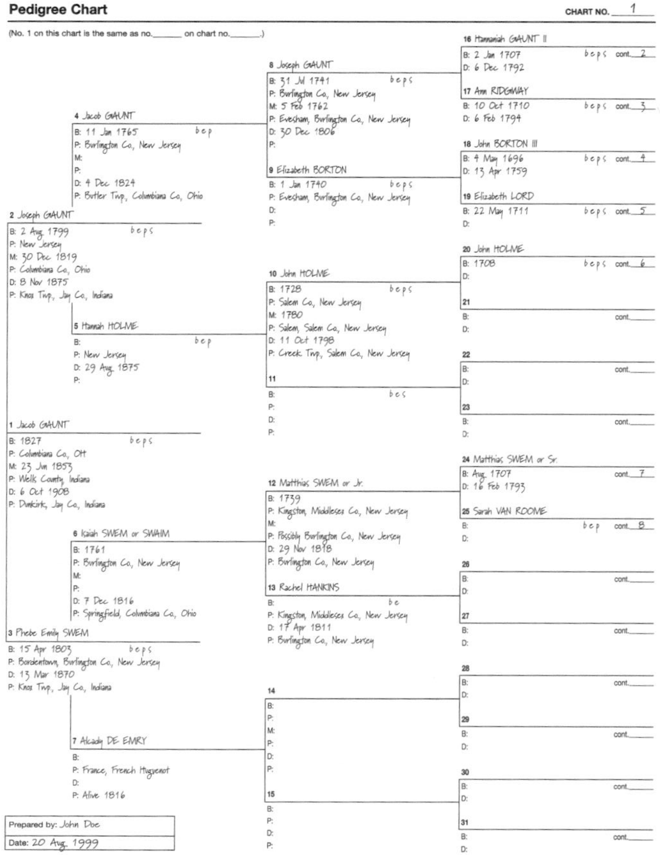

Family Group Records

Family Group Record SHEET 1 PAGE 1 OF 1

HUSBAND: Hannaniah GAUNT II		OCCUPATION:		SOURCES:	
BD	2 Jan 1707	BP	Germantown, Philadelphia, Philadelphia Co, Pennsylvania	Church Rcds.	
MD	10 Jul 1730	MP			
DD	6 Dec 1792	DP			
BRD		BRP	Friends Graveyard, Tuckertown, Burlington Co, New Jersey	Cemetery Rcds.	
FATHER: Daniel GAUNT (b 1 Sep 1688)		MOTHER: Hannah SHOURDS			
OTHER MARRIAGES:					
RELIGION:		MILITARY:		SS	29 Mar 1977 SLAKE
B	13 Apr 1988 JRIVE	E	25 Aug 1988 JRIVE	SP	16 Sep 1988 JRIVE

Family Group Record SHEET 1 PAGE 1 OF 2

HUSBAND: Jacob GAUNT		OCCUPATION:		SOURCES:	
BD	1827	BP	Columbiana Co, OH		
MD	23 Jun 1853	MP	Wells County, Indiana		
DD	6 Oct 1908	DP	Dunkirk, Jay Co, Indiana		
BRD	Oct 1908	BRP	Winters Cemetery, Hwy 1 & 26, Knox Twp, Jay Co, Indiana		
FATHER: Joseph GAUNT (b 2 Aug 1799)		MOTHER: Phebe Emily SWEM (b 15 Apr 1803)			
OTHER MARRIAGES:					
RELIGION:		MILITARY:		SS	10 Aug 1972 ARIZO
B	3 Jul 1971 ARIZO	E	16 Oct 1971 ARIZO	SP	11 Aug 1972 ARIZO

Family Group Record SHEET 1 PAGE 1 OF 2

HUSBAND: Joseph GAUNT		OCCUPATION:		SOURCES:	
BD	31 Jul 1741	BP	Little Egg Harbor, Burlington Co, New Jersey		
MD	5 Feb 1762	MP	Evesham, Burlington Co, New Jersey		
DD	30 Dec 1806	DP			
BRD	Dec 1806	BRP	Baptist Church Cemetery, Evesham Twp, Marlton Co, New Jersey		
FATHER: Hannaniah GAUNT II (b 2 Jan 1707)		MOTHER: Ann RIDGWAY (b 10 Oct 1710)			
OTHER MARRIAGES:					
RELIGION:		MILITARY:		SS	29 Mar 1977 JRIVE
B	19 Nov 1993 JRIVE	E	24 Feb 1994 JRIVE	SP	20 Sep 1994 SLAKE

Family Group Record SHEET 1 PAGE 1 OF 1

HUSBAND: Joseph GAUNT		OCCUPATION:		SOURCES:	
BD	2 Aug 1799	BP	New Jersey		
MD	30 Dec 1819	MP	Columbiana County, Ohio		
DD	8 Nov 1875	DP	Knox Twp, Jay Co, Indiana	Jay Co, IN Death Rcds.	
BRD		BRP	Winters Cemetery, Hwy 1 & 26, Knox Twp, Jay Co, Indiana		
FATHER: Jacob GAUNT (b 11 Jan 1765)		MOTHER: Hannah HOLME			
OTHER MARRIAGES:					
RELIGION:		MILITARY:		SS	12 May 1972 SLAKE
B	1 Sep 1972 SGEOR	E	4 Nov 1972 SGEOR	SP	7 Dec 1972 OGDEN

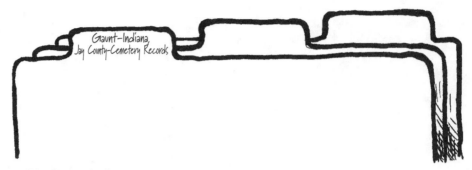

Clear Labeling

Always label everything from the broadest division to the smallest division. Print. Use ink or a felt-tip marker. Colored folders or colored pens can be another means of quickly identifying a surname, location, or topic.

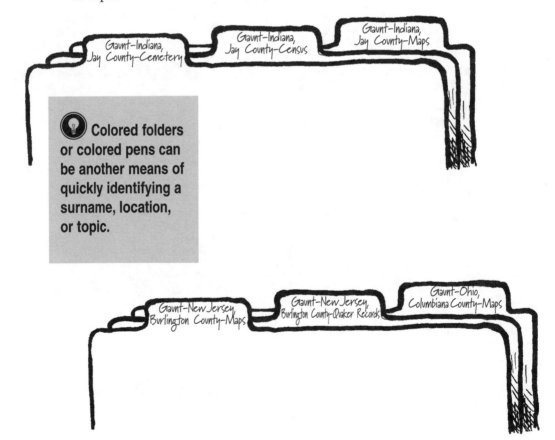

> 💡 **Colored folders or colored pens can be another means of quickly identifying a surname, location, or topic.**

Other Important Forms

(?)   A **descendancy chart** starts with one ancestral couple and creates a list of all of their descendants. All the children of this couple with their spouses, plus all of the grandchildren of this couple with their spouses, are included, and so on for each generation (if known). A descendancy chart gives a broad view of a family and is especially helpful when planning a family reunion or working with a family history association. Most family history computer software programs can easily create a descendancy chart. (See Figure 5.)

> (💡) **Use your computer to help keep your family history organized.**

(?)   A **kinship report** is a list of family members and their relationship to one particular ancestor. Again, these reports are valuable in planning a family reunion or working with a family history association and are easily generated by most family history computer software programs.

Figure 5

Descendants of Jacob GAUNT   20 Aug 1999

```
1-Jacob GAUNT (1827-6 Oct 1908)
sp: Melvina F. Bennett (4 Jun 1833-11 Aug 1891)
    2-Joseph R. GAUNT (-10 Aug 1866)
    2-Viola V. GAUNT (May 1854-10 Aug 1855)
    2-infant GAUNT (1855-Jun 1855)
    2-David Clinton GAUNT (13 May 1856-2 Dec 1920)
    sp: Martha Sophronia HARTMAN (2 Feb 1861-20 Oct 1943)
        3-Joseph Harley GAUNT (29 Sep 1881-11 May 1969)
        3-Charles Lee GAUNT (1 Sep 1883-13 Feb 1958)
        3-Orlan Fay GAUNT (27 Jul 1888-11 Jan 1974)
        3-Floyd GAUNT (22 Jul 1891-23 Apr 1968)
        3-Ora Myron GAUNT (31 Jul 1894-1984)
        3-Edith Jemima GAUNT (15 Jul 1902-22 May 1994)
    2-Arthur Lee GAUNT (2 Mar 1858-19 Nov 1935
    sp: Rachel Lovena STUTSMAN (-Mar 1910)
        3-Harry Mark GAUNT (27 Mar 1893-25 Aug 1957)
        3-Edward Lee GAUNT (31 Jan 1889-)
    2-Charles Dalton GAUNT (1 Oct 1861-16 Nov 1929)
    sp: Laura Ellen MARTIN (8 Oct 1865-31 Jan 1960)
    2-George Wise GAUNT (Apr 1863-9 May 1920)
    sp: Julia SPAHR (Nov 1863-1900)
        3-GAUNT (-7 Nov 1894)
    2-John F. GAUNT (Apr 1867-18 Jun 1877)
    2-Harry Swain GAUNT (1870-)
    sp: Lulu SAWYER (1874-)
    2-Willard Warren GAUNT (28 Aug 1872-10 May 1924)
    sp: Lora Opal WRIGHT (1874-)
```

Want to Know More?

- Copies of pedigree charts and family group records are available on your family history computer software program, at your Family History Center, or at the end of this book in the section called Forms. Your ward family history consultant may also have these forms.

- You can order charts and forms from many places, including:

  a. Ancestry, Inc., P.O. Box 476, Salt Lake City, UT 84110-0476 or on the Internet at **www.ancestry.com**.
  b. Everton Publishers, Inc., P.O. Box 368, Logan, UT 84321 or on the Internet at **www.everton.com**.

Try This

❑ 1. Fill out the first three generations on your pedigree chart.

❑ 2. Fill out two family group records: (1) one with you as a child and (2) one with you as a parent.

❑ 3. Print out your pedigree chart and a family group record for every couple on your pedigree chart.

❑ 4. Arrange your pedigree charts and family group records in a 3-ring notebook.

❑ 5. Check to be sure each name, date, and place is documented.

❑ 6. Try printing out a descendancy chart or a kinship report using your family history computer software program.

❑ 7. Think about how much your family means to you and tell them.

Write the names, dates, and places that identify your ancestors so the information won't be forgotten.

CHAPTER 3

Getting Your
Computer's Help

★ **IN THIS CHAPTER**
✔ Advantages of family history computer software
✔ Twelve things your computer can do for you
✔ Learn what a GEDCOM file is

George's Story: Why Travel by Horse and Buggy When You Can Go by Jet?

I learned to type in the ninth grade on a Smith Corona manual typewriter. Back then it was a major crisis to make an error, especially if you were using carbon paper. Well, thank goodness all that has changed. I stil make an eror on about evry other werd that I tipe but with the computer such errors don't matter. Now I just push a button or two to run my spellchecker, and my work is perfect.

But for years I thought that computers were only for secretaries. I wrote all my books on yellow paper with a ballpoint pen, and then my secretary typed it into the computer.

One Saturday I was in the middle of a sentence when my ballpoint pen went dry. I frantically searched for another pen but there was none in my desk. My secretary wasn't in, and her desk was locked. What could I do? I looked at my computer, which I had never really used. I was desperate. I turned it on and began to type, and I've never looked back.

How about you? If you already have a computer, great! But if you aren't using one, I say to you, "Come on! Get with it! A computer can become your number one ally in your family history research." (Of course, if you can't afford a computer right now, you can use one of the computers at your local Family History Center.)

I remember when I got my family history computer software program. I was as excited as I am on Christmas morning. I was tempted to have my son come over and load it onto my computer for me. That's what I always do when I'm confronted with a high-tech challenge—call for help. But I didn't. I had decided that I was going to do this myself or die trying.

With trembling hands, I opened the box. I was certain that if I did the wrong thing, it would explode in my face. Inside, I found two books and two disks and some papers. The smaller of the two books was titled "Getting Started," so I opened it. Since I'd never actually loaded a program onto a computer, I followed the step-by-step directions as if my life depended on it. After just four steps, I saw the words "Installation Complete." I had done it! It seemed to me that I had been quickly transformed from clueless to brilliant. My confidence was growing. I thought to myself: "Look out, Bill Gates! There's a new kid on the block."

Now it was time to put the information about the Durrants that I had found on Ancestral File at the Family History Center onto my computer. The volunteer at the Family History Center had helped me to create a **GEDCOM** file of my family history and to save it on a disk. With that disk in hand, I was ready to begin. Now I knew I was ready to go to the big book—after all, big tasks require big books. I opened the cover and carefully read the Table of Contents until I found the chapter on how to import a GEDCOM file. I put the disk in the only place where it would fit into my computer, and then step-by-step I followed the instructions.

When the computer program asked me to name my file, I typed in "Durrant." (Very original.) Then *voila!* The message on the screen told me that all the records had been imported. I wanted to call my son and tell him what I had done. In the twinkling of an eye, I had gone from having no names on my computer to having thousands of names. These names, with their dates and places, were all linked together into one great big family.

With new confidence, I began to experiment with the myriad of computer tools I now had at my fingertips. I felt that I was invincible. I tried this and that, moving my mouse with gusto and pushing one key after another.

In the process, I tried to print out some things onto paper, but I couldn't because my printer wasn't selected. But I even figured out how to do that. And I tell you, if I can do it, you can do it. Of course, some of you are saying, "Why the big fuss? It's no more complicated than riding a bike."

In 1915, the Hopmans of Hammond, Indiana, traveled in style in their new "Hupmobiles."

Twelve Things Your Computer Can Do for You

⭐ Your computer—loaded with a family history software program—has the power to do many tasks quickly and easily that would otherwise be difficult and time-consuming for you.

1. A computer allows you to store all of your information in an organized manner and out of sight. While you will still have a lot of paper, the bulk of your family history will be stored electronically in a very small space. If you have a laptop computer, you can easily take everything with you when you go to the library, visit Aunt Gertrude, or travel to your ancestral hometown. Plus, you can share your data with others using a small disk.

2. Computers can sort information and print it out in many different formats, including: (1) pedigree charts, (2) family group records, (3) descendancy charts, (4) kinship lists.

3. Depending on your software program, you can create any or all of the following lists: (1) Possible Problems, (2) Duplicate Names, (3) To Do List, (4) Source List, (5) Facts without Sources,

(6) Individuals without Parents, (7) Individuals without LDS Ordinances, (8) Address List, (9) Birthday and Anniversary List, (10) Multimedia List, (11) Unlinked Individuals List, (12) Marriage List, (13) Place List, and so on. (You get the idea.)

4. You can also print blank forms: (1) pedigree charts, (2) family group records, (3) correspondence logs, (4) research logs, and so on.

5. Documentation of facts can be more complete with the aid of your family history software program. Once you have entered the full source citation, you never have to retype it again. The full citation can simply be linked to each new fact as it is added to your family history.

6. Some family history software programs provide plenty of space to add notes or stories.

Ch. 9

7. Most family history software programs have a date calculator, a relationship calculator, and a **Soundex** calculator.

8. Most family history software programs have the ability to merge duplicate records of the same person together into one record.

9. A computer allows you to transfer information electronically: no more photocopying information or copying it by hand. By importing and exporting GEDCOM files, volumes of detailed information are available with the click of a few keys.

10. For Latter-day Saints, use your computer to create a GEDCOM file for TempleReady. You can also create a GEDCOM file to add your family history to Ancestral File or to preserve your genealogy through the **www.familysearch.org** site on the Internet.

11. Of course, with the growing use of the World Wide Web, your computer becomes the tool that connects you with the world of family history in cyberspace. Not only can you download information from the Internet for your own use, but you can create a Web site to share your information with others. You can query others on specific ancestors. You can even find how-to materials or order forms, books, and other materials online.

12. A family history software program can help you compile and print your family history. It helps you add photographs to your text. If you want to print a descendancy family history, it will automatically number the individuals using a commonly used system, such as **Ahnentafel** or **Modified Register**.

So take time to become friends with your computer and learn how to use your family history software program. By doing so, you will gain a powerful tool.

What Is a GEDCOM File?

GEDCOM is an acronym that stands for GEnealogical Data COMmunication. This file format, developed in 1987 by The Church of Jesus Christ of Latter-day Saints, makes it possible to transfer family history data between different family history software programs. It has now become the standard.

Most, if not all, family history software programs allow users to import and export GEDCOM files. GEDCOM is even compatible between Macintosh computers and DOS or Windows-based computers.

To convert your data into GEDCOM format, simply follow the instructions in your manual. It is not difficult.

GEDCOM files can be attached to e-mails.

GEDCOM files can also be converted to **HTML** so that they can be placed directly onto the World Wide Web.

Which Family History Software Program?

Right about now you are probably asking yourself, How many family history software programs are there? And how do I know which one to buy?

There are nearly forty family history software programs on the market. Ask family and friends which program they are using and why. There is an advantage to using the same program as those with whom you are likely to exchange information.

Personal Ancestral File, developed by The Church of Jesus Christ of Latter-day Saints, became one of the most widely used programs because it sold for only $15. At the time of the printing of this book, Windows-based Personal Ancestral File 4.0 (PAF) is available free at **www.familysearch.org**. In early 2000, it will also be available on CD-ROM for $5.00 at The Church of Jesus Christ of Latter-day Saint's distribution centers worldwide (1-800-537-5971).

The following is a brief listing of a few family history computer software programs (Macintosh and Windows) with their Internet addresses:

- Ancestral Quest **www.ancquest.com/** (Windows)

- Cumberland Family Tree **www.cf-software.com/** (Windows)

- Family Origins **www.familyorigins.com/** (Windows)

- Family Treasures **www.famtech.com/** (Windows)

- Family Tree Maker **www.familytreemaker.com/** (Windows)

- Legacy **www.legacyfamilytree.com/** (Windows)

- Reunion **www.leisterpro.com/** (Macintosh)

- WinFamily **www.winfamily.com/** (Windows)

Organizing Computer Files

Want to reduce your stacks of paper? Then use your computer to organize your family history information. Remember that the goal of a good filing system is to have quick access to each piece of information through the use of logical divisions and clear file names. Go from the broadest division to the smallest division: first by surname, then by topic. Group all records together by surname. By using the first three letters of the surname as the first three letters of the file name, your files will automatically be grouped for you.

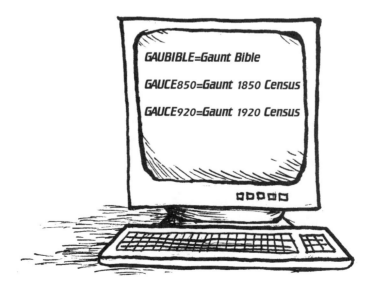

Create a Correspondence File

Summarize each letter as it comes in so that your correspondence file remains current.

Consider creating a separate correspondence file on your computer so that you can throw away the handwritten letters and have the ability to search quickly for a specific name. Summarize each piece of correspondence. Include all essential data: name, address, phone number, e-mail address, date of letter, details of query with all genealogical information contained in the letter. Also include a summary of your response to each letter. This project will take several hours to create, but once it is in place you will be grateful for the ease with which you can access the information and for the increased space in your filing cabinet.

Want to Know More?

- Read Matthew and April Leigh Helm, *Genealogy Online for Dummies,* Foster City, CA: IDG Books Worldwide, Inc., 1998.

- Visit with sales people in a variety of computer stores before buying a computer. Compare.

- Check computer periodicals at your local library.

Try This

❏ 1. Practice exporting a GEDCOM file to a disk using Ancestral File and TempleReady.

❏ 2. Take time each week to learn one new facet of your computer hardware or family history software.

❏ 3. Learn the difference between notes and sources. Practice adding notes and sources.

Ch. 4

❏ 4. Learn to document your family history information. Make sure every source is cited in full. You can cite more than one source for each fact, if necessary.

❏ 5. Learn to attach a GEDCOM file to an e-mail.

> Hammond Ind.
> Oct. 30th. 1918
>
> Dearest Aunt Josephine and all : —
> You surely must think we have forgotten you but we have'nt. We think of you and speak of you so often; but you know how letter writing is. I suppose you received the telegram saying uncle Fred was dead. He took sick on Friday night Sept 27th. he had'nt been feeling well for several days before then but he did'nt want to give in. He had the Spanish Influenza which is very bad in Hammond and it turned to pneumonia, he was very sick. The

Preserve fragile old family letters by transcribing them into your computer.

PART TWO:
Gathering Information

If you love to put puzzles together, you'll love family history research. As you look through the records, you'll gradually uncover piece after piece of information until you have enough pieces to put them together into a complete picture of each of your ancestors. It's thrilling to get to know them and to discover how they fit into history. And don't be surprised if you find some similarities between you and them—after all, you do share the same DNA.

Maybe you will be the one who discovers an important record that puts part of your family history together. Any record upon which you find information about the birth, marriage, or death of one of your ancestors will feel like a sacred record to you. It is no wonder that the Maoris of New Zealand insist on washing their hands before they handle the genealogical records of their people.

In This Part

- You'll learn the research cycle and how to document information.

- You'll learn how to gather previously compiled family history by asking family members, checking compiled sources, using FamilySearch™, and searching the Internet.

- You'll learn all about Family History Centers.

- You'll learn how to verify what you've found and how to find new information by searching original government records such as censuses, vital records, or military records.

- You'll discover the wealth of information awaiting you in the cemeteries, libraries, and churches of your ancestor's hometown.

- And George's stories will give you confidence and courage to do original research.

Utilizing the Research Cycle

George's Story: Take Aim

I recall duck hunting with my father and my Uncle Dick. A flock flew right over us. My Uncle Dick emptied his gun, but no ducks fell. Those were the only ducks we saw that day. As we rode home, my father asked Uncle Dick how he could have missed such easy shots. Uncle Dick replied, "I guessed I aimed at the whole flock instead of just at one duck. Somehow I hit only the places where the ducks were not."

In family history, we don't aim for the whole "flock" of ancestors— we aim for just one.

The Research Cycle

Understanding and using the research cycle is vital to solving family history challenges. The six steps in the research cycle are:

1. Choose a specific goal.

2. Find possible records.

3. Search the records.

4. Document your search.

5. Evaluate.

6. Integrate New Information. Return to step #1.

Research Cycle

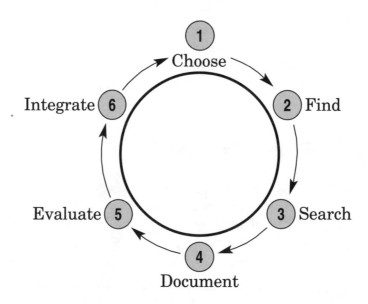

Step One: Choose a Specific Goal

Always search from the known to the unknown. Begin by looking at your own pedigree charts and family group records to find your next research goal.

Let's take a simple example. Your name is number one on your pedigree chart. Everything is fine with your information and with your parent's and grandparent's information. Now you look at your paternal grandfather's name and notice his birth date and birthplace are missing. Now you have a specific research goal.

It is a good idea to have two or three additional research goals in case you have time to move on to one of them.

Step Two: Find Possible Records

Using the Family History Library Catalog (FHLC) on FamilySearch™, create a list of records that may contain your great-grandfather's birth date. Your list could include church records, birth records, Social Security Death Index, census records, death records, obituary, or a family Bible.

> 💡 When searching an index, search for all variations of the spelling of your surname. Also check for variations of the given name, including the middle name as the first name, and initials only.

What you find will depend on what records were created for that time period. The information available can vary from the exact birth date to the approximate year to nothing.

Step Three: Search the Records

> 💡 When visiting a records office, use a pencil so that you do not accidentally get ink on the original documents. Remember to handle original documents carefully; they are often old and brittle.

Locate each document on your list and then search it for your specific goal: your great-grandfather's birth date. In the process, you may find other important information on your family. Gather it also. Searching records for your ancestors is thrilling and filled with surprises. Maybe the book or film you research will have an index or maybe it won't. Maybe you'll find what you are looking for—plus information on many other family members—or maybe you'll come up empty-handed. As you search each record on your list, you won't want to miss anything. Even if your great-grandfather's birth date isn't there, at least you know one place that it is not. That's important, too.

Step Four: Document Your Search

As you search each source, make a note in your research log of your findings. Good researchers make notes of what they did and did not find in a particular record. Thus they will never have to search the same record twice.

If you find the information you are seeking, make a photocopy of the material. If you must transcribe it, print slowly and carefully. Be sure to proofread it for accuracy.

Make sure to cite the full source on your copy, including the author, title of the book, page number, call number or film number, and place of research.

Step Five: Evaluate

After you have searched each record on your list, evaluate the information to determine whether or not it meets your research goal chosen in step #1. Don't jump to conclusions until you have studied the information. Discrepancies may appear. Be logical as you analyze it. Ask yourself: (1) Is the information complete? (2) Does the information conflict with what I already have? (3) Is the source credible? If you are unsure of your findings, try to find the information in at least two other sources. Remember, family folklore has a way of creeping into both printed and oral histories.

Minimum identification for each person is:

* Name
* Birth Date
* Birthplace
* Names of Parents

Death date and death place or marriage date and marriage place can also uniquely identify a person. Sometimes the names of siblings can also uniquely identify a person.

Step Six: Integrate New Information. Return to Step #1

If you found your great-grandfather's birth date then you achieved your goal. Integrate it into your records. Make sure you cite the source of the information each time you add it to a pedigree chart or family group record. With another piece added to your family history puzzle, you are ready to begin again with step #1.

Genealogical research is something you learn by doing. Anyone who has the desire to do family history research and who will follow the research cycle outlined here can, in time, become successful.

Appendix I
As you research your surnames in their particular locations and time periods, you will learn the geography and migrations and customs of the lands of your family's past. You will become an expert in the records that specialize in those areas and time periods and that contain the vital details of your ancestor's lives. (See Appendix I for an example of one beginner's research.)

Research Logs

Keeping a research log is essential in family history research. It is impossible to remember every record you search and what you find or don't find there. A research log remembers these details for you and keeps you from duplicating your research. (See Figure 6.)

Forms
A sample research log is located at the end of this book in the section titled Forms. Photocopy it or create your own. A good research log provides plenty of room to include the name of the researcher; the date of the search; the record searched; the results of the search, even if you find nothing; and the location of the source plus the call number or film number.

Primary Sources vs. Secondary Sources

Sources can be divided into two main groups: primary and secondary.

- A **primary source** is a document, oral account, photograph, or any other item created at or near the time an event occurred. Information for the record was supplied by a person who witnessed the event.

- A **secondary source** is a document, oral account, or any other record that was created some time after an event took place or with information that was supplied by someone who was not an eyewitness to the event.

Primary sources are more valid than secondary sources because the information was recorded at the time of the event. You should gather your names, dates, and places from primary sources whenever possible.

Some sources are both primary and secondary. For example, a death certificate is a primary source for the death date and death place but a secondary source for the birth date and birthplace. Try to verify names, dates, and places found in secondary sources with reliable primary sources or from two independent sources.

Figure 6

Research Log

Goal: Locate the wife of Joseph Gaunt	For (Name): GAUNT
	Researcher: Jane Doe

Date	Call Number / Repository	Source	Results
Jun. 10, 1995	640,981 / FHL	Marriage records of Burlington Co., NJ	NIL
Jun. 10, 1995	733,000 / FHL	Quaker records, NJ	NIL
Jun. 10, 1995	640,982 / FHL	Family Bible of Jacob GAUNT	Joseph Gaunt and Phebe Swem married 30 Dec 1819

Where Do I Look Next?

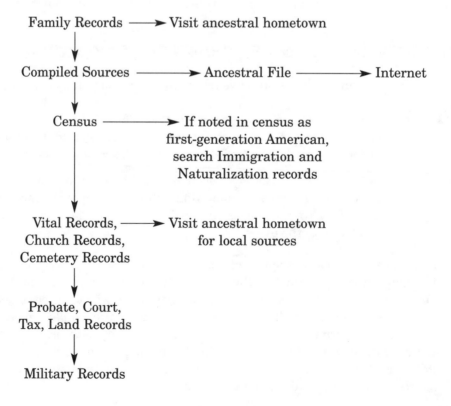

Family Records ⟶ Visit ancestral hometown

Compiled Sources ⟶ Ancestral File ⟶ Internet

Census ⟶ If noted in census as first-generation American, search Immigration and Naturalization records

Vital Records, Church Records, Cemetery Records ⟶ Visit ancestral hometown for local sources

Probate, Court, Tax, Land Records

Military Records

There is a logical order to searching for your ancestors and the research cycle should be applied at each step.

Ch. 5

1. Visit with your extended family to find family histories, scrapbooks, photos, letters, Bibles, and so on. Interview family members who have firsthand knowledge. It's always a good idea to tape or videotape your interview. (If you can, visit your ancestral hometown and search local sources.)

Ch. 8

2. Check compiled sources:
   a. Check FamilySearch and other large genealogical databases on the Internet to discover if your ancestors are listed on Ancestral File or International Genealogical Index (IGI).

Ch. 6

   b. Check published materials, such as family histories, county histories, and biographical directories, to see if someone has already researched your ancestor and written about his or her life.

Ch. 9, 15

3. Check federal census records to locate the town, county, and state where your ancestors lived. If they were first-generation Americans, then search immigration and naturalization records. From there, search homeland records.

Ch. 10, 11, 12

4. Once you find out where your ancestors lived, check the state records and the local records of the town and county by searching vital records, church records, and cemetery records. These will give you birth and death dates. If you can, visit your ancestral hometown and search local sources.

> *Remember, if after thorough but reasonable research dedicated to finding a specific ancestor, you still cannot find him or her, then move on to another line.*

Ch. 13

5. Check other records, such as probates, wills, deeds, court records, and other less-used sources.

Ch. 14, 15

6. If your ancestor served in the military or immigrated to the United States, check those federal records.

Appendix C

7. Remember to document everything you find that pertains to your family. Set high standards for yourself. With something as important as family history, be thorough, honest, and exacting. It is worth doing well.

8. Take each newly found ancestor through each step of this flow-chart.

Remember, if after thorough but reasonable research dedicated to finding a specific ancestor, you still cannot find him or her, then move on to another line. No need to spend all your time looking for one ancestor who seems to be deliberately hiding, while neglecting the 99 others.

Value of Estimating Dates

For the purpose of research, it is a good idea to estimate birth, marriage, and death dates for each of your ancestors if you cannot find an exact date. Use the term "about" when doing so. If your estimation falls within a range of years, use the term "between." Having an approximate date helps you know which time periods to search.

Clues for Estimating Birth Dates:	Clues for Estimating Marriage Dates:
Early census records give ages or age categories.	The age of the first child. Simply count backward two years and use that as the approximate date of the wedding.
Children were generally born two years apart. This can be used as a starting point in the absence of other information.	Add twenty years to the birth date of the bride or groom.
Age of majority was usually 21 for males and 18 for females. Guardianship records or marriage records (if the bride or groom needed permission to marry) mean that your ancestor had not reached the age of majority.	
Cemetery records often list the age of the deceased in terms of years, months, and days: 66y 4m 22d. Most family history computer software programs can quickly calculate the birth date from this data.	

Finding Specific Facts

Specific Question	Where to Look
When and where was my ancestor born?	Census records, cemetery records, church records, family Bible, military records, newspapers, obituaries, tax records, vital records
Where did my ancestor come from and when?	Biographies, census records, church records, compiled histories or genealogies, emigration and immigration records, military records, naturalization and citizenship records, newspapers, obituaries, vital records
When and where did my ancestor die?	Cemetery records, church records, family Bible, land records, military records, newspapers, obituaries, probate records, vital records
What if my ancestors divorced?	Court records, divorce records, newspapers, vital records
How do I find a maiden name?	Census records, church records, compiled histories or genealogies, family Bible, land records, military records, newspapers, probate records, vital records
How can I find the members of a family?	Census records, church records, compiled histories or genealogies, emigration and immigration records, family Bible, land records, newspapers, obituaries, probate records, vital records
How can I find out what religion my ancestors were?	Cemetery records, church records, compiled histories or genealogies, family Bible, obituaries
How can I find where my ancestors lived?	Census records, compiled histories or genealogies, land records, military records, newspapers, obituaries
Where can I find county boundary lines and parent counties?	Maps, gazetteers

Resolving Discrepancies

When you have conflicting names, dates, places, or relationships, compare the information and ask yourself where it came from. Remember to value:

1. Primary sources over secondary sources.

2. Original documents over a transcript of the document.

3. Two independent sources over one source.

4. Actual dates over estimated or calculated dates.

5. Logical over the illogical.

6. Historically accurate over the historically inaccurate.

Missing Limbs on Every Family Tree

Don't ever fall for the old falsehood, "Our genealogy has been done already." It's true that some family lines, perhaps your own surname line, have been extended back as far as archival records will allow. But undone ancestral lines are a heritage each of us has in abundance. And to those lucky ones whose relatives have never tapped their ancestral reservoir, you are like the military group who was surrounded by the enemy and told they were lucky because they could fire in any direction and hit the target. So take aim, the skies are full of ducks.

Remember, no matter how much research has been done on your lines, there are some ends of some branches that are still untouched. Go out on a limb and discover what still needs to be done.

HEY!... I'VE BEEN LOOKING FOR YOU!

FAMILY TREE

Want to Know More?

- Val D. Greenwood, *The Researcher's Guide to American Genealogy,* 3rd ed., Baltimore, MD: Genealogical Publishing, Co., 1999.

- Loretto Dennis Szucs and Sandra Hargreaves Luebking, *The Source: A Guidebook of American Genealogy,* revised ed., Salt Lake City, UT: Ancestry, Inc., 1997.

- *The Handybook for Genealogists,* 8th ed., Logan, UT: Everton Publishers, Inc., 1991.

- *Family History SourceGuide* on CD-ROM from LDS distribution centers. Also available at the Family History Library and at Family History Centers.

Try This

❑ 1. Set a simple research goal.

❑ 2. Review documentation in Appendix C.

❑ 3. List five primary sources and five secondary sources.

❑ 4. Check your pedigree chart for ends of maternal lines. Now that more records are available, you may be able to find the maiden name of one of your great-grandmothers and open up a whole new surname line.

❑ 5. Review the *Family History SourceGuide* for "A Guide to Research" and "Discovering Your Family Tree."

❑ 6. Review *Family History SourceGuide* and locate the research outline and summary for the state or county where your ancestors resided.

Finding Family Sources

★ **IN THIS CHAPTER**
  ✔ How to gather family history from your immediate family
  ✔ How to write a letter asking for family history
  ✔ How to interview a family member

George's Story: You Can Go Home Again

I recall a day some years ago in Nashville, Tennessee, when my wife and children and I were at an amusement park called Opryland. The sun had just gone down and, being a bit weary, I found a seat in a little outdoor theater. Some country-western singers were providing entertainment on the stage. I was in a most reflective mood as they began to sing, "Country road, take me home." Those words caused a dream to begin to unfold in my heart and mind, and I began to reminisce.

In my mind, I walked the old Alpine Road again as I had done so many times as a child coming home from Harrington Elementary School. I passed through Old Mill Lane that wound its way though the trees. I stopped on the bridge and looked down into the water. There was always a rainbow trout there. He never swam for cover. It seemed that he liked seeing me as much as I liked seeing him.

One more block and I was home. Soon I saw the old adobe house surrounded by green grass. Growing up from the lawn were three giant cedar trees. I smelled the lilacs that bowed the limbs low with the weight of their blossoms. I could see into the big bay window that was in the corner of our large kitchen.

I saw my father looking at me through the window where he sat in his rocking chair. He was dressed in his bibbed overalls. I opened the door. My mother, who was standing by the pots and pans that covered the hot end of our old coal range, smiled and greeted me but continued with her cooking.

All seven of my brothers and sisters were home as we sat down for dinner. Mother placed her delicious cooking before us and, after a prayer, we ate. My mother was up and down many times as she served us one of her unforgettable meals.

My country road had taken me home again. It was so good to be there and to see my father and my mother and my family.

Suddenly someone shouted, "Daddy!" and I was no longer in the home of my childhood. I was back in Opryland. My dream had ended.

My little daughter Sarah called out my name again and came running to me. I took her in my arms and hugged her close. Oh, how I hoped that her memories of home would someday be as dear to her as mine are to me. My dream of home made me want to hold my wife and each of my children close. Life felt so good.

An In-House Project

   Once you've decided to seek out your roots, the first thing you need to do is to gather up the information already within your immediate family. Look for family history information around your own home. If your mom and dad are still around, make a special visit to their home. Let them know in advance that you want to talk to them about family history. Ask them to locate birth certificates, marriage licenses, old family pictures, a family Bible—any records that might shed light on the past. Such a visit can be among the most satisfying and love-filled times you have ever had as a family.

So with your pedigree chart in hand, start talking family history with your relatives. If they live nearby, visit them in person. If not, then call them on the phone or send them a letter or e-mail. Involve everyone—your children, brothers, sisters, cousins, uncles, aunts, and grandparents. Remember, your ancestors are their ancestors.

Tips for Interviewing Family

1. Ask open-ended, leading questions that cannot be answered with a yes or no. Have your questions written down on a paper to serve as a guide. This will give the interview a focus. When the person begins to talk freely, do not interrupt until he or she seems to need another question. If the person skips from one time period to another or from one story to another, let them

continue. You can reestablish the chronology when you transcribe the tape.

2. Ask permission to tape the interview. Once the interview is underway, the person will forget about the tape. However, you must remember to keep an eye on it so you can turn the tape over or change it.

When the person wanders too far off the topic, politely interrupt and ask your next question.

3. Keep your interviews to two hours. Usually people are tired by then. If you aren't finished, simply make arrangements to come back another day.

4. If you are relaxed yet intensely interested, the person will sense it and give you their most interesting information and deepest feelings.

5. Seek out your oldest living relatives. They carry a lot of family history in their heads and hearts and usually love a visit. Share old family pictures with them since photos have a way of triggering memories. Also ask to see any old pictures they might have. Talking with them can be a joyful time for you and them.

Ch. 16

6. If other relatives have family records, make arrangements to visit them and see what they have. Don't ask for copies unless you are willing to do the work of getting the copies made and to pay the expenses. If they are reluctant to let old photographs or family records out of their hands, offer to go with them to have them copied.

Don't press for details if Grandma is reluctant to talk about a particular time in her life. Respect her privacy.

Ch. 3

7. If you and your relatives both keep your family history on a computer, offer to share information using a GEDCOM file.

Asking about an Ancestor

❏ 1. What was Grandma's name? What did they call her?

❏ 2. Where was she born? When?

❏ 3. What were her parents' names? Her mother's maiden name? Where were they born and when?

❏ 4. What were the names of her brothers and sisters? When and where were each of them born? What about her early life?

❏ 5. How did she meet Grandpa? Where did they get married and when? Who performed the marriage?

❏ 6. Where did they live? Did they own land? Did they move around?

❏ 7. What did Grandma look like? Do you have any pictures of her?

❏ 8. How did they earn a living?

❏ 9. What were the names of their children? Where were they born?

❏ 10. Where did the family go to church?

❏ 11. What were her hobbies? Was the family involved in sports or music or things like that?

❏ 12. Does anyone in the family have any heirlooms?

❏ 13. What are the most interesting stories that you have heard about her?

❏ 14. What sort of traditions did the family have?

❏ 15. When and where did she die? Where is she buried?

You get the idea of the kind of questions to ask. Follow your own inclinations and inspiration. Ask the same questions about Grandpa that you asked about Grandma.

Transcribing the Interview

If you can type, you will find great joy in the several hours it takes to transcribe the tape. A transcribing machine with a foot pedal will make the job easier. If you cannot do it, hire a typist or get a family member to do it. The final transcript will be a family treasure forever.

Writing Letters

Writing letters to family members is another way to gather family history. Use 8½" x 11" paper with wide margins and space between paragraphs. Type or write clearly. Include your full name and full address on the letter. Always include a self-addressed, stamped envelope.

Make sure that your letters are easy to read and not too long. Don't ask for too much information at a time. It is better to write several letters over time than to ask for too much in one letter.

Sample Letter

Dear (Name of relative),   (Date)

I have learned through (the way you found out this person is related to you) that we are related. My name is (list full name). I live in (list city and state).

I am researching my family history, and I'm interested in (list name here).

I know (include summary information here).

I'm not able to find (specific information you seek).

Can you help me? I've enclosed a self-addressed, stamped envelope. If you have pictures or documents and would be willing to make copies for me I'd be grateful. Let me know how much this will cost and I will send you a money order.

If I learn more about this ancestor, I would be happy to share this information with you. Thank you for your help.

Sincerely,
(name)
(full address)
(telephone number)
(e-mail address)

Keeping a Correspondence Log

Keep a record of all of your queries, responses, and replies on a correspondence log. Make a separate log for each surname for ease of filing. (See Figure 7.)

Note the date and the name and address of the person to whom the letter was sent. Make a note of the information you are requesting.

When you get a reply, note the date and a brief summary of the response.

Figure 7

Correspondence Log — GAUNT

Date Sent	TO: (Name and Address)	QUESTION	Reply Date	ANSWER
Oct. 10, 1990	John Doe 1234 Main St. Dunkirk, IN 55555	Who are the parents of Jacob Gaunt?	Nov. 20, 1990	Joseph Gaunt is father. Mother unknown.
Apr. 20, 1991	Mary A. Smith 32221 State St. Annapolis Royal, CA 55555	Who is the wife of Joseph Gaunt?	May 10, 1991	Unknown
Jun. 5, 1991	Mrs. John Jones 320 Elm Reedsville, MO 55555	Who is the wife of Joseph Gaunt?	Jun. 25, 1991	Unknown

This record of your correspondence will increase in value as time passes. It will remember details that you will forget. It will save you duplication of work and provide a paper trail to the sources of some of your information.

A sample correspondence log is located at the end of this book in the section titled Forms. Photocopy it or create your own. A good correspondence log provides plenty of room to include the date of the incoming letter, the address of the person writing to you, their question, the date of your reply, and your answer.

Finding Family Treasures

When you start visiting family members, always ask if they have any heirlooms, photos, or papers. You'll be thrilled with what others have in their attics, basements, trunks, and closets.

1. ***Family Bibles.*** This is often the only written record of some families. The names of family members along with their births, marriages, and deaths are usually recorded in it. Locations are not always recorded. Sometimes dates are copied from an earlier Bible into the new Bible. Because the family Bible contains

this important family history, it is usually passed onto the next generation. Try to find the names of each owner of the Bible, and in the process, you will find more of your family.

Appendix
E

2. ***Letters, deeds, and personal papers.*** Though they may be faded and hard to read, these papers have bits and pieces of your ancestors' lives captured on them. Letters especially reveal relationships between family members as well as the family news. Family newsletters, birth or wedding announcements, baby books, school records, address books, and account books will all be filled with valuable information and clues to help you build the story of your family. Some families have actual birth, marriage, or death certificates among their personal papers. Military records may turn up. Remember to look at the envelopes for clues, too.

3. ***Old family photographs.*** One of the best things about visiting family members is the opportunity to see old family photos. Actually seeing the face of one of your ancestors draws you to them and helps family history come alive.

4. ***Journals.*** Among the most treasured finds is the diary or journal of a family member. Nothing reveals a person's life like their own written feelings about their life events. Most journals capture the important life events, but some devoted journal keepers also write of day-to-day life, hence revealing the fascinating details of their lifestyle.

Ch. 17

5. ***Newspaper clippings, obituaries.*** Most families save obituaries of family members. They are filled with the names, dates, and places of your ancestor's life. The list of survivors helps establish family relationships. Often a photo is part of the obituary. Since newspaper is not meant to last a long time, it yellows and crumbles quickly. Transcribe it exactly or photocopy it.

6. ***Heirlooms, such as clothes, toys, jewelry, dishes, cross-stitch samplers.*** Nearly everyone is sentimental about a few mementos of their life and saves them. These become family treasures. Photograph everything, and tape record or write down the stories behind family heirlooms.

Want to Know More?

- Read "Finding Information at Home" at **www.familytree maker.com** and "Discovering Your Heritage 101—The First Steps" at **www.ancestry.com**.

- Loretto Dennis Szucs and Sandra Hargreaves Luebking, *The Source: A Guidebook of American Genealogy,* revised ed., Salt Lake City, UT: Ancestry, Inc., 1997.

- Milton Robincam, ed., *Genealogical Research: Methods and Sources,* revised ed., Washington, DC: The American Society of Genealogists, 1980.

- Laureen R. Jaussi, *Genealogy Fundamentals,* Orem, UT: Jaussi Publications, 1994.

Try This

❏ 1. Visit one of your relatives and conduct a family history interview with them.

❏ 2. Write a letter to one of your relatives asking for a specific piece of family history information.

❏ 3. Tell your children about what your life was like when you were their age.

Reviewing Compiled Sources

George's Story: "Daddy, I Found Myself!"

Once, one of my children was hiding from me. I knew where he was hiding because I could see his feet sticking out from behind a chair. I said, "I think he's hiding in the bookcase." And I took some of the books out and couldn't find him. I said, "I think he's hiding in the stereo set." And I lifted up the lid and couldn't find him there. I said, "I think he's hiding in the lamp." And I turned it off and on and couldn't find him there. Then I went over close to where he was and said in a loud voice, "I can't find him. I suppose I'll have to go buy an ice cream cone all by myself." Then suddenly he popped up from behind the chair and said, "Daddy, I found myself!"

It doesn't matter if others have found you and in finding you they have come to love you. The great discovery comes when you find yourself and come to say, "I have found myself. I'm glad I'm me." Compiling your family history can help you discover your roots, and in the process discover who you are. It can give you self-understanding, and that is the key to all understanding.

A Family History Framework

Compiled sources are an essential part of the early phase of gathering your family history. While they are secondary sources and the least accurate of all sources, they are essential because they provide existing research and a framework upon which to add data collected from other sources. Don't assume that because someone else has done so much work gathering a family history that the information in it is totally accurate and complete. Compiled sources are only as accurate as the abilities of the person compiling them and the sources from which they were gathered. Names, dates, places, and relationships should be verified whenever possible by using primary sources, such as vital records and church records, or two independent sources.

Important Compiled Sources

Ch. 16,
Appendix
G

1. *County Histories.* These books (published or unpublished) feature historical events and local genealogies of a specific area. Most were written around the turn of the century. People paid to have their biographies included in these county histories.

Ch. 19,
20

2. *Family Histories, Genealogies, or Biographies.* These books (published or unpublished) focus on a particular surname or time period and are usually compiled by an individual, family history association, or historical society.

3. *Directories.* Prior to the advent of the telephone book, many cities compiled a yearly directory. These are helpful because they identify all of the residents living at each address. Some directories have a householders index. This reverse listing by street address can help you locate neighbors of your ancestors. Local libraries house the collection of directories, some printed as early as 1800.

4. *Magazine and Newspaper Collections.* A great deal of useful historical and genealogical information can be found in the periodicals of a specific area. Many local county libraries have small collections of newspapers and historical society periodicals.

Ch. 17,
Appendix
G

The Allen County Public Library, P.O. Box 2270, Ft. Wayne, IN 46801, has the largest collection of periodicals in the country. They developed the Periodical Source Index (PERSI) as a means of searching their more than 2,000 periodicals. They have also indexed about 500,000 articles by topics. Articles are also indexed for surname, locality, and research methodology. Copies of the PERSI are available in many public libraries.

Ch. 7

5. ***Family Group Records Collections.*** These collections of family group records are usually housed in the library of a historical society or a family history association. One of the largest collections of this type is located on the fourth floor of the Joseph Smith Memorial Building (JSMB) in Salt Lake City, Utah. These eight million family group records were submitted by members of The Church of Jesus Christ of Latter-day Saints during two different time periods: (1) Archive Section (pink tags) submitted between 1940 and 1971 and (2) Patrons Section (yellow tags) submitted between 1975 and 1984.

Ancestral File on **www.familysearch.org** is an electronic collection of family group records.

Appendix D

6. ***The Internet.*** This powerful technology is the fastest growing source of compiled family history. It is also the most accessible. Nearly 90 percent of the family history information on the Internet has been compiled from a variety of sources by individuals just like you and me. As a result,

> Family folklore has a way of creeping into mainstream family history. Include it if you want, but make sure to note it as family folklore and not fact.

these genealogies are of varying quality. Nevertheless, the Internet provides a wealth of information as well as the names of others who are working on the same lines as you. Corresponding by e-mail provides quick and easy communication on the Internet with the compilers of family histories.

Avoiding Duplication

Once you decide which surname you want to research, you should do a survey of existing family histories to see what may have already been compiled on your line. This prevents duplication of work. It is discouraging to do a lot of work only to have someone say, "Oh, I could have told you all that if you had asked me." Asking relatives and gathering compiled sources are the two best ways to avoid duplication of time, energy, and money.

Remember, survey only one surname line at a time. Start with:

1. A **pedigree chart** showing the surname line.

2. **Family group records** for each family listed on the pedigree chart.

3. Check with **family members** to see what they have. Make sure you locate the relative who seems to be the expert on that branch of your family.

4. Check **Ancestral File** on FamilySearch™.

5. Check **International Genealogical Index** (IGI) on Family-Search.

6. Check the **surname** listing in the Family History Library Catalog (FHLC) on FamilySearch for your surname. If there are many listings, scan them briefly and come back later when you know more.

7. Check the **locality** listing in the Family History Library Catalog (FHLC) on FamilySearch for the areas where your ancestors lived. Check for county histories or compiled genealogies of local families.

8. Check the **Internet** for compiled family histories.

9. Photocopy **maps** for the states, counties, and townships of the different areas where your ancestors lived.

Forms

10. Compile a simple chronology chart showing where the generations of your family lived between 1790 and 1920. When necessary, expand the chart to cover the needed time period. This will allow you to track the movement of your direct ancestors over time. Now you are ready to launch into original research.

Contacting Historical Societies

Most states and counties have historical societies. Since these societies are interested in gathering and preserving local history and genealogies, they are wonderful repositories of compiled sources. County histories, family genealogies, or collections of periodicals and newspapers—all specializing in the history, genealogy, or records of the area—may be housed with them. Check Appendix G for a state-by-state listing of libraries and historical societies.

Appendix G

These historical societies may also sponsor conferences where you can meet others who are interested in the same area or surnames as you. Check the telephone book or the library of the city or county in which you are interested to discover if there is an historical society and to get the phone number.

Three of the largest national societies are:

- Daughters of the American Revolution
  1776 "D" Street NW
  Washington, DC 20006-5392

- The National Genealogical Society
  4527 17th Street, North
  Arlington, VA 22207-2399

- New England Historic Genealogical Society
  101 Newberry Street
  Boston, MA 02116

Want to Know More?

- P. William Filby, *A Bibliography of American County Histories,* Baltimore, MD: Genealogical Publishing, Co., 1987.

- *Directories in Print: A Descriptive Guide to Print and Non-Print Directories, Buyer's Guides, Rosters and Other Address Lists of All Kinds,* 14th ed., 2 vols., NY, Toronto, London: Gale Research, 1996.

- "PERiodical Source Index (PERSI)" in *Family History Source-Guide* on CD-ROM, available at LDS distribution centers, the Family History Library, and at Family History Centers.

Try This

❏ 1. Check the Internet for compiled sources on one of your ancestral surnames.

❏ 2. Check with family members for unpublished family histories or genealogy.

❏ 3. Contact your local library to help you locate a copy of the Periodical Source Index (PERSI). Check PERSI for periodical collections dealing with your family surnames or ancestral hometowns.

Family photos are often included in compiled sources, like this one of Mary Ann Schow and Joseph J. Porter of Escalante, Utah, on their wedding day.

CHAPTER 7

The Family History Library and Family History Centers

George's Story: The Best Films Come from Salt Lake City, Not Hollywood

The development of microfilming during World War I led to one of the most significant breakthroughs in family history work: the ability to make readable copies of written records on film that could be reproduced and viewed. The Genealogical Society of Utah was among the first to send out photographers to microfilm genealogical data on site. At last, old records that were too fragile to be moved could be microfilmed in the churches, libraries, or government offices where they were stored.

The Genealogical Society recognized the benefits immediately. Microfilm copies of important records could be made available to family history researchers through the Family History Library. Copies of the microfilm could also be given to the parish, library, or government agency who had charge of the original records, thus further preserving the original records. The original microfilms (which are stored in the Granite Mountain Vault in Little Cottonwood Canyon near Salt Lake City) would always be available to make copies from.

Microfilm changed the way we search for our ancestors. Now we have convenient access to a growing number of previously inaccessible

THIS MICROFILM HAD SUSPENSE, MYSTERY, AND QUALITY ACTORS. WE GIVE IT TWO THUMBS UP!!

genealogical records. For us, these films are much more exciting than those produced in Hollywood.

Among the Church's microfilming pioneers was James Black. A photographer, Brother Black's first microfilming assignment was in 1941 to North Carolina. Since his early efforts, hundreds of other microfilmers have gone all over the world gathering genealogical records on microfilm. Of course, it is impossible to film all of the records containing genealogical data, but through the Genealogical Society's aggressive efforts, many important records are being filmed.

Another important event that has made family history research easier took place in 1977. The Family History Department formed a committee whose goal it was to discover ways to simplify genealogical research. The committee looked at many aspects of research. Time and time again, they came back to the same conclusion: indexing records would be the most important thing they could do to simplify research.

In the twenty-three years that have passed since that decision to create more indexes, thousands of volunteers have extracted data and typed it into computers—a time-consuming, tedious process—in order to create thousands of indexes.

Today, all of us enjoy the benefits of this massive ongoing effort to microfilm and index genealogical records.

Visiting the Family History Library

If you live near Salt Lake City or if you vacation there, you will be able to visit the incredible Family History Library of The Church of Jesus Christ of Latter-day Saints at 35 North West Temple Street. An average of 2,700 people come to this library each day to search for information about their ancestors. The doors are open 82 hours per week, including many holidays. Those using this facility have access to more than two million rolls of microfilm and 700,000 microfiche. Most of these are copies of original records found worldwide in courthouses, churches, parishes, government offices, or other archives. It has been estimated that some six billion names can be found on these films. Many of these records date back as far as the 1500s, when people first began to keep records of the "common folks."

In addition to the records, the employees in the library are among the world's leading genealogists. Within their ranks are experts in genealogy for every part of the world. Together, this team of researchers has a collective family history knowledge that is impressive and at your disposal.

Visitors from all over the world come to visit this library. People from England, Denmark, and many other countries find it easier and more productive to come to Salt Lake City to search the microfilms of the records of their countries than to go to the record repository facilities located in their own countries. In France, researchers must pay to view many of the records so, in some instances, it is less expensive to travel to Salt Lake City and view all the records for no charge than to stay in France and pay the costs.

Floor Plans of the Family History Library

The main floor houses computers with FamilySearch™ and books with genealogical data for the United States and Canada. The second floor houses the complete United States Census, including available indexes and the Soundex. Computers with FamilySearch are also available on the second floor. Most of the second floor is taken up by microfilm readers, microfiche readers, and metal cabinets filled with microfilms of genealogical data for the United States and Canada. Administrative offices and cataloging facilities are on the third floor.

Family History Library Floor Plan

Main Floor—United States and Canada Books

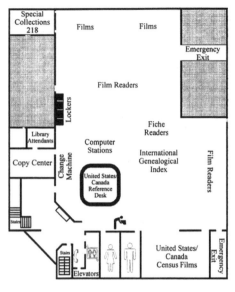

Second Floor—United States and Canada Films

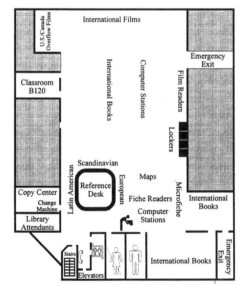

Basement 1 (B1)—Europe, Scandinavia,
Latin America, and International

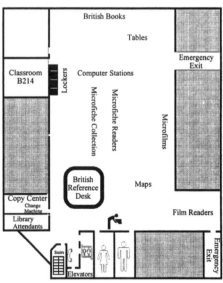

Basement 2 (B2)—British Isles

The first lower level houses books and microfilms for international genealogical records. The second lower level houses books and microfilms for the British Isles. Copy centers are available on each floor to photocopy pages from books or from microfilms.

Library Rules

1. Handle film, books, and equipment carefully.

2. Cellular phones should be used only in lobbies and other public areas.

3. Do not leave personal belongings, such as purses or laptop computers, unattended. The library is not responsible for lost or stolen items.

4. Maintain quiet so others can work. Children under twelve must be supervised by parents.

5. Food and drinks are not allowed in the FamilySearch Center or in Family History Centers. In the Family History Library, a snack room is provided on the first floor.

6. Smoking is not permitted anywhere in the building or on the grounds.

7. Do not take more than five microfilms at a time from the cabinets. Refile them when you are finished.

8. If you will be gone from your microfilm reader for more than thirty minutes, take your possessions with you so someone else can use it. You may need to find another microfilm reader when you return.

9. Use no more than five books at a time. Return them to the red shelves on either end of the bookshelves when you are finished.

10. Limit yourself to five photocopies if others are waiting.

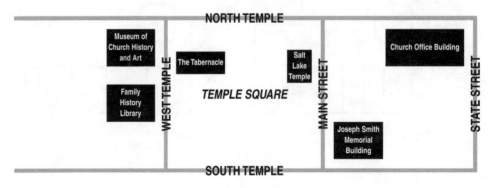

Visiting the Joseph Smith Memorial Building

While in Salt Lake City, visit the Joseph Smith Memorial Building (JSMB) located just a block east of the Family History Library.

The facilities in the JSMB are designed to help tourists and others  who are new to family history. Inside the JSMB on the main floor, hundreds of computers are located in the FamilySearch™ Center. A brief orientation to FamilySearch and the FamilySearch Center is part of each FamilySearch computer. With a trained volunteer at your side, you can use FamilySearch immediately. The probability is high that you will get at least one "hit" on Family-Search if you are a person with ancestry in the United States, the British Isles, or the Scandinavian countries.

Also located in the JSMB, on the fourth floor, are:

- More than 70,000 printed family histories inviting you to find out if one of them has the story of your family on its pages.

- A copy of the 1920 Soundex and Census.

- Eight million family group records submitted by Latter-day Saints during two different time periods: (1) Archive Section (pink tags) submitted between 1940 and 1971 and (2) Patrons Section (yellow tags) submitted between 1975 and 1984.

Welcome to Your New Office: A Family History Center

Of course, it isn't possible for most people to come to Salt Lake City to use the Family History Library. For that reason, the Church has an ongoing program to establish branches of this great library throughout the world. Currently, there are about 3,400 branches in operation. They are called Family History Centers (FHC). In these Family History Centers, you have access to FamilySearch and a trained volunteer. And through the microfilm ordering service, you also have access to copies of the vast microfilm collection of genealogical records located in Salt Lake City.

All Family History Centers are open to the public and anyone is welcome to use the facilities without charge.

They Come in All Sizes

Family History Centers vary in size, but all have a computer with FamilySearch and access to microfilms from the Family History Library in Salt Lake City. The size of the Family History Center dictates the size of its collection and the number of volunteers, microfilm readers, microfilm and microfiche, computers, and books available to you. And, as you will no doubt discover, a knowledgeable family history consultant or trained Family History Center volunteer is one of your most valuable resources.

> *All Family History Centers are open to the public and anyone is welcome to use the facilities without charge.*

Most Family History Centers are housed in a Latter-day Saint meetinghouse and have a separate entrance so they can operate independently of other activities taking place in the building. Sometimes a Family History Center is sponsored

> ☺ **If you have access to the Internet, FamilySearch is available at www.familysearch.org.**

by several stakes, so it may be larger and located in a building other than a meetinghouse. If you live in the United States or Canada, the chances are very high that a Family History Center will be within 30 to 60 minutes of where you live. If you live in a large city outside of the United States or Canada, you should still be able to find a Family History Center. If you don't have a Family History Center yet, be patient. Remember, if you have access to the Internet, FamilySearch is available at **www.familysearch.org**.

Finding a Family History Center

⭐ To locate the Family History Center nearest you, check **www. lds.org** or inquire by mail at the Family History Library, 35 North West Temple Street, Salt Lake City, UT 84150, or call (801) 240–2331.

How Do I Order a Microfilm?

One of the most powerful features provided at your Family History Center is the microfilm ordering service. You will have access to more than two million microfilms.

What	Why
Search the *Family History SourceGuide* on CD-ROM or the Family History Library Catalog (FHLC) on FamilySearch	to determine which records are available for your area of research.
A trained volunteer will be there	to help you place your order.
Once you find records that may contain information about your ancestors,	you can order them for about $3.25 per microfilm.
The microfilms must be read at your Family History Center but	can be kept anywhere from three weeks to an indefinite loan.

Want to Know More?

- Read "Early Church Information Guide," "Family History Library and Family History Centers," and "PERiodical Source Index (PERSI)" in *Family History SourceGuide* on CD-ROM available at LDS distribution centers, the Family History Library, and Family History Centers.

- Visit the Family History Center nearest you and see how they can help you.

- Review "Part 4: Ten Tens" for a quick overview of important resource materials.

Try This

❏ 1. Search *Family History SourceGuide* for information about the area where one of your grandparents or great-grandparents lived.

❏ 2. Plan a group visit to the Family History Library, Family-Search™ Center, or a Family History Center. Contact them in advance for a list of hours, services, holiday schedule, and so on.

❏ 3. If you have a current indexing project underway, you may wish to register it with the Genealogical Projects Registry, 35 North West Temple Street, Salt Lake City, UT 84150. (If you want more information about the Genealogical Registry, write to Genealogical Projects Registry, National Genealogical Society, 4527 Seventeenth Street North, Arlington, VA 22207-2399.)

❏ 4. If you would like to volunteer to help extract or index information from vital, census, or immigration records, contact the Family History Library, 35 North West Temple Street, Salt Lake City, UT 84150.

CHAPTER 8

FamilySearch™

★ **IN THIS CHAPTER**
  ✔ FamilySearch™ defined
  ✔ How to use Ancestral File
  ✔ How to make corrections on Ancestral File
  ✔ How to use International Genealogical Index (IGI)
  ✔ How to use the Family History Library Catalog (FHLC)

George's Story: Your Family History Tool Kit

Have you ever tried to fix your car engine with only one wrench? To do a job, you have to have the right tools. And have you ever noticed that most tools seem to have just the right name? For instance, *hammer* is the perfect name for a hammer. The name sounds just like what it does—ham-mer!

Well, when it comes to family history there is an incredible tool kit available to help you find your ancestors and it is perfectly named— FamilySearch! Just hearing the name of this amazing tool kit tells you what it does; it helps you search for your family.

Where can you get this great tool kit? It is available at the Family History Library, at the Joseph Smith Memorial Building (one block east of the library in Salt Lake City), and at the more than 3,400 branches of this library called Family History Centers—most of which are located in Latter-day Saint meetinghouses. All of these buildings are open to the public. FamilySearch is also available on the Internet at **www.family search.org**.

I decided to visit a Family History Center myself and try out Family-Search. When I arrived, I told the volunteer that I was writing a book for beginners and wanted her to treat me as if I had never done any of this before. We sat at a computer, and she taught me how to check Ancestral File for my ancestors. Within a few minutes, we hit the jackpot—there were Durrants and Maynes all over the place! Then she taught me how to download the information on my ancestors from Ancestral File onto a disk, which saves it automatically as a GEDCOM file. The whole process took only a few minutes and the instructions on the screen led us through each step. It was really simple. She told me that I could take the disk home and import the file into my own family history computer software program.

Of course, Ancestral File is only one part of FamilySearch, so she showed me the other great resources within FamilySearch. Then she showed me everything else that was available at the Family History Center and said she would be glad to help me whenever I came. As I left, I could tell that in her I had a friend who could help in my goal to gather my family history. I tried to imagine how I would feel if I truly were a beginner. I sensed that with an ally like her and access to FamilySearch at my Family History Center, and with my own family history software program at home, I could be successful in this exciting adventure.

I think you're going to love your Family History Center and the opportunity to use FamilySearch, too.

What Exactly Is FamilySearch™?

FamilySearch is a computer operating system containing several large genealogical databases. It is like a filing cabinet with several drawers. Each drawer contains a specific file of family history information.

FamilySearch

1. Ancestral File
2. International Genealogical Index (IGI)
3. Family History Library Catalog (FHLC)
4. Social Security Death Index
5. Military Index
6. Scottish Church Records
7. TempleReady
8. Personal Ancestral File (PAF) is sometimes a part of FamilySearch.

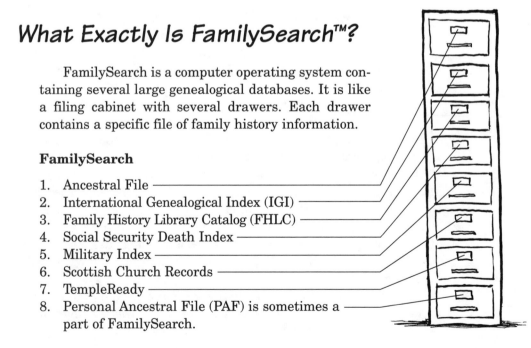

FamilySearch allows you to search quickly through millions of records and locate the names, dates, and places of births, marriages, and deaths; the names of parents, spouses, and children; and the dates of completed temple ordinances.

All information in FamilySearch can be printed on paper or copied to a computer disk by pressing F2.

FamilySearch has a tutorial that will teach you the basic computer skills needed to use it.

Ancestral File

Ancestral File is a collection of millions of names from individuals, families, and genealogical organizations throughout the world that is organized into family groups and pedigrees. For deceased individuals, Ancestral File shows the names of individuals; their family relationships and pedigrees; and the dates and places of their births, marriages, and deaths. For living individuals, Ancestral File limits the amount of information shown in order to protect the individual's right of privacy. You will find the name of the individual, their spouse, their parents, and their children, but the word "LIVING" appears where the dates and places would be. No LDS ordinance information is listed for living individuals.

▶ Using Ancestral File

The minimum information Ancestral File needs to search for a specific person is a surname and the approximate time of their birth. Of course, the full name and exact birth year allows a more narrow search.

1. F4 begins your search. Choose either similar or exact spelling.

2. Type in your ancestor's name and birth year. Press Enter or F12. This will take you to the index.

3. If the name of your ancestor does not appear, check to see if the name is misspelled or if your ancestor is listed by initials instead. Press Enter for more details that can help you determine if this is your ancestor.

4. Ancestral File also has an addendum. Check there, also, for the name of your ancestor. Pressing F9 will allow you to toggle back and forth between the main version and the addendum to Ancestral File.

5. If the name of your ancestor appears on the index, the information can be displayed as the first person on a pedigree chart (F7) or on a family group record (F6) either as a child or as a parent. You can also display your ancestor as the first person on a descendancy chart.

6. From the index, you can also press F9 for a list of submitters, a list of interested researchers, or a history of changes to the data.

▶ Contributing to Ancestral File

Once you have collected a substantial database of your family history, you may want to have it appear on the next Ancestral File update. Send your information, saved as a GEDCOM file for Ancestral File, to the Family History Department, Attention Ancestral File Contributions, 50 East North Temple Street, Salt Lake City, UT 84150.

▶ Correcting Information on Ancestral File

Because the information in Ancestral File is submitted by individuals of varying abilities and placed on Ancestral File without any changes or reviews, there are errors in the database. Everything from discrepancies in facts to typographical errors occur. When you find information on the Ancestral File that you believe is in error, submit the corrections and include the proof or source for each change you request.

The three ways to submit corrections to the Ancestral File are:

- Push the Edit F3 key while using Ancestral File. Follow the instructions.

- Use Personal Ancestral File (PAF), or another family history computer software program, to make the corrections; then submit them on disk to the Family History Department, 5th Floor, 50 East North Temple Street, Salt Lake City, UT 84150.

- Submit the corrections in writing to the above address.

It is essential that corrections are clearly identified as *changes* for the Ancestral File. If you simply submit your own correct family history for use on Ancestral File, it will not affect the incorrect information on Ancestral File. Your file will simply be added to Ancestral File as a second version of the same information. One correct version of the information should be the goal.

The information on Ancestral File is updated regularly by volunteers, but the process is slow. Do not be concerned if it takes years before your corrections appear on an Ancestral File release. Be patient. They will appear.

Oh My, the IGI!

The International Genealogical Index (IGI) is an index of some 330 million names of deceased persons for whom temple ordinances have been completed since 1970. This index has been divided into two parts: (1) the International Genealogical Index, which contains valuable genealogical information such as dates and places of births, christenings, and marriages, and names of parents, spouses, and children, as well as the sources of this information; and (2) the Ordinance Index, which lists the dates of temple ordinances performed for these deceased persons. (The Ordinance Index is not listed on **www.familysearch.org**. You must search it at your local Family History Center.)

The IGI is published by The Church of Jesus Christ of Latter-day Saints, but the names on it are not limited to Church members or their ancestors. The IGI is updated periodically. Accuracy is limited to the ability of the person entering the information into the original database and the person who recorded the information. Names are not submitted to the IGI; they appear on the IGI after temple ordinances have been performed for them.

▶ Using the IGI

This index is sorted first by region and second alphabetically by surname in two groups: Individual and Marriage.

1. F4 begins your search. Chose the region where your ancestor was born, married, or died. You may need to search all three locations if they are different.

2. Select the type of search: Individual Index (F6), Marriage Index (F7), or Parent Index (F8). The Individual Index lists an individual including name, dates, and places; the Marriage Index lists a couple and their marriage date and place; the Parent Index groups all individuals with the same parents together.

3. Type in your ancestor's name. Remember to use a woman's maiden name. Search for the information using F10 or F12.

4. The IGI has an addendum, so be sure to also search it for the name of your ancestor. To do so, press F9. This will allow you to toggle back and forth between the main version and the addendum to the IGI.

▶ Where Does the Information on the IGI Come From?

Information on the IGI comes from three major sources:

- Birth, christening, and marriage records extracted from church or civil records dating from as early as 1500 to as late as 1875.

- Records submitted by members of The Church of Jesus Christ of Latter-day Saints for temple ordinance work. Some records come from selected temple records of completed temple ordinance work.

- Some membership records of The Church of Jesus Christ of Latter-day Saints.

▶ Batch Numbers

Whenever you locate a name in the IGI, a batch number is listed with the genealogical data. This number will lead you to the original submissions, which will have the name of the person submitting the names and the sources from which the submitter gathered the information to identify each individual ancestor.

Names are submitted for temple work in batches of one hundred. Each batch is given a seven-digit batch number. Each sheet in the original batch is numbered in order from 1 to 100 in the upper right-hand corner and that number is added to the end of the seven-digit batch number after a hyphen. For example: 7773453-15.

The original sheets in the batch are microfilmed in order. Tracking the batch number is a three-step process:

❑ 1. Write down the batch number listed on the IGI next to the name of your ancestor. For example: 7773453-15.

❑ 2. Locate the appropriate microfilm for your batch number.

Batch numbers are listed in numerical order. Once you locate your batch number, copy down the call number of the microfilm that shows the original submissions in your batch.

❑ 3. Using the call number, locate the microfilm, then search for the batch number. For example, for batch number 7773453-15 you will locate batch number 7773453. Then follow the numbers in the upper right-hand corners of the original sheets until you come to your number, which in this case is 15.

The Family History Library Catalog (FHLC)

The Family History Library Catalog describes all the materials held by the Family History Library in Salt Lake City. The call number and a summary of contents are listed for more than three million books, microfilms, microfiche, maps, and other materials. Records can be searched by title, subject, surname, and locality. The catalog will guide you to family histories; birth, marriage, and death records; census records; church registers; and many other records that may contain information about your ancestors. This catalog is a part of **www.family search.org**. This information can be printed to paper or copied to a computer disk.

The Social Security Death Index

This index lists the names of several million deceased people who had social security numbers and whose deaths were reported to the Social Security Administration from 1937 to 1997. To search the Social Security Death Index, all you need is the name of your ancestor.

If your ancestor is listed in the index, you will find:

• The state where your ancestor lived when the social security number was issued. (This could be important if your ancestor is not buried in the same town where he or she died. Remains of deceased persons are sometimes returned to their home state to be buried.)

• Where the death benefit payment was sent. A spouse or child may still be living there.

• Birth and death dates.

• Last place of residence.

- Social security number. Once you know the social security number, you can write to the Social Security Administration and get more information.

The United States Social Security Index is also available on the Internet at **www.ancestry.com** and **www.everton.com**.

The Military Index

This is an index of almost 100,000 U.S. servicemen and women who died in the Korean War from 1950 to 1957 or in the Vietnam War from 1957 to 1975. Casualties included in the Vietnam War Index may have occurred in Cambodia, Communist China, Laos, North Vietnam, South Vietnam, or Thailand.

The minimum information needed to search this index is the name of your relative and if he or she served in the Korean or the Vietnam War.

If your relative is in this index, you will learn:

- Birth and death dates as well as death place.

- Home residence and country at time of enlistment.

- Rank, serial number, and branch of service.

- For the Vietnam War Index only: religious affiliation, marital status, race, and the Vietnam War Memorial plaque number.

Scottish Church Records

This index of nearly ten million names has been gathered primarily from the Church of Scotland (Presbyterian) parish registers dating from the late 1500s through 1854, with a few later entries. This includes as much as 60 percent of the population of Scotland during that time period. When available, records of other Scottish churches have been included.

The minimum information needed to search this index is the name of your ancestor. Searches are available for individuals, marriages, and parents.

If your ancestor is listed in this index, you will find his or her birth, christening, death, and marriage record. Sometimes the names of the parents are also on these records.

Always check the original source cited on the microfilm. It may contain additional information.

TempleReady

TempleReady is a computer program that helps Latter-day Saints provide temple ordinances for their ancestors. For a complete explanation of TempleReady, see Chapter 22. TempleReady is not listed on **www.familysearch.org**.

Personal Ancestral File

Personal Ancestral File (PAF) is a family history computer software program designed to help you organize your family history into family groups. It can be purchased for home use through the Salt Lake Distribution Center, 1999 West 1700 South, Salt Lake City, UT 84104-4233. As of June 1999, a Windows version of PAF can be downloaded for no charge at **www.familysearch.org**. For those who do not have a computer, the PAF program has been installed on the FamilySearch computers at Family History Centers for your use.

Want to Know More?

Several documents about FamilySearch appear on the *Family History SourceGuide* on CD-ROM. The following documents are also available at the Family History Library or Family History Centers for a minimal fee:

- For Ancestral File: "Using Ancestral File," "Contributing Information to Ancestral File," and "Correcting Information in Ancestral File."
- For the International Genealogical Index: "Using the International Genealogical Index."

Try This

❏ 1. Locate the Family History Center nearest you. Check **www.lds.org** or inquire by letter at the Family History Library, 35 North West Temple Street, Salt Lake City, UT 84150.

❏ 2. Review "Part 4: Ten Tens" for a quick overview of important resource materials.

❏ 3. Check for one of your surname lines on Ancestral File.

TempleReady, a part of FamilySearch, can help you provide temple ordinances for your ancestors, as it did for this couple at the San Diego California Temple.

Census Records

George's Story: In Their Home for a Moment in Time

I'm clueless when it comes to census records, yet after just a little instruction from my ward family history consultant, I was able to move forward. I recall finding my mother and father on the 1900 census. In my mind, I could see the census taker in American Fork, Utah, at the turn of the century riding on his horse to the home of Willard Albert "Bert" Durrant and Marinda Elizabeth Mayne and their children. I can see him coming in, sitting down, and asking all about the family. Reading the census made me feel like I was there with them in their home for that moment in time.

Opening the Door to the Past

In the United States, an official count of the population by the federal government has been taken every ten years since 1790 in order to determine the number of representatives to the U.S. Congress for each state. The resulting census is one of the most basic and valuable research tools available to the genealogist.

The person taking the census was called an **enumerator** and traveled from door to door within an assigned area. The quality of the censuses reflects the varying levels of ability and handwriting of the enumerator.

The goal of the census is to count the population for the entire county on one specific day. Even though the enumerator may not have gotten to everyone's house on that specific day, he listed the family members as if it were that day. Births or deaths near the specific date of the census were treated strictly as if the enumerator had been there on that date. So if a family member was alive on the specific date of the census, but dead two weeks later when the enumerator actually came to the house, the deceased was listed as if he or she were alive. The same was true for births. If a baby had not been born by the specific date of the census, but was alive two weeks later when the enumerator came, the baby was not listed.

Use the census early in your research. It won't give you the dates of your family's births, marriages, or deaths, but it will give you a framework of the family structure and their location at one point in time. It will also provide you with leads to other records.

Track each ancestral family through all possible censuses. Start with the census just prior to the death of your ancestor and track backward. Each census will provide new information and in the end you will have learned many important things about the family. Compare information from census to census. Are there discrepancies in ages or birth places? Comparing the census information over a fifty-year time period may help resolve differences.

Forms

Recognize that mistakes in the census often came as the result of human error. Some people really did not know exactly how old they were, a child could have given the information, or the enumerator could have written it down wrong. But for the most part, enumerators did the best they could. Often they knew the people they were counting and that added to the accuracy. Occasionally, the enumerator added a comment in the margin about someone. A few people were missed, but most were not.

Censuses are an important record for genealogists in spite of human errors, skipped pages when microfilming, and faded text. Use them often.

Census Summary 1790–1920

Census records provided varying amounts of information. The federal government decided what information would be requested in each census based on what information it needed for future planning. Generally, the more recent the census, the more information it contains. The following chart summarizes the data available in each federal census taken between 1790 and 1920:

Year	Contents and Categories	Miscellaneous Information
1790	Head of household was listed by name. Two groups of males: Free white males 16 and older; free white males under 16. Free white females. Slaves. Censuses exist for: Connecticut, Maine, Maryland, Massachusetts, New Hampshire, New York, North Carolina, Pennsylvania, Rhode Island, South Carolina, and Vermont.	The destroyed 1790 censuses are: Delaware, Georgia, Kentucky, New Jersey, and Tennessee. The Virginia census was destroyed, but reconstructed from tax lists.
1800–1810	Head of household was listed by name. Free white males: under 10, 10–16, 16–26, 26–45, 45 or older. Free white females were grouped into the same age categories. Number of other free persons (did not include Indians because they were not taxed), number of slaves, and place of residence.	The names are listed in the order the enumerator took the information. This keeps the proximity of families living near each other intact and allows you to assume that families with the same surname living in close proximity are likely part of the same family.
1820	This census was the same as 1800–1810 except it now had a category for males 16–18. Notice that this overlaps the category for males 16–26.	New information included: number of individuals not naturalized; number in agriculture, commerce, or manufacturing; number of "colored" persons; number of other persons (did not include Indians because they were not taxed).
1830–1840	These two censuses expanded the age groups into smaller divisions. The categories for the males and females were the same: under 5; 5–10; 10–15; 15–20; then in 10-year increments to 100; and over 100. The number of those who were "deaf, dumb, and blind" and the number of aliens were	The 1840 census added a column for the names and ages of military war pensioners (usually Revolutionary War), those who could not read and write, the number of insane, and

(continued)

Year	Contents and Categories	Miscellaneous Information
	listed. In addition, the number of slaves and free "colored" persons were included by age categories.	several other categories.
1850	Finally, the name and age of each person in the household was listed. In addition, the following was included: gender, color, occupation, value of real estate, birthplace, whether married within the year, attended school within the year, and whether they could read or write (if over 20). Also, anyone deaf-mute, blind, insane, "idiotic," or convicted was identified. A separate schedule for slaves was included in this census.	Be sure to study the names and ages of each person listed to discover how they were related to each other. An older resident could be a parent or sibling of the husband or wife. Alternately, some of the residents could be boarders or laborers. 💡 Remember to look at the five families on either side of your ancestors. Often brothers, married sisters, or parents lived nearby.
1860–1870	These censuses were nearly the same as the 1850 census, but added columns for the value of personal property and paupers. The 1870 census added columns for foreign-born parents. When a child was born within the year of the census, the month was included.	
1880	Similar to the 1850–1870 censuses, but added the relationship of each person to the head of the household. Also added were columns for the birthplace of the father and the mother (even though these are not always correct) and the addresses of those who lived in cities.	Only families with children under the age of 10 are listed in the 1880 Soundex because the government needed a way to determine who was eligible for Social Security benefits. *All* people, however, were

(continued)

Year	Contents and Categories	Miscellaneous Information
		listed in the actual census.
1885 State Censuses	Five states and territories took a census: Colorado, Florida, Nebraska, Dakota territory, and New Mexico territory.	These are available in the National Archives. Colorado and Nebraska are the only two that have been microfilmed.
1890	This census was almost entirely destroyed by a fire on 21 January 1921. All that survived was a part of a special census taken for Union soldiers and their widows.	It is available on the National Archives micropublication M407.
1900	The month and year of birth were added to this census. Also added were columns for the following valuable information: number of years married, how many children born to the mother, and how many children still living.	Immigrants were tracked closely. The year of entry, the number of years in the United States, and whether an individual was naturalized were all recorded.
1910	This census added a column for Civil War veterans.	Unfortunately, this important census does not have a complete Soundex, but the census is complete.
1920	The year of immigration, whether naturalized, and the year of naturalization were added to this census.	

The 1930 census will be released in 2002. Information on a deceased relative can be requested, but it will not be the full listing. To order an application for a search of the 1930 census, write to the Bureau of Census, P.O. Box 1545, Jefferson, IN 47131.

It's All on Microfilm!

Microfilms of the complete censuses 1790 through 1920 are available in the Family History Library and through the more than 3,400

Family History Centers. They are also available through the National Archives. Many state libraries will have complete sets for their state. Other libraries will have partial sets.

Luckily, Most Are Indexed

Censuses from 1790 through 1870 have indexes. Censuses from 1880 through 1920 have a special index called a Soundex, which is explained in the next section. The indexes and Soundex are created using the name of the head of the household, usually the father. If the father is deceased, then the widow is listed as the head of the household.

Most census indexes are in book form. A few are on CD-ROM. Some partial indexes are online. Check **www.genealogy.com** and **www.cyndis list.com** for possible links to online census indexes. Search by location. Also check **www.census-online.com/links/index.html** and **www. usgenweb.org** for information about transcribed census records.

Once you find your ancestor in an index, carefully write down the state, county, township, district or ward, enumeration district, house number, and page number. If possible, photocopy all the pages of the index with your surname listings.

Remember, new census indexes are constantly being added.

Human error will account for some mistakes in the indexes. If you believe your ancestor lived in a certain place but is not listed in the index, go directly to the census and search name by name.

Some States Took Censuses

Check Ann S. Lainhart, *State Census Records,* available at most libraries. Also check Loretto Dennis Szucs and Sandra Hargreaves Luebking, *The Source: A Guidebook of American Genealogy,* revised ed., Salt Lake City, UT: Ancestry, Inc., 1997. These books will help you discover if state censuses were taken in the state where your ancestors resided.

Mortality Schedules

Starting in 1850, the federal government asked the local census takers to compile a list of those who had died during the twelve months

prior to the census (1 June 1849 to 31 May 1850). These mortality schedules were taken with the 1850, 1860, 1870, and 1880 censuses, and with
a special 1885 federal census. Each schedule included the names of the
deceased, gender, age, race, whether widowed, place of birth, occupation,
the month in which the death occurred, cause of death, and number of
days ill. In 1870, the birth place of the deceased's parents was included.

For a full listing of mortality schedules and the physical location of
these important records, see Val D. Greenwood, *Researcher's Guide to
American Genealogy,* 3rd ed., Baltimore, MD: Genealogical Publishing, Co.,
1999. Also see Loretto Dennis Szucs and Sandra Hargreaves Luebking, *The
Source: A Guidebook of American Genealogy,* revised ed., Salt Lake City, UT:
Ancestry, Inc., 1997. Also see the *Family History SourceGuide.* Some of the
mortality schedules have been microfilmed and are available at the Family
History Library or through your Family History Center.

Censuses outside the United States

Starting in the 19th century, most governments began to conduct a
regular census or an official enumeration of the population in their
countries. Censuses are available for Australia, Austria, Canada, Denmark, Germany, Ireland, Italy, Norway, and the United Kingdom.

Using the Soundex

The **Soundex** is an index for the 1880, 1900, 1910, and 1920 censuses created by assigning a number to a phonetic sound of one or more
consonants to the surname. In other words, surnames that sound similar
were grouped together by the same Soundex code.
This accounts for all misspellings or purposely-
changed spellings of the same surnames.

#1	B, P, F, V
#2	C, S, K, G, J, Q, X, Z
#3	D, T
#4	L
#5	M, N
#6	R
Delete	A, E, I, O, U, W, Y, H

What's My Soundex Code?

The Soundex code for each surname consists of a letter and three numbers. For example, let's create a Soundex code for the name GAUNT.

Directions	Code
1. Write down the first letter of the surname:	G
2. Of the remaining letters, cross out A, E, I, O, U, W, Y, H:	G̶A̶U̶NT
3. Of the remaining letters, cross out any double letters:	None in this name.
4. Using the Soundex code table, assign the code number of the phonetic sound to the first three remaining letters. List the numbers to the right of the first letter:	N=5 T=3 —— G53
5. Cross out any duplicate numbers: (Duplicate numbers mean there are two or three letters in sequence with the same Soundex code number.)	None in this name.
6. If necessary, add "0"s until you have a total of three numbers to the right of the first letter:	G530

The Soundex code for GAUNT is G530, DURRANT is D653, PARKER is P626, JACKSON is J250, and BAILEY is B400.

Most libraries have a Soundex code book that lists all the surnames with their Soundex code. Ask the librarian for help. In addition, most family history computer software programs have the ability to calculate Soundex codes.

The Internet has at least three sites that will calculate the Soundex code for you.

1. National Archives and Records Administration's Soundex Machine: **www.nara.gov/genealogy/soundex/soundex.html**

2. Surname to Soundex Code: **www.rootsweb.com**

3. Surname to Soundex Converter: **www.geocities.com/Heartland/ Hills/3916/soundex.html**

The Soundex on Microfilm

Once you have determined the Soundex code for the ancestral surname, you can go to a microfilm to view the actual Soundex cards. Each name in the census has been given a Soundex code and partially extracted onto a small card. These cards were then arranged first by state, second by Soundex code, and third by given name. Because they were arranged by state and not by county, you can search for your surname by state. Once you find your surname, you will know the residence of everyone by that surname in that state. Wonderful! If you do not know which state your ancestor lived in, it is easy to check state by state until you find them.

Once you locate your family on a Soundex card, write down the exact information listed in the upper right-hand corner. The enumeration district number, page number, sheet number, and line number will assure you that you can find the exact location of your ancestor. Then you can go to the microfilmed copy of the actual census for the full description of the family. Starting with the enumeration district number (ED) will lead you to your family. Use the forms in the back of this book to help you extract the information. Copy out every detail exactly as it appears.

> **Most censuses have two sets of numbers on each page—one that is stamped on and one that is handwritten. If you don't find your ancestor on the pages listed, follow the other set of page numbers and look again.**

> **The 1880 Soundex lists only the families with children under the age of 10.**

These records are a tremendous help to researchers who know little about where their ancestors came from. You will be able to find cousins, uncles, parents, and grandparents within the same county among the Soundex cards grouped together by surname. Learn how to use this priceless tool. It is easier than it looks at first glance.

Want to Know More?

- *Century of Population Growth: From the First Census of the United States to the Twelfth 1790–1900,* reprint, Orting, WA:

Heritage Quest Press, 1989. (Original printed in Washington, DC: U.S. Government Printing Office, 1900.)

- William Thorndale and William Dollarhide, *Map Guide to the U.S. Federal Censuses, 1790–1920,* Baltimore, MD: Genealogical Publishing, Co., 1987.

- *U.S. Census Bureau's Gazetteer* available on the Internet at **www.census.gov**.

- "Research in Census Records," in Loretto Dennis Szucs and Sandra Hargreaves Luebking, *The Source: A Guidebook of American Genealogy,* revised ed., Salt Lake City, UT: Ancestry, Inc., 1997, 104–46.

Try This

❏ 1. Check **www.firstct.com/fv/uscensus.html** for a summary of the contents of each United States census and suggestions on how to use them.

❏ 2. Locate your grandparents in the 1920 census.

❏ 3. If you have an ancestor listed in the 1910 census who was a Civil War veteran, check for pension records.

❏ 4. Figure out the Soundex code for your own surname.

Starting with the 1850 census, the name, age, and birthplace of every family member is listed.

CHAPTER 10

Vital Records

★ **IN THIS CHAPTER**
- ✔ How to find courthouse addresses
- ✔ Why vital records are so important
- ✔ The forgotten divorce records

George's Story: Hidden Treasures in the County Courthouse

County courthouses are a treasure house for family historians. I remember my first visit to the Utah County courthouse with my friend Noel Barton. Once inside the beautiful marbled halls of the courthouse, I followed closely behind Noel—he was the expert, after all. Our first stop was the county clerk's office.

"Can I help you?" the clerk asked.

"Yes, I'd like to look for the marriage license of my mother and father, Willard Albert Durrant and Marinda Mayne," I said.

The clerk quickly returned with a microfilm, inserted it in the machine, and turned the handle to move the film forward. Before long, there it was! What a thrill to read:

Utah County Marriage License.
Bert Durrant of American Fork and Marinda Mayne of Alpine.
23 yrs. old, 21 yrs. old.
Lic. 12 March 1912.
Married same day at Provo . . . Judicial District Court. . . .

Then we asked for a copy of my grandparents' marriage license, too. It was there!

I ordered copies of these marriage certificates for only a few dollars. I now own copies of these documents, which are sacred to me.

Next we visited the recorder's office and found the records of the land my parents and grandparents owned. That, too, was amazingly interesting to me. Just seeing these marriage certificates and deeds gave me quite a case of family history fever.

You'll want to go to the courthouses where your people once stood to get the license to wed or to buy land.

After we left the courthouse, Noel and I also visited the schools in which I attended class, the mortuary that saw the burial of three generations of my ancestors, the state penitentiary where twice my great-grandfather had a room, and the state archives. Is it any wonder why those who do family history find it so exciting and fun?

Searching Vital Records

Vital records are government documents that record the most basic events in people's lives. They are of vital importance to the genealogist. Not only do they contain the date and place of an event, but relationships are often established because of these records. They are considered primary sources because they were created at the time of the event.

Most governments keep records of births, marriages, and deaths. They are listed under "Vital Records" in the United States and Canada. For other countries, they are listed under **"Civil Registration."** Church records, cemetery records, and newspapers may also carry these important dates. They are not government records, but church records are also considered a primary source while cemetery records and newspapers are considered secondary sources.

Vital records are often kept in chronological order. Sometimes they are in chronological order within alphabetical order.

Ch. 4,
Appendix
C

Because vital records are such an important source, be sure to document the location of the records and the book, page, and record numbers. Record the information slowly and carefully. Print clearly and large so that others can relocate these records, if needed.

Sometimes when the page for a particular letter of the alphabet is filled, the clerk goes to the end of the book and starts another page for that letter. Watch for that if your surname starts with a common letter such as "S."

Original vs. Transcript

Original vital records may be kept at the county courthouse, state archives, or health department. Transcripts of vital records may be kept in historical society or family history libraries. Try to use the original records, if possible. Clues may appear when you can see the original records in relationship to other records, such as unusual notes, or other names, places, or relationships associated with the record. Transcripts, of course, still have value, but be aware that mistakes can be made when copying records. When you use a transcript, include that fact in the citation of your source.

Some Web sites are beginning to provide transcripts of vital records. Check **www.usgenweb.org** and **www.worldgenweb.org**.

Birth Records

Birth records will provide the name of the baby, date and place of birth, and the name of the mother and the father. Other information that may be included: birthplace of the parents, ages of the parents, occupation, address at the time of the birth, and whether the mother had given birth before. Some records may include the marriage date of

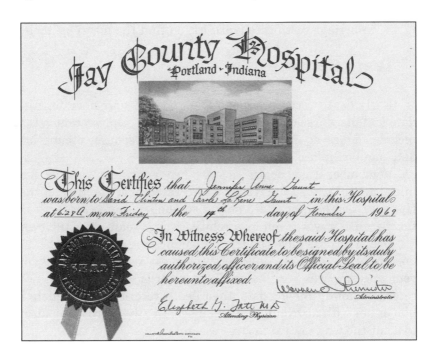

Don't assume that a marriage took place because you find a marriage bond, banns, or license. People changed their minds back then, too.

the parents and the names and ages of previous children, but that is rare. In some countries, the names of the grandparents may also be recorded.

Marriage Records

Marriage records provide the names of the bride and the groom, as well as the date and place of the marriage. They often include the ages of the bride and groom. If either are under age, then the signature of the parent giving permission for the marriage will be on the license. Other information may include the birthplaces of the bride and groom, names of witnesses, occupation, parents' names and birthplaces, and previous marriages. These records may be indexed under the groom's name or there may be two indexes—one for the grooms and one for the brides.

Four records associated with marriage are:

- Marriage bonds (financial guarantee of intent)
- Marriage banns (intent to marry)
- Marriage license (permission to marry)
- Marriage certificate (verification that the marriage took place)

Death Records

Early death records provide the name of your ancestor, the death date and place, residence, and cause of death. More recent records also include names of the parents, name of the spouse, occupation, birth date and birthplace of the deceased.

Remember that death records are a primary source for death information because the record was created near the time of the event. However, death records are only a secondary source for birth information because it was given by a relative many years after the event.

Death records have the advantage of being created at the end of an ancestor's life and are therefore the most recent record available. If your ancestor was born before birth records were kept and no church record or family Bible exists, then death records can uniquely identify him or her with an event date and place. Death records may also be able to point the way toward future research.

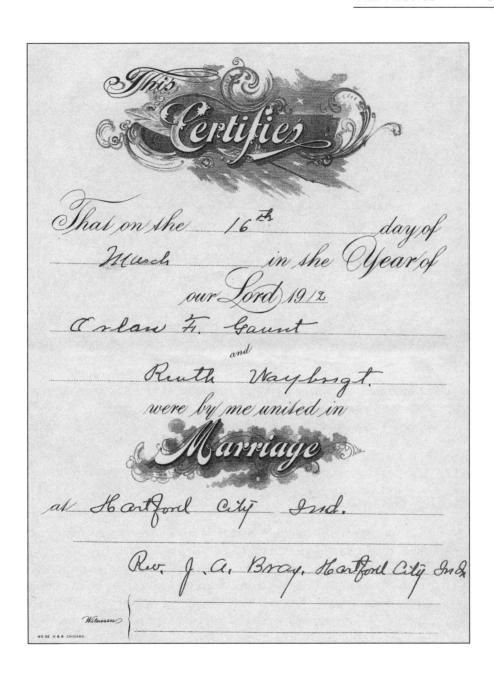

This Certifies

That on the 16th day of March in the Year of our Lord 1912 Orlan F. Gaunt and Ruth Waybright were by me united in Marriage at Hartford City Ind.

Rev. J. A. Bray, Hartford City Ind.

Witnesses

NO 35 N & B CHICAGO.

```
                    JAY COUNTY BOARD OF HEALTH
                          PORTLAND, INDIANA
                    CERTIFICATE OF DEATH
    This Certifies, that according to the records of the Jay County Board of Health Department
              Name _____Jacob Gaunt_____
            October  6, 1908                    Dunkirk, Ind    Jay County
    Died on_____ at ____ C.S.T. at _____
           [month]   [day]  [year]       [time]     'street, hospital or rural'
```

| SEX M | COLOR OR RACE White | MARRIED, NEVER MARRIED WIDOWED, DIVORCED [specify] | AGE [In years] 81 | Mo. 8 | Days 6 | Hours Born in 1821 | Min. |

```
    Primary cause of death given was _____Cancer_____
        son of Joseph Gaunt and Phobæ Swain Gaunt. He was bron in Ohio
    --------------------Parents in Delware (State)-----------------------------------
    Certified by_____F. M. Replogle M.D/___Dunkirk, Ind.
              Physician or Coroner                     Address
    Place of burial or removal ____Center_____Greene Twp. Jay County_____
                              Cemetery                   Address
    Date of burial__no date___G. W. Cook____no address___ ____
                          Funeral Director      Address
    Record was filed_no date_____ Book No. _D CH 5 Page No. _____1_____
                   Date
                                            E. M. Gillune    M.D
        SEAL                                  Local Health Officer
                              Issued on _July 9,_____19_76_
```

Divorce Records

Divorce records provide the name and age of the petitioners, birth-place, address, occupations, names and ages of children, property, and grounds for divorce. These records are not always readily available but can provide important information. If you know your ancestors divorced, and you are having a hard time finding information about them, divorce records may be your answer.

State or County?

By the turn of the century, states provided for the registration of vital statistics. Check by state first.

Counties often kept vital records long before the states required it. Generally speaking, check with the county clerk in the county where your ancestors resided after you have checked state records.

In order to determine when vital records started in the county and in the state of your ancestor's home, check one of the following sources:

- *The Handybook for Genealogists*
- *Ancestry's Red Book*
- Thomas Kemp's *International Vital Records Handbook*. This book includes a copy of the order form that you can photocopy and use when requesting records.

- For an online list of vital record repositories in each state, check the National Center for Health Statistics at **www.cdc.gov/ nchs/**.

Finding the County Courthouse Address

Three sources for the addresses of county courthouses are:

- *The Handybook for Genealogists*
- *Ancestry's Red Book*
- **www.usgenweb.org** Click on state, and then county. The address will appear.

Sample Letter

When writing to a county clerk, keep your requests separate—one request per letter—unless you know that they are going to the same office. For example, vital records and probates are kept in different offices so they require different letters. However, a request for two or three marriage records would go the same office and can go in one letter.

> **Telephone the courthouse before you write and ask the cost for the service and for a copy of the record. Enclose a money order or a check for the total amount.**

> (Date)
> Dear Friends,
> I'm seeking a marriage certificate for (name of groom here) and (name of bride here). I believe they were married in your county in about (year).
> Would you please check for their marriage certificate and, if you find one, send me a copy? I have enclosed a (check or money order, list which one) to cover the cost, and a self-addressed, stamped envelope for mailing.
> Thank you for this service.
> Sincerely,
> (Your name and address here.)

Want to Know More?

- *The Handybook for Genealogists,* 8th ed., Logan, UT: Everton Publishers, Inc., 1991.

- Alice Eicholz, Ph.D., *Ancestry's Red Book,* Salt Lake City, UT: Ancestry, Inc., 1992.

- *Where to Write for Vital Records: Birth, Death, Marriage, and Divorce,* No. [PHS] 87–1142, Superintendent of Documents, U.S. Government Printing Office, Washington, DC 20402.

- Elizabeth Petty Bentley, *The Genealogist's Address Book,* 3rd ed., Baltimore, MD: Genealogical Publishing, Co., 1995.

- "Parish and Vital Records" in *Family History SourceGuide* on CD-ROM, available at LDS distribution centers, the Family History Library, and Family History Centers.

- Thomas Jay Kemp, *International Vital Records Handbook,* 3rd ed., Baltimore, MD: Genealogical Publishing, Co., 1994.

- "Where to Write for Vital Records," in Loretto Dennis Szucs and Sandra Hargreaves Luebking, *The Source: A Guidebook of American Genealogy,* revised ed., Salt Lake City, UT: Ancestry, Inc., 1997, 736–56.

Try This

❏ As you can afford it, send for the appropriate birth, marriage, and death records for you, your children, brothers, sisters, and parents.

Cemeteries

George's Story: She Called Me Georgie Porgy

Although I lived in American Fork, Utah, I had never been to the local cemetery except on Memorial Day to take a bouquet of purple irises to my parent's graves. I knew all the Durrants in town, but with my new interest in family history, I decided it was time to get better acquainted with the Durrants in the cemetery.

Since my brother Stewart was older and knew the cemetery better than I did, I asked him to come with me. He agreed, saying that being 78 years old, he now had more friends up in the cemetery than he did down in town. And so we went.

Stewart found the resting place of our family before I did. He exclaimed, "Here they are!" The sun was on our backs as we stood looking down at the gravesites of our beloved mother and father. For a few seconds we were silent. Then I read the tombstone inscriptions aloud. Doing so caused me to hesitate as a deep sense of love and appreciation came into my heart. I looked at Stewart and sensed that he felt the same as I did.

I copied all the words and dates inscribed on the tombstones onto a notepad. Stewart took pictures of them. As we stood there talking about Mom and Dad, it almost seemed like they were there with us. All sorts of sweet memories of days gone by started flowing into my mind. I didn't want to leave, but there were other Durrants beckoning us to visit them.

After a short walk, Stewart declared, "Here's one we are looking for."

Sure enough, it was my grandfather's and grandmother's gravestone. I had never known my grandfather Durrant because he died before I was born. However, I had studied his life, and I loved him. I could remember Grandma. She called me Georgie Porgy. If others called me that I got mad, but I didn't get mad at her. I had said the prayer at her funeral, and I remembered crying when I did. I sure did love her and warm emotions came flooding back into my heart as I read her name and her birth and death dates out loud. What a thrill it was to be there with them.

Next, we visited the cemetery in Alpine, some six miles north of American Fork, where my maternal grandparents were buried. Part of the Alpine cemetery is located on a beautiful little hill. We drove up the winding road and from the top we could see a beautiful view in every direction.

Up there, among the sixty or so burial sites, we found the graves of two little girls, each of whom had died within a week of her birth. They were buried there side by side on the brink of the hill. These little ones were my mother's two baby sisters. I cannot ever visit them without feeling both joy and sorrow—sorrow because of the sadness their deaths brought to my mother and grandmother, and joy because I know that they still live.

We left the hill and went down into the lower portion of the cemetery. Soon we stood at the graves of Grandmother and Grandfather Mayne—my mother's parents. Each of them had died before I was born, but I felt like I knew them personally because I had read about them. I love them because I have felt their influence in my life. Again reading the tombstone inscriptions aloud and thinking of them brought me the same deep sense of love and appreciation that I had felt earlier when I stood at the gravesites of my Durrant grandparents. These cemeteries have become holy places to me.

Finding Cemeteries

Large, well-maintained cemeteries are easy to find, but not all cemeteries fall into that category. Cemeteries in small towns sometimes fall into disrepair when finances run out. Family cemeteries on rural farmland are usually abandoned when the last descendants die or move away. Some cemeteries are even moved when public works projects, such as dams or highways, get the right-of-way.

Check the listings under "cemeteries" in the yellow pages of the telephone book to locate the cemeteries in your area. To discover the location of cemeteries no longer in use, check your local library. Look for topographical maps, which may show the locations of all cemeteries in your area. County histories may include cemetery information.

The Internet can help identify the location of topographical maps, county histories, cemetery records, and so on.

The Family History Library Catalog (FHLC) is one of the best sources and is available through **www.familysearch.org** or at your Family History Center. These books and microfilms often have the address of the cemetery as well as the names and dates of those buried there.

Who Owns the Cemetery?

Traditionally, cemeteries are owned and maintained by one of the following groups:

Group	Maintenance	Available Records
Government	Uses taxpayer money.	Records are open to the public and usually found at the courthouse, city hall, or in an office on the cemetery grounds.
Business	Maintains private cemeteries or memorial parks for profit.	Their records are private, but most owners are willing to share the information.
Family	Burial plots on family farmland are often the most difficult to find. If they were abandoned long ago, all visible signs of the cemetery may be gone.	If records exist, they may be in the library, with the historical society, or in the home of the local sexton.

(continued)

Group	Maintenance	Available Records
Church	Cemeteries are generally located near the church, but some may be located elsewhere.	Records may be at the local church, at a regional church archive, or in a university collection. They could be with the current minister or have been taken by a previous minister or clerk.
Fraternal organizations, such as the International Order of Odd Fellows (I.O.O.F.)	They may have a section within or adjoining an existing cemetery.	

Sexton's Records

A **sexton** is the person whose job it is to maintain the cemetery and prepare for burials. If the cemetery is small, the sexton may do everything from digging the graves to keeping the records. Likely, the records will be at his home. Ask around town, at the courthouse, historical society, or library to find out the name of the sexton. If he has lived in the town for a long time, he becomes a valuable resource to you as he will probably know quite a bit about your family's history.

If the cemetery is large, then the sexton's name and telephone number should be listed in the telephone book or on a sign at the cemetery.

Sexton's records should include burial registers, **plats** (a map of the cemetery showing the locations of each grave and who owns it), **plots** (a card with the name of the plot owner, date of purchase, and names and dates of those buried there), and deeds for the plots. They will also tell you if more than one person is buried in a plot (common if a mother and infant die in childbirth, or if twins or triplets all die at birth), and if a body has ever been exhumed and moved to another cemetery or plot. You may discover the names of ancestors buried in the cemetery without a marker. If a married daughter buys the burial plots for her parents, you could discover her married name.

Check with funeral homes and morticians. Many recognize that they possess important genealogical records and carefully preserve them.

Be Prepared

Even if you know the death dates and burial places of your ancestors, visiting the cemetery can yield important finds. Be prepared before you go. Compile a list of those you know are buried there. Ask other family members to tell you exactly where the graves are located, especially if the cemetery is large. Remember that over the generations, family members will likely be buried in several groups throughout the cemetery.

Take several photographs of each marker. Also take photographs of groupings of markers. Remember to take several general shots of the cemetery from several different views. See Chapter 16 for a list of basic camera equipment.

Ch. 16

Be sure you have a pen and paper. Write down every detail from the tombstones. Print slowly and clearly and proofread everything. Write using large letters. Use plenty of paper and leave space so that your work is easy to read.

Make a drawing of the area where your family is buried and label the location of each grave with the name of the person buried there. Indicate the location of the family graves on an overall sketch of the cemetery.

Visit the cemetery on Memorial Day, if possible. Hopefully you will meet other family members who have come to remember your common ancestors.

Tombstones—More than Just Names and Dates

Tombstones may contain a wealth of genealogical information. They can provide:

- Full names, birth dates, and death dates.

- Often, the only reminder of children who died as infants. The marker may include the names of the parents, but if it doesn't you may still be able to determine who the parents are by the location of the graves. Sometimes these children carry an unusual given name that will help tie them to a family.

- A mark of military service or a fraternal organization, which may suggest other records to check.

- Clues to help determine relationships of family members. Take some time to look around and note the proximity of graves to each other. Are there several children who died on the same day or within the same week? It could indicate a diphtheria epidemic. Was one of your ancestors among those who died?

- These epitaphs often suggest relationships, such as "mother," "loving son," or "Phoebe, wife of Jacob Gaunt." They also add insight into your ancestors and, sometimes, humor to your visit to the cemetery.

Abandoned Cemeteries

Dress appropriately when visiting an abandoned cemetery. Wear long sleeves and long pants to protect against poison oak, poison ivy, or bug bites. Wear boots or sturdy shoes. An abandoned cemetery is a welcome home to chiggers, ticks, snakes, and mice. High grass may be filled with burrs. The ground could be uneven with fallen tombstones as added obstacles. Use caution if the cemetery is in an isolated area.

Some markers may be difficult or impossible to read because they have broken off, fallen down, or sunk into the ground. Small markers may be under weeds and tall grass. Dirt or lichen may cover the names and dates. If the stones are dark, patting white talc or chalk over a dry stone with an eraser can make the letters and numbers easier to read. Come prepared with clippers, a stiff plastic brush, lots of rags, and clean water. Clean the stones gently. Resist the temptation to take a rubbing off the tombstone. Pictures will give you a better visual record without harming the stone.

It is heartbreaking to see the state of some cemeteries—inscriptions worn smooth by the weather, and markers painted or flipped over by vandals. Tombstones may be stacked on top of each other under a tree or in a corner of the cemetery, but don't try to move them. They are usually too heavy. Instead, photograph and record what you can.

Don't stay away because of these things. Any difficulties will fade in importance as you touch the aged tombstone of your great-great-grandmother or see the small marker of infant children of whom you had no record.

Want to Know More?

- To locate funeral directors and morticians nationwide, check your local library or funeral home for the following directories: (1) *National Yellow Book of Funeral Directors,* Youngstown, OH: NOMIS Publications and (2) *National Directory of Morticians,* Youngstown, OH: National Directory of Morticians. Both are published annually.

- Read Appendix E on photography.

Try This

- ❑ 1. Take your children to visit the graves of their ancestors. Read the inscriptions on the markers out loud. Tell the children all you know of these family members. If your ancestors' burial sites are far from where you live, plan a family vacation to visit them. It will be an unforgettable experience for you and for your children.

- ❑ 2. Check the Family History Library Catalog (FHLC) on FamilySearch™ to see what cemetery records in your geographic area are available on microfilm.

Church Records

George's Story: Film #596,744

I'll never forget the day nearly twenty years ago when my friend Noel Barton took me to the Family History Library in Salt Lake City and helped me find my Durrants in the Hertfordshire, England, parish records.

Back then, we checked the card catalog, though today we'd check the Family History Library Catalog on FamilySearch™ (isn't technology wonderful!), and then Noel led me to row after row of metal file cabinets containing microfilms. He searched the many numbers on the cabinets.

"What is the exact number?" he asked.

"It's 596,744," I replied, pleased that I was helping.

Noel plucked out one of the hundreds of little white boxes. On the other side of the library we found a microfilm reader that was unoccupied. Noel gave me the box.

I held the roll of microfilm in my hand, eventually threaded it onto the microfilm reader, and sat down to search the record. But alas, to my disappointment, the record was upside down. For a moment I thought I was going to have to stand on my head to read it. No, just kidding. I had just loaded the film wrong. We all do that. Anyway, threading the reader was the most intimidating part of the trip for me. Noel kindly gave me a few instructions (and so will the workers at the library), and soon the film was in the machine. We flipped on the light and turned the handle until we found the words, "Bishop's Transcript, 1604 to 1850, Bovingdon, Hertfordshire, England."

As we scrolled through the records, we could see that the original pages were old and decayed. Some of them seemed to be unreadable.

I almost panicked when I saw the condition of the record get worse and worse as we searched the microfilm for the year we needed. Then I had a most unforgettable thrill. "There!" I shouted. "Noel, that's it! That's it!"

Before my eyes lay the photograph of a partially decayed page. The borders of the original document were gone, but the information was legible: "ohn, son of William and Mary Durrant of Bovingdon, father a laborer." The "J" was missing, but this was my John.

"Noel, this is one of the greatest experiences of my life," I said. "This is a photo of the actual record. Look at the handwriting of the minister."

"Let's carefully copy down what it says, exactly as it is on the film," Noel said. "Then we can look for other members of the family."

For the next few minutes I was in a different world. We found the birth records of many Durrants. Somehow I usually spotted them before Noel did. The name Durrant seemed to jump right out at me.

What a thrill! My heart was filled with love for these people to whom I suddenly felt connected as I read the records of their births.

Where Did My Ancestors Go to Church?

Check the following sources to discover the religion of your ancestors:

- Family tradition.

- County histories or compiled histories.

- Obituaries.

- Marriage records, which may indicate the name of a pastor who performed the ceremony and provide a clue to the couple's religion.

- Time period and location can be a clue. Religion provides a strong bond among people. Traditionally people of the same religion not only worshipped together, but they migrated in groups. If a religious family moved alone, they sought out the same religion in their new place of residence. Explore the local history of the time period and area where your ancestors lived. Determine the available and dominant religions. Which church was closest to where your ancestors lived? If your ancestors are buried in a cemetery next to a church, then likely that is the church they attended.

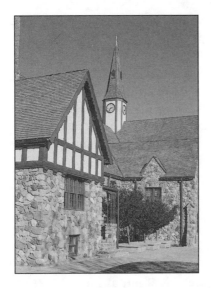

- Nationality can also be a clue to the religion of immigrants. Many countries had an official or dominant religion. For example: Germany—Lutheran; England—Church of England; Mexico and South America—Catholic, and so on. Your ancestry may follow that pattern.

What Will I Find in Church Records?

Church records contain christenings, baptisms, confirmations, marriages, and burials. Here you will find names, dates, relationships, and the location where the parents lived. Sponsors in christening records and witnesses at marriages were often family members.

Sources of Records for Major Religions

Church records are among the most difficult to locate. Usually maintained by the minister and housed at the church or the minister's home, the records often succumbed to fire, moisture, rodents, insects, or time. Some records became lost when ministers moved and took the records with them.

Some records did make their way into the central repository of that particular religion. The records of your family may be there. Check with the libraries and archives of the religion favored by your ancestors. Most of these libraries or archives are open on a limited basis, so call ahead and get their schedule.

An extensive listing of record repositories for major religions appears in *The Source: A Guidebook of American Genealogy* by Loretto Dennis Szucs and Sandra Hargreaves Luebking. Many are listed in Elizabeth Petty Bentley's *The Genealogist's Address Book,* pages 457–77. Check with your reference librarian for these books or for other known sources.

The Family History Library Catalog (FHLC) on FamilySearch is an excellent source to discover which church records are available for the area and time period of your ancestors. Check by locality and also by religion. The FHLC on FamilySearch is available at the Family History Library in Salt Lake City, Utah, and its 3,400 branches called Family History Centers. It is also on the Internet at **www.familysearch.org**.

Microfilm copies of these records are easily accessible through Family History Centers.

Web Sites

Many religious groups maintain a Web site that may provide leads to records repositories as well as information about that religion.

- Anabaptists: **www.gty.org/~phil/anabapt.htm**
- Catholic: **www.onr.com/user/cat/**
- The Church of Jesus Christ of Latter-day Saints: **www.lds.org** and **www.familysearch.org**
- Huguenot: **www.rootsweb.com/~ote/hugres.htm**
- Hutterite: **feefhs.org**
- Lutheran: **www.aal.org/lutheran_roots/**
- Jewish: **www.jewishgen.org**
- Mennonite: **www.ristenbatt.com/genealogy/mennonit.htm**
- Methodist: **rylibweb.man.ac.uk**
- Moravian Church: **www.moravian.org/**
- Quaker: **www.rootsweb.com/~quakers**
- United Church of Canada Archives: **www.library.utoronto.ca/utarms/index.html**

Remembering Grandparents

Some religions encouraged members to follow a specific pattern when naming their children, usually for deceased relatives in a specific order. This can be helpful if you know that your ancestors followed a naming pattern suggested by their church.

1. Some named the first boy for his maternal grandfather and the first girl for her paternal grandmother.

2. Some named the first boy for his paternal grandfather and the first girl for her maternal grandmother.

Want to Know More?

- Elizabeth Petty Bentley, *The Genealogist's Address Book,* 3rd ed., Baltimore, MD: Genealogical Publishing Co., 457–77.

- Loretto Dennis Szucs and Sandra Hargreaves Luebking, *The Source: A Guidebook of American Genealogy,* revised ed., Salt Lake City, UT: Ancestry, Inc., 1997.

Try This

❏ 1. Choose an ancestor whose religion you know. Check the Family History Library Catalog (FHLC) for the church records available for the time period and area where that ancestor lived. Take a look at the records.

❏ 2. If your ancestor is buried in a cemetery near a church, visit both. Take your camera, pedigree charts, and family group records. Talk with the minister, if possible. He may have or know of the location of church records.

CHAPTER 13

Less-Used Government Records

George's Story: "One Cow and One Bay Mare"

My co-author LaRene Gaunt is fascinated with wills and the intimate glimpse they give into family relationships. In handwritten wills, the clerk's penmanship is often spidery but each sentence is straight and even. The faded words, filled with flourishing capital letters, all say something similar in the first few lines: "In the name of the benevolent Father of all, I Joseph Gaunt of Jay Co. and state of Indiana being of sound mind and memory do make and publish this my last will and testament as follows viz Item 1 I direct that after my decease that my remains be decently interred and all my funeral expenses be paid. Item 2 I direct that all my just debts be paid."

After that, the words open a window into the feelings—good and bad—among family members as well as into the family's economic situation. The above Joseph Gaunt, a widower, divided his land equally four ways among his four living children, but he left personal items to his grandchildren: "My bureau" to Phebe, "My bed and bedding" to Mary Emily, and "Twelve dollars" to Harry S.

My husband's fourth great-grandfather, Emanuel Coble, has nearly two pages praising his wife Rachel and making arrangements for his youngest son, Henry, to care for her. He left her "all my household good, and kitchen furniture and one cow and one Bay mare, the one we generally drive in the carriage and the carriage and harness." All seems well in the three-page will until the last paragraph when Emanuel indicates that one of his daughters should "receive fifty dollars more than my other heirs," and another heir should "receive fifty dollars less." I wonder why?

A poignant story surrounds the probate of my second great-grandfather Levi Hartman dated July 1865. Levi, age 38, and his brother, Joseph, age 37, signed up with the Union troops and went to war. On 27 January 1865, Levi died on Hilton Head Island, South Carolina. Four months later, on 30 May 1865, Joseph died in Nashville, Tennessee. Levi left a widow, Jemima, and six children, ages 15 to 1; Joseph left a widow, Catherine, and five children, ages 12 to 5. The two Hartman families lived near each other in Knox Township, Jay County, Indiana. What would they do? The probate of "Levi S. Hartman, dec'd" says that he "died intestate" and that the personal assets of the estate amounted to about $540, while the debts of the estate amounted to $1,500, showing an "insufficiency" of $960. The probate also notes the 80 acres of land in Knox Township, Jay County, Indiana, was worth $1,500. After identifying Levi's widow and each of his children by name and age, the probate simply states: "Sell said land at public sale."

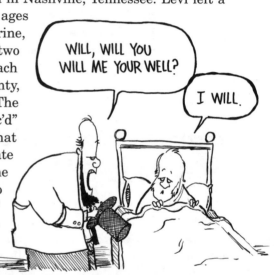

I have often wondered what happened to these two widows and the 11 children left fatherless because of the Civil War. A search of the land records would tell me if Levi's land was sold, and a look at the 1870 census for Knox Township, Jay County, Indiana, would tell me if they moved in with aging parents, but I will always wonder how these two families managed after that tragic year of 1865.

The Reasons Vary

There are some records that contain genealogical information, but are not often searched. The reasons vary. Some records yield inconsistent family history information, other records are difficult to locate and search, and still other records, such as wills, exist for only part of the population. Here we will briefly discuss three less-used sources: wills and probates, land records, and tax records. We suggest that beginners wait until they have some experience before they search these records.

Wills and Probates

Records created at the time of an adult parent's death, like wills or probates, are filled with important genealogical information, especially if he or she had property. They primarily contain the names of family members with their relationships. They also contain a listing of the deceased's possessions at the time of his or her death.

When a person dies and does not leave a will it is called **"intestate,"** and the court appoints an administrator to handle the distribution of property. When a person dies and leaves a will it is called **"testate,"** and an executor handles the distribution of property.

Either way, if the deceased has enough property, then the distribution of the property will show up in courthouse records.

Intestate

During the time of our ancestors, most people died without a will unless they had a lot of property. When this happened, a family member usually went to the courthouse and asked to administer the estate of the deceased. All of the papers generated by this process were compiled into a packet called an administration packet. These packets were given a file number but they were not always indexed.

Testate

The process of submitting a will to the proper legal authorities is known as probate. Once proved, the will is transcribed into a will book, which is kept in the courthouse, and each book usually has its own index. The original will and all the other papers are collected into a packet called a probate packet and are filed in the courthouse. Each probate packet has a file number and is indexed.

When you find a probate packet for one of your ancestors, it is important to photocopy each paper in it. Studying the papers in the probate packet may yield important clues about this family. In addition, it is important to locate the will in the will book and abstract it.

Ten Steps for Abstracting a Will

- ❑ 1. Write down the name of the testator (the person making the will) exactly as it is written.

- ❑ 2. List the residence and occupation of the testator. Include the burial place, if listed.

- ❑ 3. List all the bequests for real and for personal property. Write down all names exactly as they appear.

- ❑ 4. Include any references to relationships, such as "my daughter, Jane," or "my uncle." Also include any noteworthy information, such as "land I received from my father."

- ❑ 5. List the names of the executors or administrators.

- ❑ 6. Note any provisions for orphan children, mention of a specific religion, or references to apprenticeship of children.

- ❑ 7. Note the signatures. Record the exact spelling of the name. Mention if the signature is simply a mark.

- ❑ 8. Record the names of the witnesses exactly as they appear. Include the residences of the witnesses, if listed.

- ❑ 9. Record the date of the will and the date the will was probated in court.

- ❑ 10. Document the will. Include the county, state, book, page, and so on. Note if it is the original will or a clerk's transcribed copy.

Guardianship

- • When the court appoints a guardian for a minor, the records show up in the probate office of the county courthouse.

- • A minor refers to one who has not reached legal age or "the age of majority." This age differs from state to state and within different time periods, but it is usually 21 for a male and 18 for a female.

> 🚫 The term "infant" in guardianship records refers to any child who had not reached the age of majority.

- Children over 14 could choose their own guardian.

- Guardianship records may show that a minor child inherited property from his or her deceased mother. Review these papers carefully. They may reveal the mother's maiden name.

Land Records—Deeds

Land was a measure of success among our ancestors—the more you owned, the more successful you were. The promise of land was usually the motivation for emigration to a new country or, for our American ancestors, motivation to move west.

How do you discover if your ancestors owned land? Census records can help; the 1850, 1860, and 1870 censuses listed the value of real estate. Tax records can also help. If your ancestor paid tax on real property, it means he had land. If your ancestor paid tax only on personal property, it means he did not have land.

Land records provide the means to track the migration patterns of our ancestors, especially prior to the 1790 census. However, searching land records can be complicated and difficult. There are multiple levels of government involved in keeping land records and many kinds of land transfers and records generated. The following is a brief description of the most common type of land records: **deeds**.

A deed is a legal document proving the transfer of land. These records are the most accessible land record available to the beginning researcher. To find local land records for your ancestors, you need to have an idea of where they lived and know something about the history of the area.

Most deeds were kept on the county level and many have been microfilmed and are available in the Family History Library and its 3,400 branches, called Family History Centers. Check the Family History Library Catalog (FHLC) on FamilySearch™ at the Family History Library, at a Family History Center, or at **www.familysearch.org** to see if the deed you need has been microfilmed. The FHLC remains one of your best sources for locating the most accessible land records available in the area where your ancestors resided.

When you want to visit in person or write to a county courthouse, check the following sources for the addresses of county courthouses:

- *The Handybook for Genealogists,* 8th ed., Logan, UT: Everton Publishers, Inc., 1991.

- *Ancestry's Red Book,* Salt Lake City, UT: Ancestry, Inc., 1992.

- **www.usgenweb.org** Click on state, then county, and then the address will be listed.

Deeds are usually filed in chronological order and indexed by grantee (buyer) and grantor (seller). Always check both indexes. However, there were other indexing systems used in the past which seem illogical and unfamiliar to us today. Ask for help if you need to understand how to read the index.

Bring a magnifying glass to help read difficult handwriting.

Deeds provide the name of the grantee and grantor, a description of the land (which often includes the names of the owners of adjoining property), and the date of sale. Sometimes these records will indicate where your ancestor lived before purchasing this land, the name of his spouse, children, grandchildren, parents, or siblings.

When you locate a land record for your ancestor, be sure to make an abstract of it.

Ten Steps for Abstracting a Deed

❑ 1. Identify the type of deed, such as gift, trust deed, warrantee deed, and so on.

❑ 2. List the exact names of the grantors (the ones selling the land) and the grantees (the ones buying the land). Also include their residences and occupations, if listed.

❑ 3. Locate the "consideration" or amount paid, or reason for transfer of ownership.

❑ 4. Describe the boundaries of the property and include the names of any adjoining property owners. List the number of acres, if mentioned.

❑ 5. Include any distinguishing comments that would provide new information, such as "land I received from my father."

❑ 6. Note the signatures. Record the exact spelling of the name. Mention if the signature is simply a mark.

❑ 7. Record the names of the witnesses exactly as they appeared.

❑ 8. Record the name of the person who acknowledged the deed in court. Include the dower release, if listed.

❏ 9. Record the date and place the deed was acknowledged in court. Also include the date of the deed and the date the deed was recorded.

❏ 10. Document the deed. Include the county, state, volume, page, and so on.

There are many other types of land records, usually involving the transfer of title from some level of government to an individual. They are often more difficult to use. Information about them may be found in: *Family History SourceGuide* on CD-ROM, available at LDS distribution centers, the Family History Library, or Family History Centers; Val D. Greenwood's *The Researcher's Guide to American Genealogy;* Loretto Dennis Szucs and Sandra Hargreaves Luebking, *The Source: A Guidebook of American Genealogy; Genealogical and Biographical Research: A Select Catalog of National Archives Microfilm Publication;* or in a number of other such resource references. You may want to consider hiring a professional genealogist to help you with land records.

Tax Records

Tax records are among the earliest records available. In the absence of other records, the value of tax records increases. They place your ancestor in a specific place at a specific time. They also reflect his economic status. Since tax rolls are compiled each year, it is best to use them as a series instead of as a single event. It is possible to track the length of time your ancestor lived in a particular area. Establish when your ancestor first appeared on the tax rolls of a specific area. Then follow his name through the tax lists every year until you find the last year your ancestor's name appears. Remember, there may be gaps in the tax lists so don't stop searching until you are sure that your ancestor is no longer being counted. When your ancestor's name disappears from the tax list, it means he moved, died, or became blind or poor.

Most taxes were collected and kept on a local level, but in modern times these records have been turned over to state or county archives. Original tax records are not indexed, but abstracted tax records usually are. Many of the tax records and tax indexes have been microfilmed and are available at the Family History Library and through the Family History Centers. Check the Family History Library Catalog (FHLC) on FamilySearch (**www.familysearch.org**). The FHLC remains one of your best sources for locating the most accessible tax records available in the area where your ancestors resided.

Want to Know More?

- *The Handybook for Genealogists,* 8th ed., Logan, UT: Everton Publishers, Inc., 1991.

- Alice Eicholz, Ph.D., *Ancestry's Red Book,* Salt Lake City, UT: Ancestry, Inc., 1992.

- Wade E. Hone, *Land and Property Research in the United States,* Salt Lake City, UT: Ancestry, Inc., 1997.

- "Land and Tax Records," in Loretto Dennis Szucs and Sandra Hargreaves Luebking, *The Source: A Guidebook of American Genealogy,* revised ed., Salt Lake City, UT: Ancestry, Inc., 1997.

- Val D. Greenwood, *The Researcher's Guide to American Genealogy,* 3rd ed., Baltimore, MD: Genealogical Publishing, Co., 1999.

- E. Kay Kirkham, *The Handwriting of American Records for a Period of 300 Years,* Logan, UT: Everton Publishers, Inc., 1981.

Try This

❏ 1. Compile a chronological listing of the places where your ancestors resided. Arrange the residences by surname. Display these migration patterns on a map using pins or string.

❏ 2. Review E. Kay Kirkham's book, *The Handwriting of American Records for a Period of 300 Years.* Becoming familiar with the differences in handwriting will be an important skill to have when abstracting wills and deeds.

❏ 3. Take time to browse the FHLC for the land records available in the area where your ancestors resided. If possible, view actual deed indexes and deeds. Take time to become familiar with this difficult, but helpful, source.

❏ 4. Check the Internet for land record sites. Begin with **www. rootsweb.com**.

In the agrarian society of our ancestors, life was linked to land. Deeds can be informative in establishing family units and tracking family migration.

Military Records

George's Story: Through Conflicts and Carnage

My daughter-in-law Julie is a newcomer to family history research and she has great enthusiasm for it. Her second great-grandfather, William Mink, was a farmer in Idaho, but he also fought in the Civil War. His obituary in the *Daily Wood River News* from 26 November 1903 tells about his military service:

"In May 1861, when the first call to arms was made by the Old Dominion, in the great civil war between the north and the south, William H. Mink was one of the first to respond, enlisting in the 50th Virginia Infantry, C.S.A. volunteers. He was immediately mustered into active service and followed the fortunes of his command through all the conflicts and carnage of the Army of the Potomac. Where duty called, William H. Mink was always found. He served with distinction and signal bravery through the battles of Ganley Bridge, Donaldson, Seven Pines, Williamsburg, Cold Harbor, Leesburg, Winchester, Manassas, Antietam, Fredericksburg, the Wilderness, Chancelorsville, the Seven Days' Battle before Richmond, Gettysburg, and finally laid down his arms at Appomattox, when Lee surrendered. In the army, as in civil life, he was very quiet and unassuming, and for cool nerve, marksmanship, and bravery he was detailed as a sharpshooter and scout for the last two years of his service. . . . At the close of the war he returned to his home and was as loyal to his country until his death."

Julie learned that her second great-grandfather was a man who was true to his convictions, conservative toward his enemies, and never betrayed a friend. He was full of that chivalry that is the boast of Virginians. She can't wait to meet him on the other side, and neither can I.

How Do I Know If My Ancestor Joined the Military?

Check the following records to discover whether any of your ancestors served in the military:

- Obituaries and family sources.

- Tombstones may have a flag or marker.

- County histories or compiled histories may mention military service for wars prior to 1900.

- National Archives micropublication M233 titled *Registers of Enlistments in the United States Army, 1798–1914* lists men who served in the army.

- Daughters of the American Revolution (DAR) and Sons of the American Revolution (SAR) publishes pedigrees of applicants who are descendants of Revolutionary War soldiers.

- 1890 special federal Civil War census may list your ancestor.

- 1910 federal census identifies veterans of the Civil War.

- Military Index on FamilySearch™ lists 100,000 U.S. servicemen who served in the Korean War or the Vietnam War.

What Can I Find in Military Records?

Military records contain the names of those who served in the military, or who were eligible to serve. The two major divisions of military records are **service records** and **pension records**.

1. Service records provide an account of a soldier's military history. Here you will find the unit in which he or she served. This information can open the door to locating other military records. Limited genealogical information can be found, including age, whether they enlisted or were drafted, the discharge date, pay records, and whether any injuries were sustained while in the military.

2. Pension records are among the richest of military records. Birth date, birthplace, marriages, residences following the war, and sometimes information about children and other family members are some of the important genealogical data to be found. On occasion you will find touching stories surrounding the death or discharge of your ancestor as well as stories surrounding the widow or recipient of the pension. These are records worth obtaining.

PRIVATE JONES REPORTING FOR DUTY!

FAMILY HISTORY LIBRARY

OH GREAT! HE'S BACK TO LOOK AT MORE MILITARY RECORDS!

Compiled Military Service Records

Fires in the War Department in 1800 and 1814 destroyed most of the records of the American army and navy. This great loss gave rise to an 1894 project to compile a packet of records on each soldier using other sources, such as muster rolls, pay rolls, rank rolls, returns, hospital records, and prison records.

These packets became known as **Compiled Military Service Records.** They contain the name of the soldier, his rank, military unit, date of entry into the service, and whether he was discharged, deserted, or died. Age, place of birth, and residence at time of enlistment may also be included.

Compiled Military Service Records (Revolutionary War, War of 1812, various Indian wars, the Mexican War, and the Civil War) have been indexed and most have been microfilmed. They are available to the public. You need to know:

Information for a Compiled Military Service Record in Order Needed	Your Ancestor's Information
1. War or time period of service	1.
2. State from which he or she served	2.
3. Military unit	3.
4. Name of your ancestor	4.

How Can I Get a Copy of Military Records?

Ch. 7, Appendix H

The National Archives has the most complete collection of military records for service prior to 1900. (See Appendix H for more about the National Archives.) Most of these records are available on microfilm, which may be available at National Archives branches or through your Family History Center. (See Chapter 7 to learn how to order microfilms from a Family History Center.)

The most important catalog to help you locate military records is titled *Military Service Records: A Select Catalog of National Archives Microfilm Publication.* It has the listings for the thousands of rolls of microfilm, including indexes, service records, unit histories, post returns, pensions, and so on. This catalog is available at branches of the National Archives and in most libraries. It is also available on the Internet at **www.nara.gov**.

Military records that have not been microfilmed can be accessed in person in Washington, DC, or by ordering photocopies by mail for a fee.

> The original military records prior to World War I, which have not been microfilmed, can be viewed at the National Archives. They are not available at the National Archives branches.

> **Remember, your Family History Center is your most convenient resource to obtain and view military records on microfilm.**

To request military records before 30 June 1917, use the NATF Form 80 available from General Reference Branch (NNRG–P), National Archives and Records and Administration, Seventh and Pennsylvania Ave. NW, Washington, DC 20408.

To request military records after 30 June 1917, use NATF Form 13043 available from National Personnel Records Center, 9700 Page Boulevard, St. Louis, MO 63132. Both forms are also available at the larger Family History Centers or you can e-mail for information at **inquire@arch2.nara.gov**.

Remember, your Family History Center is your most convenient resource to obtain and view military records on microfilm. Locate the records using the Family History Library Catalog (FHLC) on Family-Search at your Family History Center or at **www.familysearch.org**.

The Revolutionary War

Men of all ages enlisted in the Revolutionary War. The promise of land enticed males as young as sixteen years old and older men as well.

The Index of Revolutionary War Pension Applications in the National Archives, Arlington, VA: National Genealogical Society, 1976 (available on microfilm and in book form) will help you determine if your ancestor applied for a pension.

National Archive micropublication M804 titled *Revolutionary War Pension and Bounty Land Warrant Application Files, 1800–1906* lists 2,670 rolls of microfilm that can help you determine if your ancestor received bounty land.

The Civil War

> Photocopy every paper in the file so as not to miss any important genealogy clues.

Brothers fought brothers during this war between the states. Emotions ran high then and are still surprisingly high in some areas of the United States today. If your ancestor lived in a border state such as Tennessee, Kentucky, Arkansas, or Missouri, he could have served in the Confederate army and later in the Union army or vice versa for any number of reasons.

▶ **Confederacy**

For service records of Confederate soldiers, search National Archives micropublication M253, *Consolidated Index to Compiled Service Records of the Confederate Soldiers*. These 535 rolls are arranged by surname in alphabetical order. Once you have the index information, check the state records of Confederate Compiled Service Records. You will need the regiment, unit, and surname.

Confederate pension records are also filed on the state level, not with the National Archives. Indexes are located in the state archives or state historical society. Check for both the name of the soldier and the widow. Check each state where the veteran lived until you locate the records. Photocopies are available.

Micropublication M347, *Unfiled Papers and Slips Belonging to Confederate Compiled Service Records* is also a fine source of Confederate records.

▶ **Union**

The only indexes that exist for service records of Union soldiers are on the state level. Locate your ancestor and copy down his unit, regiment, and other information exactly. Then check the *Military Service Records: A Select Catalog of National Archives Microfilm Publication* to locate the microfilm with the correct military unit.

Union pension records are available at the National Archives. Micropublication T288, *General Index to Pension Files, 1861–1934* will help you locate your ancestor's records. They are arranged by surname, then by the state from which the soldier served. Extract all the information listed in the index about your ancestor. You will need it when ordering the file by mail or viewing it in person at the National Archives.

Bounty Land

Between 1776 and 1855, the government offered free land to some as an inducement to serve or to remain in the military. Called bounty land, it was also sometimes used as a reward for military service.

Many Revolutionary War bounty land records were destroyed by fire. The surviving records were combined with pension records and can be accessed through micropublication M804 at the National Archives.

Bounty land records for the War of 1812 have been microfilmed and indexed, and are available through micropublication M848 at the National Archives.

The majority of bounty land records have not been microfilmed or indexed; however, they are a wealth of genealogical information: marriages, family Bible records, death records, and so on. If you believe your ancestor received bounty land, fill out NATF Form 80 and check the box for bounty land file.

Want to Know More?

- *Military Service Records: A Select Catalog of National Archives Microfilm Publication,* Washington, DC: National Archives Trust Fund Board, G.S.A., 1984. (Available on the Internet at **www.nara.gov**.)

- *"Military Service Records in the National Archives,"* General Information Leaflet 7, available from National Archives and Records Administration, Room G-7, Seventh Street and Pennsylvania Avenue, NW, Washington, DC 20408.

- "Research in Military Records," in Loretto Dennis Szucs and Sandra Hargreaves Luebking, *The Source: A Guidebook of American Genealogy,* revised ed., Salt Lake City, UT: Ancestry, Inc., 1997.

- James C. Neagles, *U.S. Military Records: A Guide to Federal and State Sources, Colonial America to the Present,* Salt Lake City, UT: Ancestry, Inc., 1994.

- *Guide to Genealogical Research in the National Archives,* Washington, DC: National Archives, 1982, Chapters 4–9, Pages 71–145.

- Virgil D. White, *Genealogical Abstracts of Revolutionary War Pension Files,* 4 vols., Waynesboro, TN: The National Historical Publication Co., 1990.

- Lloyd DeWitt Bockstruck, *Revolutionary War Bounty Land Grants: Awarded by State Governments,* Baltimore, MD: Genealogical Publishing, Co., 1996.

Try This

❏ 1. If you have living family members who served in the military, talk to them about their experiences. Be sure to tape your conversation. There may be stories you would like to pass on to other family members or include in your family history.

❏ 2. Create a list of your ancestors who served in the military. Include their rank, serial number, and unit. Frame the list and display it in your home.

❏ 3. Order a copy of *Military Service Records: A Select Catalog of National Archives Microfilm Publication,* Washington, DC: National Archives Trust Fund Board, G.S.A., 1984. (Available on the Internet at **www.nara.gov**.)

Pension records often provide information about the whole family.

Immigration and Naturalization

George's Story: Measles, Measles, Measles

My co-author LaRene Gaunt has an immigration story to share with you: "Our Boyers, Mohlmanns, and Hoppmanns were part of the great immigration into the United States around the turn of the century. As friends and family, the Boyers and Mohlmanns left their homes in the small German community of Mehringen, and the Hoppmanns left their home in Hoya for America.

"I can imagine them as they sorted through their possessions, looking at each thing and deciding if it would go with them or if it must stay behind. Yes, to a few clothes and small family heirlooms. No, to nearly everything else. Did the children cry? Perhaps they were afraid to leave the familiar landscape and their cozy home. But perhaps, instead, some of them were adventuresome and felt excited about crossing the ocean to a new land. When it came time to go, how long did the hugs last between family members who knew they would never see each other again?

"Of course there was strength and courage in numbers. So these families, who had joined together for this life-changing event, turned and left behind everything they had known or loved—their families, homes, farms, and animals. But along with their few possessions, they no doubt brought abundant hope for a better life. Together they made the long and crowded journey across the Atlantic Ocean to a new country, a new language, and a new life.

"When they arrived at last in Forest Park in New York in 1883, three-year-old Anna Boyer (back row, left, of photo below) and her sister

were both sick with the measles and had to be detained. Anna's mother and the other sisters stayed behind in New York while Anna's father took the boys and went on to Tinley Park, Illinois, a German community just outside of Chicago. Two weeks later, the girls were over the measles and they took the train to Tinley Park.

"Anna grew into a young woman and got a job in Chicago cleaning the home of a wealthy doctor who had an office off Michigan Avenue. It was here that Anna gained polish and education. She learned to write English, and she lost her German accent. She developed an appreciation for fine music and nice clothes.

"In 1902, she married Frederick Hopman (whose family dropped the extra letters to become Hopman). The Boyers and Mohlmanns kept their names the same. Anna and Frederick moved to Hammond, Indiana, not far from Tinley Park, Illinois. Frederick established a dry-cleaning business and became active in politics. They, like thousands of others, put their culture and language behind them, took the oath of allegiance and became naturalized citizens of the United States— successful, contributing, first-generation Americans."

Immigration

Immigration records show when a person **arrived in** a country to reside. One of the best sources for immigrant records prior to 1820 is the eleven-volume index compiled by P. William Filby and titled *Passenger and Immigration Lists Index and Supplements*. Published naturalizations and oaths of allegiance are also included. There are several other indexes for pre-1820 immigrants. Ask the librarian or check the Family History Library Catalog (FHLC) on FamilySearch™.

Passenger Lists

After 1820, passenger arrival lists are the best source of immigration information. They provide the name of the passenger, name of the ship and port from which it left, and the dates of departure and of arrival. Many of these lists are indexed. Check with the librarian for help locating them.

Passenger lists prior to 1882 list the name of the passenger, age, occupation, country of origin, and place of intended settlement.

Beginning in 1882, passenger lists (which had been originally created for customs) were created to meet new immigration laws. In order to use these lists, you need to know the ship on which your ancestor crossed the ocean and the date it arrived.

🚫 Ship lists sometimes record the port where the ship sailed as the country of origin for the passengers, when in fact the passenger may have traveled to that port from Europe or Scandinavia before sailing to America.

Passenger lists after 1882 contained more information than earlier lists and included the name, address, and relationship of the relative they were going to meet in America. Later, the lists even included a physical description of the immigrant and the name and address of their closest relative in their country of origin.

Passenger lists are available on microfilm at the National Archives, or they can be ordered through the Family History Library or any of the 3,400 branches, called Family History Centers.

Port Cities

Between 1820 and 1920, 35 million immigrants arrived at U.S. ports, and 82 percent of them came to New York. The other main ports of entry were Boston, Baltimore, Philadelphia, New Orleans, Key West, Mobile, Charleston, Savannah, New Bedford, New Haven, Providence, Gulfport, Pascagoula (MS). San Francisco, Galveston, Seattle, and Port Townsend (WA) were also main ports, but the records are missing.

Censuses Can Help

The federal census may help you locate the date your ancestor arrived in America and the name of the ship.

Year	What Is Listed
The 1870 federal census	has a column regarding citizenship.
The 1900 federal census	lists the year of immigration and the number of years the person has lived in the United States, as well as if the person is naturalized.
The 1910 federal census	lists the year of immigration and if the person is naturalized or an alien.
The 1920 federal census	lists the year of immigration, if the person is naturalized or an alien, and the year the person became naturalized. When you know the year a person immigrated, you may be able to find your ancestor on the ship lists for that year.

Emigration

Emigration records are located in the land **from** where your ancestor left or, in other words, your ancestral homeland. If you know where your ancestors lived, the date they left, and where they left from, you can search these records. Clues to this information can be found in family records, census records, immigration records, passenger lists, and naturalization records. Some of the emigration records for some areas have been microfilmed, for example, the Hamburg passenger lists and the Copenhagen Police Lists.

Consider hiring a professional genealogist to help you locate the family of your immigrant ancestor in his or her homeland.

The search for this information—locating your family across the ocean—is one of the most challenging in family history research.

Naturalization

Naturalization is the process of becoming a citizen of a country other than the one where he or she was born. In America, most people were naturalized between 1790 and 1952. Prior to 1922, when a man was naturalized, his wife and minor children also became citizens.

As part of the process of becoming an American citizen, you must swear an **Oath of Allegiance** wherein you renounce allegiance to any foreign government. These records tell you the country from which your ancestor emigrated. Later immigrants filed a **declaration of intent.** Five or more years after emigrating, immigrants petitioned for naturalization.

Naturalization records are held in the court of record where they were processed—that could be in a federal, state, county, or municipal court. Start with the municipal court and work your way back to the federal court.

Naturalization records prior to 1920 do not give the birth date or birthplace. After 1920, these records include the place and date of birth for the immigrant and other family members, port of arrival, vessel name, and date of arrival.

Remember, your Family History Center is one of the best resources for immigration and naturalization records on microfilm. Locate those records using the Family History Library Catalog (FHLC) and then order the microfilm through your Family History Center.

Let's Change Our Name

Many immigrants changed or shortened their names when they arrived in their new country. Often they did this to make their names easier to spell or so they sounded less foreign. On occasion, the immigration clerk purposely shortened, or accidentally misspelled, the name upon entry to the country and the immigrant kept the change.

In some instances, names were changed when brothers argued and parted company. One brother may have changed the spelling of his surname, or taken on an entirely new surname, to avoid being linked to his estranged brother. For example, the Saunders brothers fought and one changed his name to Sanders.

In other instances, children may have changed their surname slightly as a way of honoring their deceased parents. Such was the case with the children of Zebulon Gaunt who added an extra "t" to their surname to honor their father after his death. Gaunt became Gauntt among his descendants, who are now linked together by the new spelling of their surname.

Remember, when searching an index, look for as many variations of the surname as you can conceive. Errors in the index may occur as a result of misspelling or bad handwriting in the original source from which the index was compiled. Keep a list of variations for your particular surnames when searching an index or records. Add each new surname variation to the list.

Of course, changing the spelling of a name does not affect relationships. Brothers and sisters and cousins are all still related even if their surnames are spelled differently. Remember that fact when searching backward, since the knowledge that a surname had been changed may have become lost over several generations. One of your pedigree surnames could contain a spelling change, so remain open to that possibility as you search backward. Nevertheless, if it occurs, make sure you prove the relationship beyond a doubt.

Want to Know More?

- *Immigrant and Passenger Arrivals: A Select Catalog of National Archives Microfilm Publication,* Washington, DC: National Archives Trust Fund Board, G.S.A., 1983. Available on the Internet at **www.nara.gov**.

- John P. Colletta, Ph.D., *They Came in Ships,* revised ed., Salt Lake City, UT: Ancestry, Inc., 1993.

- John J. Newman, *American Naturalization Processes and Procedures 1790–1985,* n.p.: Indiana Historical Society, 1985.

- Christina K. Schaefer, *Guide to Naturalization Records of the United States,* Baltimore, MD: Genealogical Publishing, Co., 1997.

- Michael Tepper, *American Passenger Arrival Records: A Guide to the Records of Immigrants Arriving at American Ports by Sail and Stream,* updated and enlarged, Baltimore, MD: Genealogical Publishing, Co., 1993.

- For information from the National Archives on naturalization, check **www.nara.gov/genealogy/natural.html**.

- "Tracing Immigrant Origins," in *Family History SourceGuide* on CD-ROM, available at LDS distribution centers, the Family History Library, and at Family History Centers. Also on **www.familysearch.org**.

Try This

❏   1. Compile a list of your immigrant ancestors. Include the year and the country from which they emigrated. Perhaps you could compile this information on a map and hang it in your home.

❏   2. Try to locate any family heirlooms that came from the "old country." If you find one, photograph it and get the story behind it. Then make copies of the photograph and story for members of your family.

CHAPTER 16

Visiting Your Ancestral Hometown

George's Story: This Old House Is Getting Dearer

My good friend Jimmy Parker tells of the time he moved his mother into a retirement center: "My sister and I went to clean out the old family home. In a drawer, we found the original marriage license of my great-grandparents who were married in Yakima in 1902. Somehow, my mother had never shown it to me.

"I also found the glass negative of my grandmother as a baby, sitting on her mother's lap. I already had a copy of this picture, but finding the glass negative was a real thrill since this picture had quite a story behind it. On the long-ago day when it was taken, the baby cried unless she was on her mother's lap. The mother felt that she was not appropriately dressed to have her picture taken, so she agreed to hold the baby on her lap only if they put her behind the lace curtain. So the picture shows the baby clearly, however, the mother is hidden behind the curtain. Knowing that story and holding the glass negative made me feel as though I were there with my grandmother and great-grandmother on the day the picture was taken.

"I also found the diary my mother kept during the time she and my father were courting. She made an entry every day. Once she broke up with my dad and a new suitor's name appeared. But soon my dad's name returned, and that was the last of the other guy.

"Being there in the old house and reading that journal was an unforgettable experience for me. I also found many obituaries and other treasures. I left the old home with a suitcase full of old family pictures and documents."

If you are able to return to your ancestral home, you'll find treasures that will be just as valuable to you as Jimmy's treasures were to him. Even if your family has been gone from the ancestral home for a long time, just being there and seeing it, imagining what it was like when your ancestors lived there, will bring a special feeling into your heart. So enjoy your trip home.

What a Vacation!

I KNEW MY ANCESTORS WERE SMALL STATURED PEOPLE BUT THIS IS RIDICULOUS!

Combine your visit to the city of your roots with a family vacation. Take your children to the cemetery and let them help you find the tombstones of your ancestors. Visit the old home or farm and talk about what life would have been like when your ancestors lived there. Find the church and the library. Seek out distant cousins. A vacation like this will give you and your family more than a good time—it will help you develop a love for your past.

Clues in the Telephone Book

Listing	What You May Find	Miscellaneous
Ancestral surname	A distant cousin who has stories or family records.	(See Chapter 5.)
Name of person living in old family home	If the person living in the old family home knew your family, they may have stories.	They may have things they found in the home that belonged to your ancestors.

(continued)

Listing	What You May Find	Miscellaneous
Names of older folks still in the neighborhood	Neighbors usually have plenty of great stories.	
Local churches	See if you can determine where your ancestors worshipped.	If you already know where they attended church, visit with the pastor. (See Chapter 12.)
Cemeteries	Visit the cemetery. Visit with the sexton, if possible.	(See Chapter 11.)
School	See if the school records of your ancestor are available.	
Businesses	If your ancestor was a businessman, there may be information or photographs of his or her contributions.	
Doctor or hospital	Medical records, if available to you, would have a wealth of information.	Medical records may include the name of an insurance company that would also have information.
Mortuary or funeral home	These are records rich in information.	To locate funeral directors and morticians nationwide, check your local library or funeral home for the following directories: (1) *National Yellow Book of Funeral Directors,* Youngstown, OH: NOMIS Publications; and, (2) *National Directory of Morticians,* Youngstown, OH: National Directory of Morticians. Both are published annually.

Treasures in the Local Library

Ch. 6

1. Ask about compiled sources, such as local county histories, directories, or unpublished genealogies. They contain local history and are an excellent way to learn of the events that affected the lives of your family and may contain information about your ancestors.

Ch. 17

2. Ask about local newspapers on microfilm. They may be available at the library or the newspaper office. Perhaps there are scrapbooks created from newspaper obituaries and other genealogical data.

Appendix G

3. Ask about a historical society or people in town who value local history and genealogy.

Appendix B

4. Ask about old maps of the area. They may show the location of your ancestral home or family burial plots.

Photograph Everything

The pictures you take of your trip will also create a photographic history of your ancestral hometown. Photograph heirlooms, cousins, the old family home, cemetery tombstones, the library, the courthouse, the church and pastor, old-timers who remember your ancestors, the farm or business where your ancestors worked, Main Street, and so on. Take pictures of you and your family at these sites, too. Now you have visual images of the current generation with part of their past.

These photos will bring back the feelings of the love you developed for your ancestors by being in the places where they once lived. When you get home, put your photos together so that you can easily review them. Share them with your children and other family members.

> *Take pictures of you and your family at these sites, too. Now you have visual images of the current generation with part of their past.*

▶ What You'll Need for Photos

❑ 1. Minimum: A 35-mm camera with a normal lens.

❏ 2. Important: A flash for indoor shots. Many 35-mm cameras have a flash built in already. Always use the flash when taking photos of people outdoors to soften the shadows on their faces and put a highlight in their eyes.

❏ 3. Essential: Film and lots of it. Use print film if you want to make copies of your photos for other family members. Use transparency film (slides) if you want to create a slide show for the family.

❏ 4. Nice, but not essential: A telephoto zoom lens so that you can take close-up photos of people. (An 80-mm to 110-mm is a good portrait range.) A telephoto zoom lens will also allow you to get tight shots of tombstones or old photographs.

▶ **Copying Old Photos On-Site**

When you cannot take old photos to a professional business to make a copy, you can get a reasonable "homemade" copy without too much trouble.

❏ 1. Lay the old photograph on a flat, clean surface outside in the shade.

❏ 2. If the weather is bad, lay the old photograph on a table next to a window in natural light.

❏ 3. Stand directly over the old photo, or mount your camera on a tripod.

❏ 4. Adjust your zoom lens until the old photograph fills the frame.

❏ 5. Make sure it is in focus and press the shutter.

❏ 6. Don't use a flash. It will leave a bright spot of light on the copied photograph.

Subscribe to the Newspaper

If the descendants of your ancestors still live in the hometown area, subscribe to the local newspaper. You'll be surprised how much you'll learn about the area and your distant cousins. Use the classified ads or "Letters to the Editor" in the newspaper to query for help. The following is a sample "Letter to the Editor."

Dear Editor,

I am [insert relationship here] of John Doe, who lived in [insert town here] for many years. His obituary lists three daughters—Mary, Elizabeth, and Sarah—and a son, Edward. I am interested in contacting them as I am compiling a family history. Please respond if you know where I can reach them.

Thank you,
[insert name, address, phone number, e-mail]

Visiting Via the Internet

When you can't visit your ancestral hometown, see what you can find on the Internet using geographic-specific Web sites. They contain information about a specific town, county, state, or country. For example, you may find (1) genealogical and historical societies, (2) government agencies and courthouses, (3) cemeteries, (4) civic organizations, (5) local histories, including biographies of prominent residents, (6) churches, or (7) links to other sites. Try **www.genealogytool box.com** or **www.genealogysitefinder.com**.

Want to Know More?

- Alice Eicholz, Ph.D., *Ancestry's Red Book,* revised ed., Salt Lake City, UT: Ancestry, Inc., 1991.

- *The Handybook for Genealogists,* 8th ed., Logan, UT: Everton Publishers, Inc., 1991.

- Read the guide for the area of your ancestral home in the *Family History SourceGuide* on CD-ROM, available at LDS distribution centers, the Family History Library, and Family History Centers.

- "Research in Newspapers," in Loretto Dennis Szucs and Sandra Hargreaves Luebking, *The Source: A Guidebook of American Genealogy,* revised ed., Salt Lake City, UT: Ancestry, Inc., 1997, 414–38.

Try This

❏ 1. Visit your ancestral hometown. Seek out cousins or others who may remember your ancestors.

❏ 2. Visit the home of your parents, grandparents, or whoever may have family heirlooms. Photograph the treasures. Write down or tape record the stories.

❏ 3. Using **www.mapquest.com** or **www.yahoo.com/recreation/ travel**, locate your ancestral home on a map. Plan a vacation there.

Ancestral home of Joseph Jared Porter in Escalante, Utah.

CHAPTER 17

Newspapers

> ★ **IN THIS CHAPTER**
> ✔ Where you'll find early newspapers
> ✔ How to read an early newspaper
> ✔ What you can expect to find in the newspaper

George's Story: A "Gold Mine" in Jay County, Indiana

My co-author LaRene Gaunt had a remarkable family history research experience using newspapers. I'll let her tell you all about it: "When I left San Francisco in 1968 to get married and live in Dunkirk, which was a small town in Jay County, Indiana, I thought I had been caught up in a time warp and transported back in time. I found myself living in the rural Midwest and it was a shock after spending nearly all of my life in California. But I quickly came to love the friendly people, the miles of fields filled with corn or soybeans, and the brilliant autumns.

"It was here that I first felt the desire to seek out my husband's roots. His ancestors had settled Dunkirk in 1837 and were buried in the old cemetery. I loved to go there and read the tombstones and imagine what it had been like when they were alive. My desire to learn more about these early people began to consume me.

"It wasn't long before I made my first trip to the county courthouse and the public library in Portland, Indiana. I didn't really expect to find much, since it seemed to me everything was thirty years behind the times. Imagine my overwhelming surprise when I discovered that the library had original newspapers dating back to the time of the Civil War! What a treasure! From then on, I spent day after day in the library poring over newspapers, fascinated by the advertisements, news, and abundant genealogical information. I read of the Civil War as if it were the weekly news. The words, drawings, and photos on the fragile, yellow pages of these newspapers transported me as historical event after historical event passed before my eyes.

"On another occasion, I read the newspapers for the entire year of 1918 trying to find the death date of an ancestor. Coverage of the Spanish flu epidemic that swept the United States following World War I filled the pages of the newspapers with increasing frequency. Stories of the deaths and quarantines were everywhere. I found myself weeping as I read of coffins stacked high at the train stations, burials without funerals because of the quarantine, and even multiple deaths within the same family. I'll never forget that experience or the way I felt connected to those long-ago people.

"Of course, between the pages, I found a lot of genealogical data. My husband had several pioneer ancestors who came to the area early and their ancestors had stayed for generations on the original farmland.

"Jay County happened to be one of those places with the good fortune of having a couple of local residents who devoted their lives to preserving the county history. Luckily for me and my genealogical research, they had written an ongoing column in the local newspaper detailing the history of these counties and their early settlers. The librarian had clipped each of these columns and compiled them into scrapbooks. Here was my gold mine! I found family after family chronicled in the newspaper clippings of these scrapbooks. When the Gaunts finally showed up in the columns, I was rewarded with the surname pedigree back four generations into the Quakers of colonial New Jersey. From there, it was an easy step to find the Gaunts in the Quaker records of New Jersey, and from there back to Peter Gaunt who came to America in 1637.

"But I didn't stop reading those early newspapers even after I had gathered most of my husband's genealogy. I kept going back to the yellowed pages of those newspapers and allowing myself to be transported back in time."

Where Can I Find Early Newspapers?

Before the days of television, radio, and the Internet, newspapers played an important role in the lives of people. They were filled with news and genealogical information.

Though many newspapers are no longer in print, back issues are often available on microfilm. In the *Gale Directory of Published and Broadcasting Media,* which was formerly *Ayer Directory of Publications,* you will find the names of newspapers currently in print and information about their predecessors. Check *Ayer* for information about newspapers that are out of print.

Newspaper collections may be located in state libraries, local libraries, or newspaper offices. Many 19th-century newspapers have been indexed. Some of the state historical societies have produced guides to newspapers. Check their libraries and look under *state* and then *newspapers.* One of the largest of these indexes is Stephen Gutgesell's *Guide to Ohio Newspapers 1793–1973,* published by the Ohio Historical Society. There are others, including unpublished indexes that may be with the collection.

Your librarian can help you determine which newspapers were published in the area of your ancestral home, where they are currently located, if they are indexed, and if you can view them on microfilm on interlibrary loan.

The Family History Library Catalog (FHLC) on FamilySearch™ can help you locate newspapers. FamilySearch is available in the Family History Library in Salt Lake City, Utah, and in more than 3,400 Family History Centers. Check **www.familysearch.org** as well. You can order microfilms from a Family History Center and view them there.

Times Were Different Then

Early newspapers have a very different look to them than today's newspapers. Events were often combined into one story that ran for several columns with no headings to indicate the change in topic. Some newspapers reported weekly news from one particular town or another under a special heading. Review several issues of the newspaper to figure out how it's formatted and where the information you are looking for might be found.

Articles most likely to contain genealogical data are: (1) obituaries, (2) birth, marriage, and death announcements, (3) church news, (4) land sales or estate notices, (5) court summons or citations, (6) unclaimed mail at the post office, (7) letters to the editor, and (8) general interest news that may include the names of families moving west or visiting from out of town.

News traveled slowly in those days. If you don't find an article on the day you expect, check several issues beyond that date. It could show up a week later. For example, a death may be mentioned in one issue and then later an obituary may appear.

Obituaries

Obituaries are one of the greatest treasures in old newspapers. They are often filled with rambling details, such as the fact that Uncle George went west to find gold. They are also a great place to find the married names of the women.

Likely the church and cemetery locations will be listed.

Marriage dates, occupations, military service, political offices held, and even the names of family members who have died previously may be included. This is especially true of small town papers where everyone wanted lots of details and there was always room to print them.

Survivors and their relationships to the deceased will help establish pedigrees. You may even find distant cousins with whom you can communicate.

In addition to obituaries, look for a "Card of Thanks" published after a funeral. These generally included a long list of the names of living relatives.

Births, Marriages, and Deaths

Families usually had to pay to have birth, marriage, or death announcements printed, so don't be concerned if the vital records information about your ancestors is missing. Birth and christening announcements included the name of the baby, birth date, birthplace, the names of the parents, and the church. Wedding announcements included the names of the bride and groom as well as the wedding date and place. Wedding anniversary celebrations also included the names of family members and relationships.

Church news included not only baptisms and confirmations but also the activities of the members. Perhaps you will find the names of your ancestors among those who are mentioned and discover which church they attended. With that information, you can search church records in more depth. If there is a cemetery located near the church, you may find more genealogical information there.

Other Tidbits

Legal notices, court summons, or citations also appeared in print. Legal notices appeared in the newspaper more often then they do now. Separation or divorce brought with it notice to others that the husband would not be responsible for his wife's debts. These notices are called Bed and Board Notices.

The sale of land often found its way into the pages of the newspaper, sometimes with invaluable detail.

Among the most interesting reading in early newspapers are the advertisements. They sometimes provide a few laughs and often provide insight into the times. If your ancestors were in business, then they may provide valuable information.

The post office published a list of unclaimed letters. These lists are valuable because they may indicate when or where your ancestor moved.

Want to Know More?

- Clarence S. Brigham, *Historical and Biographical American Newspapers, 1690–1820,* Worcester, MA: American Antiquarian Society, 1975.

- Winifred Gregory, *American Newspapers, 1821–1936: A union list of files available in the United States and Canada,* New York, NY: H. W. Wilson, 1937.

- Stephen Gutgesell, *Guide to Ohio Newspapers 1793–1973,* Columbus, OH: Ohio Historical Society, 1974.

- "Research in Newspapers," in Loretto Dennis Szucs and Sandra

Hargreaves Luebking, *The Source: A Guidebook of American Genealogy,* revised ed., Salt Lake City, UT: Ancestry, Inc., 1997, 414–38.

- Pettengill's newspaper directory and advertisers' handbook for 1878 comprises a complete list of the newspapers and other periodicals published in the United States and British America, also the prominent European and Australian newspapers.

- George Presbury Roswell's American newspaper directory contains a description of all the newspapers and periodicals published in the United States and territories, Dominion of Canada and Newfoundland, and of the towns and cities in which they are published, together with a statement or estimate of the average number of copies.

Try This

❑ 1. Transcribe or photocopy newspaper obituaries in your possession so that the record will remain long after the newspaper fades and crumbles.

❑ 2. Use newspaper directories at a local public library to determine what newspapers are or were published in your ancestral hometown. List the names of the newspapers and where copies can be found.

❑ 3. Telephone the newspaper offices in your ancestral hometown. Ask if they have early newspapers on microfilm. If they do, ask where they are located and when they are available to be viewed by the public. Go take a look.

Hiring a Professional

George's Story: The Grapes of "Wath"?

Hiring a professional genealogist is an excellent way to discover family roots that are too deep for you to dig. Many years ago, my cousin hired a professional genealogist in England to go to the church in Bovingdon, where our Durrants lived, and look at the actual parish records. This visit really paid off because the researcher found five generations of Durrants, dating back to 1673. Can you imagine finding such a genealogical treasure in one record? Such a find rivals the 1847 discovery of gold at Sutter's Mill.

Later, these parish records were microfilmed by The Church of Jesus Christ of Latter-day Saints and copies of the microfilm are now available. I have even searched them myself at the Family History Library in Salt Lake City, Utah.

Of course, by now you know that you don't have to live in Salt Lake City to be able to check their catalog or to use their microfilms. You can go to your local Family History Center and check the Family History Library Catalog (FHLC) there, or you can log onto the Internet to **www.familysearch.org** and check the FHLC from the comfort of your own home. If the films are listed in the FHLC, you can order them through your local Family History Center and search them there.

However, professional researchers find a lot of things that we sometimes miss. After all, they know more—they are professionals. And since they are familiar with the records, they know which records to search and can search them faster.

My mother and some of my aunts and cousins spent years working to find information about my mother's side of the family. Finally, they pooled their money and hired a professional genealogist to help them. They had remarkable success on almost every line. Unfortunately, they hit a dead end on my mother's grandfather's line in Wath, England.

I looked at a map of England and found two Waths. I figured all I needed to do was to find the Wath where grapes are grown. Get it? The Grapes of Wath. Pretty bad, huh? See why I'm not a professional?

You May Want to Hire a Professional If . . .

- You've searched everywhere and haven't been able to find what you want.

- You don't have time to do research yourself, but you want to find your ancestors.

- You don't think you have the aptitude for it.

- You can't travel to a distant area.

- You don't have access to the records you need, either in person, from a library, or through the Internet.

- You want your family history compiled into a book.

- You want help setting up a family history Web site.

- You want to join the Daughters of the American Revolution, Sons of the American Revolution, or other societies that require a pedigree.

- You want to find your biological parents or siblings, if you are adopted.

- You want to determine if you have Native American ancestry.

- You want someone to lecture to a group or teach a class on a family history topic.

- You need someone who can do research in a foreign language.

- You need research on medical projects or legal cases.

Finding a Professional Genealogist

Organization	Contact
The Family History Library in Salt Lake City, Utah, has a list of genealogists accredited by them.	Send a SASE to: 35 North West Temple Street, Salt Lake City, UT 84150. Or you can get a list from your local Family History Center.
Association of Professional Genealogists	Check your local library or archives for the *Directory of Professional Genealogists,* published by the Association of Professional Genealogists, P.O. Box 40393, Denver, CO 80204-0393.
Board for Certification of Genealogists	Check your local library or archives for the *Certification Roster,* published by the Board for Certification of Genealogists, P.O. Box 14291, Washington, DC 20044.
County Courthouses	Some counties have a list of researchers who will search their records for others. Check *The Handybook for Genealogists* or *Ancestry's Red Book* for addresses of every county courthouse in the United States.
Genealogical Research Companies	In a few cities, such as Salt Lake City, there are companies that employ professional genealogists. Check the phone book or the Internet.

Finding a Professional Genealogist Online

❏ 1. Go to **www.genealogytoolbox.com**.

❏ 2. Choose Genealogy SiteFinder.

❏ 3. Click on Supplies and Services.

❏ 4. Click on Research Services.

❏ 5. Study the services. Identify the ones that work in your area of interest. Visit the Web pages of those companies or people.

Asking the Right Questions

❏ 1. How long have you been a professional genealogist?

❏ 2. By whom are you certified or accredited?

❏ 3. What is your area of expertise?

❏ 4. What do you charge? How do you prefer to be paid?

❏ 5. When can I expect the first report from you?

❏ 6. Can you do research in any language other than English?

❏ 7. What is your educational background?

❏ 8. Are you willing to limit your research to the authorized amount?

What to Expect

- A neat, well-documented report summarizing the research. It may include a copy of the research logs listing all records searched. It should include photocopies of everything that the researcher has found, such as censuses, vital records, and so on.

- You will need to pay for photocopying, postage, parking, long-distance phone calls, and loans of books or films.

- Professionals generally specialize in specific geographic areas, ethnic groups, or time periods. Some prefer to prepare family histories for publication in a book or on a Web site.

- Some professionals will provide consultation, if you prefer. They can make suggestions on where to look; you can do the research; they can help you evaluate it and then make suggestions on where to look next.

- Some professionals are self-employed, but others work for a company, library, or county.

- Most professionals charge by the hour: $15 to $100, with the average being between $20 and $40. Payment can follow three patterns: (1) payment in full up front; (2) payment in full at the end; (3) pay a retainer up front with the rest at the end. You can expect a financial statement detailing charges.

> 🚫 **If problems arise, get in contact with the organization that certified the genealogist. Most organizations will mediate disagreements.**

- There is no guarantee that a research goal can be met within a certain length of time or even met at all. You pay for the time spent researching, not the amount of information found.

What Do All Those Acronyms Mean?

Accrediting Organization	Acronym and Title	Function
Accredited by the Family History Library of The Church of Jesus Christ of Latter-day Saints	**AG** Accredited Genealogist	Specializes in specific geographic areas.
Certified by the Board for Certification of Genealogists (BCG)	**CAILS** Certified American Indian Lineage Specialist	Determines descent from an historical Indian tribe indigenous to North America.
Certified by the Board for Certification of Genealogists (BCG)	**CALS** Certified American Lineage Specialist	Reconstructs a single line of descent and prepares hereditary society applications.
Certified by the Board for Certification of Genealogists (BCG)	**CG** Certified Genealogist	Proficient in all areas of research and analysis. Experience in the compilation of family histories.
Certified by the Board for Certification of Genealogists (BCG)	**CGI** Certified Genealogical Instructor	Conducts courses on all aspects of genealogical methodology and sources.
Certified by the Board for Certification of Genealogists (BCG)	**CGL** Certified Genealogical Lecturer	Gives public addresses on genealogical topics.
Certified by the Board for Certification of Genealogists (BCG)	**CGRS** Certified Genealogical Records Researcher	Searches original and published records. Specializes in specific areas. Reports on records examined.

▶ **Recognition and Honors**

FASG
Fellow, American Society of Genealogists

FNGS
Fellow, National Genealogical Society

FSG
Fellow, Society of Genealogists, London

FUGA
Fellow, Utah Genealogical Association

▶ **Organizations**

APG
Association of Professional Genealogists

ASG
American Society of Genealogists

FGS
Federation of Genealogical Societies

FHL
Family History Library of The Church of
    Jesus Christ of Latter-day Saints

NGS
National Genealogical Society

SOG
Society of Genealogists, London

UGA
Utah Genealogical Association

Want to Know More?

- "Hiring a Professional Genealogist," Family History Library, 35 North West Temple Street, Salt Lake City, UT 84150. Also in *Family History SourceGuide* on CD-ROM, available at LDS distribution centers, the Family History Library, and Family History Centers.

- Request a free brochure, *So You're Going to Hire a Professional Genealogist.* Send a SASE to Association of Professional Genealogists, P.O. Box 40393, Denver, CO 80204-0393. Or download the brochure from **www.apgen.org/~apg**.

- "Certification of Genealogists," on the Internet at **rootscomput ing.com**.

Try This

❏ 1. Talk to someone who has worked with a professional genealogist about the advantages and disadvantages of having professional help.

❏ 2. Log on to the Internet to **www.apgen.org** to see the code of ethics for the Association of Professional Genealogists.

❏ 3. Log on to the Internet to **www.genealogy.org/~bcg/** to see the code of ethics for the Board for Certification of Genealogists.

Discovering a woman's maiden name can be challenging. A professional researcher may be helpful.

PART THREE:
Giving Family History Back to Your Family

$\mathbf{M}$any great histories have been written. Now is the time to write the histories of the simple folk—not those that have occurred on the battlefront or in Parliament, but those that have taken place within the walls of our own homes. Write warm family histories that, when read, could make kings say, "I wish I could have lived that way." These kinds of histories form a seedbed from which all other histories grow.

Such will be your family history—a history of the heart. Compiling it is creating the revered and exceptional story of your people—the literature of your family, if you will.

Spencer W. Kimball, president of The Church of Jesus Christ of Latter-day Saints between 1973 and 1985, said of this "family literature," namely family histories and journals: "What could you do better for your children and your children's children than to record the story of your life, your triumphs over adversity, your recovery after a fall, your progress when all seemed black, your rejoicing when you had finally achieved?

"Some of what you write may be humdrum dates and places, but there will also be rich passages that will be quoted by your posterity" ("The Angels May Quote from It," *New Era,* October 1975, 5).

In This Part

- You'll learn how to compile your family history so it can be printed or put onto a Web page.

- You'll get ideas on how to write your own personal history and how to keep a journal.

- You'll learn how to plan a family reunion and how to organize family members so they can share the joy of doing family history research.

- And George's stories will touch your heart and set an inspiring example for you to follow.

CHAPTER 19

Compiling a Family History

George's Story: "Bread Was Very Scanty with Us"

Many of us have a stronger interest in our surname family line than we do the other lines. I must admit that I'm a greater authority on Durrant history than I am on my other lines. That doesn't mean that I ignore the other lines; I just try to be a credit to my name and my name is Durrant.

My great-grandfather John Durrant wrote that he was born in Bovingdon, Hertfordshire, England, and "went to infant school a little while, say a few years, with my sister, Mary, until she was burnt to death in the year 1844, on Feb. fourteenth. She was buried in the Bovingdon Parish churchyard by the side of her brother. She was a good girl and her mother loved her very much."

Of his poverty, he wrote: "Bread was very scanty with us, butter put on and then scraped off again."

John's father was ill when John was still a young boy, and so he had to go to work to sustain the family. First he labored on a berry farm near his home, where one of his duties was herding the sheep. While employed there, his father died. His employer insisted that John stay with the sheep and refused to allow him to attend his father's funeral.

John wrote, "Who can tell what mother had to undergo? I have said many times, 'Mother what are you crying for?' The reply would be, 'My boy, the greatest desire I have is to live and see you two youngest boys grow up so that you can both take care of yourselves.'"

On occasion it seems that some of our ancestors cry out from the past to be remembered, like my grandmother Estella Jannette Mayne did. I recall that some time ago, as I was reading a history of my grandmother Durrant, I had a strong impression that my grandmother Mayne wanted me to learn more about her, too. I decided then and there that I'd better follow the impression. As I learned of her, I felt her love, and I found this happy and sad moment in the life of her daughter (my mother) that occurred when she left home to marry my father. My mother wrote:

"On the 11th of March my father took me down to Maggie's in the wagon as he had to go to American Fork anyway. Steve went with us. I was very unhappy when I left home for the last time as I hated to leave my father who had always been so good to me. And I hated to leave Steve as he and I were so close. I had been the only mother he had known, and although he was twelve years old, I felt he still needed me, and so did he. Tears were in my father's eyes as he kissed me good-bye, and I was almost tempted to go back home with him."

This heart-to-heart awareness of family history is my favorite part of it. I love to know about the circumstances and conditions of my ancestors' lives. Where did they live and what did they do to earn their living? How did they meet their spouse? What were their feelings, their victories, their defeats, and their faith? My thinking, speaking, and writing about my ancestors has invited them to be close to me. The same thing can happen to you.

Finding the Story in Names, Dates, and Places

⭐ When you look at records closely, you can begin to imagine how things used to be. In the provisions of a will designed to ensure that young children would be cared for until they were grown, you will feel the love of the deceased for his or her children. You'll see joy in the bold and graceful signature on a marriage license, and find great pathos in a simple epitaph. As you view a map of farms showing a community of neighbors and relatives, you'll almost hear the laughter and daily chatter of those who lived in the community.

Emotions are just below the surface of the names, dates, and places on a family group record or a certificate. By adding the local history to the facts, you can add another dimension to the story of your ancestors. For example, knowing that several of your great-great-grandparent's children died from cholera while on the trek west tells you the facts. But reading about what happens when an epidemic of cholera hits a wagon train or about the symptoms of cholera helps you understand the details of what your family experienced. So, weave the simple facts with the local history into a story that reflects the joys, struggles, and pains of your ancestors. Don't embellish. Just put the facts in juxtaposition with the history and let them speak for themselves.

Remember, a pedigree chart proves your ancestors were born. A family history proves that they lived, and because of them you can have a better life.

Who Goes in My Family History?

The number of our ancestors doubles every generation—two parents, four grandparents, eight great-grandparents, and sixteen great-great-grandparents. Suffice it to say that in nine generations back we have 512 family lines in our family history. It would take quite a book to contain the family history of all those folks, so narrow things down when you begin compiling a family history.

The following are some suggestions:

- Compile a family history of the descendants of your grandmother and grandfather. Since you have two sets of grandparents, you may want to compile two family histories, one for each set of grandparents. Or you could compile a family history of one set of great-grandparents.

- Compile a family history of the ancestors of your father or your mother. Remember, the number of names doubles as you go back, so you could limit yourself to six generations or less.

- Compile a family history on a single surname in a single area over a specific time period—for example, the Gaunts of New Jersey in Colonial times.

- If several of your lines came from the same area, you could compile a family history on those surnames in a single geographic location, such as the Speelmans, Cobles, Swallows, and Weybrights of Darke County, Ohio, between 1850 and 1890.

- Compile a family history of the descendants of one of your immigrant ancestors.

- Compile a family history of the descendants of a famous ancestor or of someone who participated in a famous event.

- Compile a family history of one surname line in the country of origin, such as the MacDonalds of Ireland, the Diazes of Spain, or the Kerrs of Scotland.

Some people have such an intense interest that they may devote many years to preparing a published family history. That is not necessary for everyone. With average diligence, over time, you can gather a great deal of information on your ancestors.

What Goes in My Family History?

Pedigree charts or descendancy charts	See Chapter 2
Family group records	See Chapter 2
Numbering system	Ahnentafel, Modified Register, or Register
Stories and local history	See Chapters 5, 6, and 16
Accurate documentation and complete citations	See Chapter 4 and Appendix C
Photographs	See Appendix E
Maps	See Appendix B
Index	Every name that appears in the family history

How Do I Publish My Family History?

- Most family history computer software programs can compile your research into a family history format. Photos can also be included. Each individual will be identified using a numbering system like the Modified Register. The computer program will also create an index of every name. Then you can print out your family history, have it photocopied, and spiral bound with a soft cardboard cover.

Ch. 18

- Hire a professional genealogist to prepare your family history research for publication.

Appendix D

- Put your family history on a Web page and link it to other genealogy sites. Again, most family history computer software programs will lead you through the steps to do this automatically.

Appendix C

- If you have an extensive family history in one genealogical area, the county historical society may be interested in helping to publish it.

- A surname or family association may have resources to help publish it.

Ch. 3

- At a minimum, send GEDCOM files of your pedigree charts and family groups records to family members who have family history software.

Want to Know More?

- Lawrence P. Gouldrup, *Writing the Family Narrative,* Salt Lake City, UT: Ancestry, Inc., 1987.

- Bob Greene and D. G. Fulford, *To Our Children's Children,* New York, NY: Doubleday, 1993.

- Joan Ferris Curran, *Numbering Your Genealogy: Sound and Simple Systems,* Special Publication No. 59, Arlington, VA: National Genealogical Society, 1992. Originally published as an article by the same title in the *National Genealogical Society Quarterly,* Arlington, VA: National Genealogical Society, 79 No. 3 (Sept. 1991):182–93.

- Elizabeth Shown Mills, *Evidence! Citation and Analysis for the Family Historian,* Baltimore, MD: Genealogical Publishing, Co., 1997.

Try This

❏ 1. Check the surname file in FamilySearch™, ask your extended family, or search the Internet for published or unpublished family histories on one of your surnames.

❏ 2. Write about your grandparents as children.

❏ 3. Match the dates and places on your parents' or grandparents' family group record with local historical events or worldwide events, such as World War I, the Great Depression, World War II, or other wars. How were your ancestors involved in these events?

❏ 4. Compile a basic family history of the descendants of your grandparents using family group records.

❏ 5. Learn how to compile and print out a family history using your family history computer software program.

❏ 6. Explore the option of putting your family history on a Web page.

❏ 7. If you publish your family history, send a gift copy to the Family History Library with permission to duplicate it for the Family History Centers.

❏ 8. Send a copy of your unpublished family history to **www.familysearch.org** on the Internet to preserve it and make it available to others.

Fill your family histories with interesting stories about family members. These sisters, Rosalie "Babe" and Ruth Weybright of Darke County, Ohio, both had 18-inch waists as young women.

CHAPTER 20

The Joy of Writing the Story of You

George's Story: Celery and Sergeants

When I was a junior in high school, I wanted to be rich. I wanted to have a car. It was 1949, and I had decided to buy the most beautiful car ever made—a Studebaker, the car that you couldn't tell the front from the back. In my dreams, I could see myself driving that car down Center Street in American Fork. Girls on the sidewalk would say, "There goes old George." Others would say, "How do you know if he's going? He might be coming. You can't tell in a Studebaker."

I knew that if I had that car I'd be popular. I found out that I could make a lot of money by growing celery. I told a farmer that if he'd buy everything, then I'd do all the work and we could split the profits. He agreed, and I got started.

At the beginning of the summer, it looked like I would make enough money to buy my Studebaker. While I hoed the celery, I imagined driving my car. While I weeded the celery, I imagined driving my car. I was never hot or tired in that summer sun because I was always dreaming of driving my car.

Unfortunately, when harvest time came, the price of celery had dipped to an all-time low. I didn't even make enough money to buy a new bicycle. But I still got my money's worth out of my celery because I had a dream all summer long and having a dream is more important than having a Studebaker.

I want my children and grandchildren all to know about my dream of owning a Studebaker. I want them to know whether I'm coming or going. I want them to know the things I hold dear in my heart—the things that I've learned through life's wonderful lessons. I can do that through my personal history, and so can you.

Let me tell you another story. When I was in the army, I had challenges even though I was never in battle. We had a real foul-mouthed sergeant who often called us names. When we were marching, I tried not to make any mistakes because I didn't want him to call me those names. Since I'm a prayerful man, I'd pray every morning that I could get through the day without being humiliated by the sergeant.

One Saturday morning we were ready to be dismissed. The sergeant was on our left. He told us to do a right-face, but I got confused and did a left-face. I was the only one that turned the wrong way. I was nose-to-nose with the sergeant, and everybody else was facing the other way. I knew it was my time to be called all those foul-mouthed names. But instead the sergeant said in a very low voice that only I could hear, "Durrant, turn around." And I did. When he said, "Dismissed," I was the only one left standing there. I was so happy that my prayers had been answered.

From this and other experiences, I have learned that if you do the right things and pray to the Lord, he will protect you. The protection isn't always against enemy bullets; it can be protection against other things that can hurt you in other ways. I want my children and grandchildren to know that, too.

I'd like to get a law passed that we can't die until we have written our personal histories. No one as wonderful as each of us should be allowed to leave this earth without telling others what happened to us while we were here. So when you write your personal history, try to do it in a way that shows your family and all the world how much God loves you. It should tell of the special things he did for you, the way he gave you strength to endure, and the gentle whisperings that he gave you to carry on. Write down all your stories. Someday you'll be glad you did—and so will everyone who loves you.

Why Write Your Personal History?

Preparing a personal history can, if you desire it, help you truly come to understand who you really are. In other words, the greatest discovery comes when you can say, "I have found myself, and I'm glad I'm me!" Writing your personal history can give you self-understanding, and that is the key to all understanding.

How to Write Your Personal History

Perhaps you feel it is hard to find time to write your personal history, but make time. You'll never do anything more important than write your life history. A birth certificate proves that you were born. A personal history proves that you lived—really lived. George remembers asking a friend if he had written his family history. The friend said, "Not yet, but let me tell you what I'm going to do." He then went on and told George about his grandiose plan. George told him he'd never do it. Shocked, the friend asked why. George said, "You're thinking too big. Just get in and write a little heartfelt story about part of your life. People don't want volumes, they just want pages. They don't need gold plates, just plain paper plates will do. But get busy and do it by writing one experience at a time."

 George is right: writing a family history seems like an overwhelming task, but writing it down one experience at a time makes it manageable. Here are some suggestions:

Ch. 5

1. You can write chronologically from birth to death. In the middle you can cover your life by subjects even though some subjects may overlap each other chronologically.

2. Make a list of things that have happened to you and then set aside a regular time to write about each thing on the list. Sunday is a good time to spend 30 minutes each week working on your life story.

3. Gather and divide. Collect your important certificates and mementos in folders in a box. Arrange the folders in a logical order, perhaps by stages of your life. You may even want to put them in a scrapbook. Then write about the events and memories surrounding each one of them.

4. Keep a tape recorder handy. You'll find bits and pieces of time to tell your life stories. Maybe you'd prefer to have a family member interview you on tape instead. Then you or some loving family member can transcribe the tapes.

5. Journals are another way to write your personal history. You don't have to write a lot—maybe three or four paragraphs a day, more if something special happens. Find the method, time, and place that works for you. Paper and pen at lunch? Small notebook on Sunday evenings? Tape recorder on the way home from work? Computer keyboard just before you go to bed? Daily? Weekly? Monthly? Only on special occasions? Whatever you decide, remember that regularity is the key.

> **❝Review your journals regularly. You'll be amazed at the insights you'll gain into yourself and into the patterns of life.❞**

Review your journals regularly. You'll be amazed at the insights you'll gain into yourself and into the patterns of life. Share journal entries with your spouse, children, or friends when appropriate. Everyone will benefit.

What Do I Write?

- A personal history is not a time to brag about your accomplishments, although they may be included. It's a time to tell of your heartbreaks, your joys, your victories, your defeats, and the lessons you have learned. It is a time to express your faith in the Lord and to express gratitude to him. It's not a time to confess your sins, but it is a time to tell of comebacks from the times you've fallen down.

- You might say, "Nothing exciting ever happened to me. I've never been very important. I wasn't student body president or a football hero. I don't have any great honors, so who cares if I never write my personal history?" The answer is that your descendants will care. To them, you are a very important person.

- You should be as accurate as possible. You'll need to be truthful and not gloss over things. You can make a positive point out of a negative event. Explain how you arrived at the solutions to the problems you have faced. Your stories should motivate people to do good. Discuss your personality and feelings. Describe the important influences in your life.

- Folklore can be included, but don't claim it as fact. Say, "This is what I feel happened."

Helping Your Parents Write Their Personal History

One of the best gifts you can give yourself and your children is the personal history of your parents. If they have not kept a journal or written a personal history, volunteer to help them and try to include your children in the project. Here's how:

☐ 1. Choose a time when you can sit down and visit with either your mother or father for about one hour without any interruptions. Try an evening, sometime on Saturday, or on a Sunday afternoon.

☐ 2. Bring a tape recorder.

☐ 3. Plan ahead what you are going to talk about. Choose a topic or time period and simply have one of your children ask your mother or father about it.

☐ 4. Turn on your tape recorder and enjoy yourself.

☐ 5. Do this each week or every few weeks until you have enough information about your mother or father to write a personal history about each one of them.

☐ 6. Transcribe the tapes and weave the stories into a chronological personal history. You can include photos, letters, certificates, and other mementos, if you like.

Interviewing Family

Whether you are writing your own personal history or helping your parents write theirs, the following guidelines will be of help.

Begin by writing down the person's full name and when and where they were born. Then ask them about: (1) early childhood, (2) elementary school, (3) secondary school, (4) marriage, (5) children, and (6) work. Remember, you won't get through all these questions in one visit. Enjoy your visit and then come back.

1. ***Early Childhood.*** Where did you live as a young child? What is your earliest memory? How was life different then than now? What do you remember about your mom and dad and things at home? What is your happiest memory of that time in your life? Who was your favorite friend, cousin, uncle, and so on? What food did you like? Did you ever get sick, lost, hurt, or anything like that?

2. ***Elementary School Years.*** What are some of your memories of your early experiences in school? Who was your favorite teacher? What subjects did you like best? Who was your favorite friend at school?

3. ***Secondary School Years.*** What was your favorite subject in junior high and high school? What did you do in the summers when you were a teenager? Did you have chores to do? What was the first job you had to earn money? Did you feel popular when you were a teenager? Did you have a boyfriend or girlfriend? How did you feel about religion in your early years? What was your greatest success? What was your greatest fear?

4. ***Adult Years.*** What did you do in the years right after high school? Did you go to college? Military? Work? How did you meet your spouse? What was your courtship like? Tell me about your marriage. Where did you work? Where did you live? What was your greatest trial? What was your greatest joy? Tell me about the birth of each of your children. What have been your goals and dreams in life?

Before long, questions will come naturally.

Want to Know More?

- Read a personal history.

- Read *The Diary of Anne Frank* to understand the value of a journal.

- Read *The Hiding Place* by Corrie Ten Boom to understand the powerful influence of one person's life.

- Read William G. Hartley, *Preparing a Personal History,* Salt Lake City, UT: Primer Publications, 1976.

Try This

- ❏ 1. Write down one of your favorite childhood memories.

- ❏ 2. Talk to your parents about when you were born.

- ❏ 3. Keep a journal for three months.

Include your joys and sorrows in your personal history. Don't be afraid to share some of your deepest feelings.

CHAPTER 21

Enjoying Family Reunions

George's Story: Becoming a Genealogical Gadfly

I recall a reunion I attended some years ago. I didn't really want to go, but my mother was ill and asked me to go instead. I said OK because I usually did whatever she asked me to do. My wife, Marilyn, and I bought some Kentucky Fried Chicken so our children would come with us willingly.

We walked into the hall and saw about 100 people sitting at tables eating. None of them paid much attention to us. I noticed that they were quite a strange-looking group. (That told me that they were indeed my relatives.)

Marilyn and I and the children sat down away from the others and ate our chicken. When we were done, I pondered whether or not we should leave. We could go, and I could still tell my mother honestly that we had attended. Instead, I got out my pedigree charts and family group records and decided to be a genealogical gadfly. I went from group to group, sat right in the midst of them, spread out my papers, and asked them how they fit into the family. Once I had taken the first step to get acquainted, everyone became very friendly. Suddenly I started liking these people—my relatives.

When it came time for the program, I found a seat right on the front row. Children mostly performed. They didn't seem overly talented, but at the conclusion of each performance I applauded generously. This greatly pleased their parents and grandparents.

Finally it was time for the big family reunion election. By now, I had met all the people who were at the reunion and liked every one of them. They elected me president. It's the only election I ever won.

The first thing I did as president was to cancel the next reunion. I explained that a family reunion of the descendants of an ancestor who is more than two or three generations back loses its warmth. I suggested that they all have reunions on the grandparent level. That way the gathering could be more meaningful and social. Of course, as distant cousins, they could still coordinate their family research for their ancestral line.

Well, everything worked out fine. So take a hint from me: when you go to a family reunion, don't wait for everyone to make a fuss over you—make a fuss over them instead. Find out who they are, what they do, where they are from, and how they fit into the family. Before long you'll love them and they'll love you back. They may even elect you president.

Family Reunions

The four kinds of family reunions are: (1) Immediate Family Reunions, (2) Brother and Sister Family Reunions, (3) Grandparent Family Reunions, and (4) Ancestral Family Reunions.

1. ***Immediate Family Reunions*** are made up of living parents and their children and grandchildren.

In a way, when we get together each Monday evening for family home evening, we are holding a "mini" family reunion. These times together allow us to develop our relationships spiritually, socially, and intellectually. One thing we can do in our family home evenings is to teach our family of their heritage—tell them of your childhood, of your parents, grandparents, and other ancestors. A more formal reunion can be held each month on Sunday evenings or on holidays.

As your children grow older, such "mini-reunions" can become treasured events.

2. ***Brother and Sister Family Reunions*** are made up of siblings and their children. These reunions form after one or both of the parents have died.

As you mature in your family and perhaps get married or move away, it is good to return home as often as possible to be with your brothers and sisters and parents. Then, when Mom and Dad have gone on, you and your siblings can still get together with the children and strengthen family ties. If you live some distance from one another, you need to plan to get together at least once a year for some quality time.

When doing family history research, join forces with your brothers and sisters, if possible. Get together and eat some pie while you go over your pedigree charts and family group records. Just talk. Encourage everyone to install a family history software program on their computers so that you can share your records. Maybe one of them has an aptitude for ancestral research and can lead the group. The rest can rally around in support. Divide up the job of typing your family history records into the computer. Decide who will send it to the Ancestral File or put in on **www.family search.org** and who will make copies for everyone else. You'll be surprised at how much working together will unify your relationships.

3. *Grandparent Family Reunions* are made up of all of the descendants of a grandmother and grandfather. These are often the most important reunions. As cousins who haven't seen each other for a long time have a chance to get reacquainted, these reunions are often the most fun.

4. *Ancestral Family Reunions* are made up of all of the descendants of a deceased couple who are listed more than four generations back on your pedigree chart. Many family reunions fall into this category, such as the family reunion in George's story, but the primary value of these reunions lies in the benefits of shared research.

Benefits of Family Reunions

Benefit	Type
They help you keep in touch with members of your family whom you may not see otherwise, and you have fun together as a family.	Immediate Family Reunions, Brother and Sister Family Reunions, or Grandparent Family Reunions are successful in accomplishing this goal.
They help you coordinate family history research.	Ancestral Family Reunions and Brother and Sister Family Reunions are successful in accomplishing this goal.

How to Hold a Family Reunion

If no one else is willing to organize a family reunion, take the initiative. You can call some of your cousins and discuss the possibilities. Form a committee of a few siblings or cousins. Serve as chairman if they need you to do so.

Immediate Family Reunions or Brother and Sister Family Reunions

Time	Place	Activities
These are the easiest family reunions to plan and hold. Usually you will see everyone invited to these reunions often. Together, choose a date for the reunion at least six months in the future.	Choose a place for the reunion that will allow plenty of room for children to play. Perhaps the reunion could double as your family vacation or a campout at a recreational area.	Appoint someone to: (1) make reservations for the place, (2) make arrangements for the food, and (3) plan the activities, including games for the kids and discussions about family history.

Grandparent Family Reunions

Time	Place	Activities
Have one of these reunions at least every three years. Choose a date at least a year away. Some people won't be able to attend no matter what date you choose, but most will be able to.	Choose a place that is as close as possible to where your grandparents resided. It is important to return to the old hometown or neighborhood, if possible.	Appoint someone to: (1) make reservations for the place, (2) make arrangements for the food, (3) plan the activities (including games for the kids and discussions about family history), and (4) advertise the reunion to all branches of the family. Appoint the most gregarious of the clan to be the Master of Ceremonies. Help everyone to get acquainted by using name tags and interactive games.

Ancestral Family Reunions

Time	Place	Activities
Choose a date at least a year away.	Choose a place that is as close as possible to where your common ancestor resided.	See Grandparent Family Reunions.

Don't Go Empty-Handed

When you learn that others are organizing reunions, do all you can to support their efforts. Attend these family gatherings and help make them successful.

1. Bring your family history notebook to show others. Let relatives update their family group records. They can give you information on their parents, grandparents, and so on. You can exchange information with others who bring their family history notebooks.

Ch. 2

2. Bring enough photocopies of the family group records of common ancestors for everyone. They will love you for it.

Appendix E

3. Bring copies of old photographs. Everyone loves to look at these treasures. No doubt family members will recognize that they have their grandmother's nose or their grandfather's eyes. It's always a lot of fun.

> YOU'RE RIGHT, GRANDPA.... BABY DOES HAVE YOUR NOSE!

4. Bring a tape recorder or a video camera. While you are visiting with family members about their lives, or the lives of their parents or grandparents, record the conversation. (Remember to ask for permission first.) People may be nervous at first, but it'll be worth it. If you are interviewing one of the older common ancestors, offer to make copies of the interview for others in the family. The interview will become a priceless treasure.

Sample Invitation

Prepare a flyer something like this one:

Dear William and Eliza Conder Durrant descendant,

When William and Eliza married on 7 June 1888, little did they know the results their union would bring. In the 110 years that have passed since their wedding, five generations of their descendants have become part of their family.

It is difficult to imagine what American Fork, Utah, would have been through the years without the Durrants living within its borders. This small family added to this interesting city. As much as any other name, Durrant is synonymous with the community of American Fork.

Some of William and Eliza's clan have left American Fork and added the special Durrant flavor to their new communities. Those of us who have remained in American Fork will forever love this place of our ancestral roots.

So let's have a really big gathering in American Fork to celebrate the joy of being part of the William and Eliza Durrant family.

Date: Saturday, July 25th, 1998
Where: LDS chapel located at 320 North 100 East in American Fork
Time: 4:00 to 6:00 PM
Honored guest: Aunt Virginia, the only living child of William and Eliza
Food: Everyone bring your own
Activities: A lot of getting acquainted, some talk of William and Eliza, fish pond and games for the children, Cosmo the Clown (he is a Durrant you know), and a basketball demonstration by the latest Durrant superstar—Blaine Durrant, a great-grandson of Uncle Clyde

The kids will love this old-fashioned reunion and so will you. Do all you can to be there because without you the gathering will not be complete.

Sincerely,
Jane Doe
456 Main Street
Any Town, UT
(801) 555-1234

Send multiple copies of the flyer to one person from each branch of the family with a letter like this one:

Dear Norma,

As you can see by the enclosed flyers, we are planning a Durrant family reunion. We would like you to notify your branch of the family of this event by giving everyone a copy of this flyer.

If you would have difficulty doing this, please call George Durrant at (801) 555-9000. Thank you so much for helping.

Sincerely,
Jane Doe
456 Main Street
Any Town, UT
(801) 555-1234

Family Reunions of the Heart

George says, "I've found that there's a portion of every heart, the entrance to which bears a sign that reads, 'Authorized Personnel Only.' To enter into that part of the heart one must be a family member. A husband or wife can enter because of a binding, loving commitment that they made to one another. Mothers, are they welcome? Oh, they're the most welcome ones of all. Father? He's welcomed with open arms. Sons and daughters can enter without knocking. Grandparents, great-grandparents are all welcome. To each family member the door to this portion of the heart is open wide. It's a big place and can accommodate a reunion of as many as will come.

"Our homes, then and now, are dear to our hearts. We often long to return to those homes. In our deepest spiritual sensitivity, we know that we have another home. We know that heaven is our home. We know that our life is a homeward journey—A journey that will take us back to the presence of God in his celestial kingdom, a journey to a home where we can live forever with our family."

Want to Know More?

- Check **www.familytreemaker.com/issue1.html** for Family TreeMaker's Online Family Reunions articles.

- Check **www.reunionsmag.com/** for *Reunions Magazine.*

- Elizabeth Petty Bentley, *Directory of Family Associations,* Baltimore, MD: Genealogy Publishing Company, 1993–94 ed.

- The March–April annual issue of the *Everton's Genealogical Helper,* P.O. Box 368, Logan, UT 84323-0398. In it you will find two important resources:
  a. "Family Associations and Their Leaders" (Family associations who have paid to be listed here)
  b. "Family Periodical Publications" (Only those who submitted their publication to Everton Publishers, Inc., during the year)

Ten Tens

- If you have difficulty locating a family association, place ads in genealogical periodicals or on the Internet. See "10 Magazines and Newspapers" in Part 4.

Try This

❏ 1. Locate and attend a family reunion.

❏ 2. Plan an Immediate Family Reunion.

❏ 3. Plan a Brother and Sister Family Reunion.

❏ 4. Plan a Grandparent Family Reunion.

❏ 5. Coordinate family history research among family members.

❏ 6. Look at the chart in Appendix A and discover your relationship to other family members.

❏ 7. Watch the Web sites of any surnames you are researching for information about a family reunion.

Family reunions, such as this one in 1920, can be as simple as a backyard picnic.

TempleReady

★ IN THIS CHAPTER
    ✔ How to use TempleReady
    ✔ How to make a submission disk
    ✔ How to manage your Family File cards
    ✔ How to keep track of ordinance dates

George's Story: Once You Have Found Them, Never Let Them Go

Feelings of discovery and joy make genealogy one of the most satisfying of all hobbies. It's not uncommon while in the large Family History Library in Salt Lake City, Utah, to hear a shout resounding from wall to wall, "There she is! I just found my great-grandmother!" Not even the librarians utter a "Shhhh!" to such exultation.

We as Latter-day Saints are like everyone else in our excitement and love of family history work. We enjoy the thrill of taking a surname line back another generation, cringe when we discover that one of our ancestors was a horse thief, and weep as we discover a family whose three children died from diphtheria in the same week. We, like everyone else, gain strength and a sense of well-being as we discover ourselves by learning of our past. We turn our hearts toward our ancestors. We become immersed in a love that stretches beyond known generations. The same is true for all who seek out their past.

But for us as Latter-day Saints, there is another reason we do family history. Our interests are doctrinally prompted. We believe that life does not end with death but that our spirits go on eternally; we continue to learn and grow.

We believe that families can be sealed together eternally through covenants we make on earth in the temple. These ordinances are, as President Gordon B. Hinckley said, "the most profound expressions of our theology" ("Of Missions, Temples, and Stewardship," *Ensign,* November 1995, 53). Even so, we recognize that our ancestors have agency after death and can choose to accept or reject these ordinances.

For us, family history is more than a passing interest; it is our religious responsibility to perform these ordinances by proxy for our ancestors who did not make the covenants in life. So, it is for this reason—our dream of being in heaven with our immediate and ancestral family—that we search for the unique identity of each individual family member. We will go to the temple and seal our family together for all eternity. For once we have found them, we will never let them go.

I once went in to see Elder Royden G. Derrick, who at the time was the managing director of the Family History Department. I asked him which was the most important—family history or temple work? He smiled broadly at my question. Then he began to sing, "Love and marriage, love and marriage. They go together like a horse and carriage. You can't have one without the other."

I got his point: family history and temple work go together like a horse and carriage. You can't have one without the other.

Family History and Temple Work

Family history and temple work share a common goal and support each other to help Latter-day Saints fulfill an exciting promise. In the end, if we live worthily, we will be linked to our ancestral families throughout all eternity.

Family history is the means by which we uniquely identify our ancestors. The Church invests substantial resources into microfilming records, cataloging the films, indexing the data, and making the information available to the entire world to help Latter-day Saints achieve that objective.

Temple work is the means by which we provide the necessary ordinances for those deceased ancestors we have identified. Temple work is flourishing today as the Church continues to build sacred buildings at an astounding rate.

Don't Rush

We have a responsibility to identify each of our unique ancestors to the best of our ability. We shouldn't just assume that the information we get from others or from compiled sources is absolutely true. We shouldn't

Don't download family history from Ancestral File and then submit it through TempleReady without verifying the information.

just submit these names for temple work without verification. Errors and unnecessary duplication of temple ordinances are the result.

Take the time to check the information you find about each ancestor. Does the information come from a primary source or a secondary source? Have you verified the names, dates, places, and relationships using two independent sources? Are the dates and places of the birth, marriage, and death logical? Would the mother have been of an age to have had each of the children listed? Do you have proof (not just circumstantial evidence) that each child is linked to the correct parents? Did the city, county, or state exist by the dates listed? Did you just estimate the dates and places when you could have found the information with reasonable research? Are there important discrepancies that have not been resolved? And so on. Study the information and ask logical, reasonable questions.

Ch. 4   Make sure you submit the most accurate information available. After all, others will rely on it—both your ancestors who desire to have their temple ordinances performed and other genealogists who will build on your research. So take the time to do it right.

Minimum Identification

Each deceased family member must be uniquely identified before their names can be submitted for temple work. Requirements include:

▶ **For Baptisms, Endowments, and Sealing to Parents**

1. Gender

2. Name

3. Birth or christening date is preferred. If unavailable, the date of another event, such as death, is acceptable.

4. Location of above event.

5. If no other way can be found, family relationships—the names of the parents and siblings—are an acceptable way to uniquely identify a person.

6. For sealing to parents—in addition to the above information, you need the names of both the father and mother. In this instance, the mother can be uniquely identified by adding Mrs. to the full name of her husband. Her relationship to her husband and their children uniquely identifies her. Remember that this is an exception to be used only after you have searched for the name of the mother and failed.

▶ **For Sealing to Spouse**

1. Names of bride and groom

2. Date of marriage

3. Location of marriage

Other Considerations

In addition to minimum identification, there are a few other things you need to remember about submitting names for temple work:

1. If you do not know the death date, submit only the names of those ancestors born more than 110 years ago.

2. If you do not know the death date, submit only the names of those couples married more than 95 years ago.

3. Do obtain permission from a common ancestor's closest living relative, if the common ancestor was born within the last 95 years.

4. Do wait the required one year after a non–Latter-day Saint family member's death before you submit their name for ordinances.

5. Do not resubmit an ancestor listed on the International Genealogical Index (IGI) simply because his or her name is spelled differently or a different event date or place has been used. The ordinances are still valid.

6. Do not be concerned with whether your ancestors will accept the ordinance work. It is our responsibility to perform the ordinances for all our deceased ancestors; it is their responsibility to accept or reject the ordinances.

7. Do not submit the names of deceased persons who are not your ancestors. (See TempleReady Guidelines on page 184.)

There Is a Method in Our Gladness

Once you have uniquely identified some of your deceased ancestors to the best of your ability and met the above requirements, you are ready to submit their names for temple ordinance work. The Temple-Ready computer program, which is a part of FamilySearch™, is the means by which we as Latter-day Saints do this.

The following is a brief summary of the main steps in this process. It is best to have help from your ward family history consultant or from a trained volunteer at your Family History Center to help you through this process the first time.

 ❏ 1. Create a submission disk. This step is done at home or at a Family History Center using a family history computer software program. Follow the directions for exporting a GEDCOM file. Choose the TempleReady format. Note: It is possible to type the information from your family group records directly into Temple-Ready, but this is a good idea only if you have one or two names to submit. If you have several names, but do not have a computer, go to your Family History Center and use Personal Ancestral File (PAF) on the computer there. A trained volunteer will help you.

❏ 2. Run TempleReady. This step is done at the Joseph Smith Memorial Building in Salt Lake City, Utah, or in any of 3,400 Family History Centers, which are the only places the Temple-Ready program is available for public use. Ask a trained volunteer to help you the first time you use this program. TempleReady checks your names against the Church submission rules, the IGI, and other data to see which ordinances have already been performed for the persons whose names you are submitting. The program will then guide you in preparing a temple submission disk containing the names of those people for whom you can perform temple ordinances.

❏ 3. Review the written report. This step can be done at the Family History Center or at home. TempleReady will automatically provide you with a written report of what appears on your disk.

It is very important for you to review this written report and note the needed corrections. If you do not have too many names, it is best to review the written report before you exit from the TempleReady computer. If you have no corrections, go to step 5.

❏ 4. Make corrections and resubmit your names. This step must be done at the Family History Center. If you have corrections, have the trained volunteer show you how to transfer them to your TempleReady file. TempleReady will automatically print another written report.

❏ 5. Take your disk to the temple. Once you are certain that your written report and disk are as you want them to be, take or send the TempleReady disk to the temple. Here Family File cards will be printed. Allow a few days for this step. (If you submit your names for the Temple File instead of for the Family File, the temple will provide proxies for all temple ordinances. You will need to wait until the next update of the Ordinance Index on FamilySearch to find the exact date the ordinances were done.)

❏ 6. Pick up your disk and Family File cards at the temple. Your Family File cards and a printed list of the cards will be given to you in an envelope. Managing the distribution of your cards is your responsibility. You and your family, serving as proxies, can perform the temple ordinances for your ancestors at your convenience in any temple in the United States, Canada, or England. (Soon this will be available in all temples.) During the process of performing the ordinance work, you will need to manage the distribution of your Family File cards.

❏ 7. Record the ordinance dates. This step is done at home. When all of the ordinance work is finished, be sure to record the dates of the ordinances on the family group records and in your family history software program immediately. Failure to do this can result in duplication of ordinance work, because it often takes a year or more for the finished ordinance work dates to appear in the TempleReady system.

TempleReady Guidelines

1. Latter-day Saints are asked to identify their ancestors and perform temple ordinances for them. Do not undertake your own extraction programs. Instead, ask your priesthood leaders about volunteering to serve in the Family Record Extraction Program.

2. Do not simply gather names from Ancestral File and then process them through TempleReady. All names should be checked against the Ordinance Index in FamilySearch and against the records of members of your extended family before submitting them on TempleReady. This prevents unnecessary duplication.

3. Do not submit the names of deceased celebrities, historical personalities, royalty, or early LDS Church leaders.

4. Do not submit the names of persons born in European countries prior to 1500 A.D. even if they are your direct ancestors. The work for most of these people has already been done, although the names do not yet appear on the Ordinance Index. If you desire to send in names counter to this policy, you must submit them to the Temple Department, 50 East North Temple Street, Salt Lake City, UT 84150.

5. Do not add Mr. and Mrs. to the surname of the person at the end of any of your pedigree lines. Since this title does not uniquely identify the individual, the practice results in duplication of ordinances.

6. List only the first and middle names on the line reserved for that information. Do not include titles, such as Miss, Mrs., Dr., Judge, Reverend, Colonel, or General. The only exception is when the name of the wife is unknown, but the name of the husband is known. The wife can be uniquely identified as Mrs. (insert full name of husband here) and can be submitted as such. For example, the unnamed wife of John Doe would be submitted as Mrs. John (on the given name line) DOE (on the surname line). Remember, this is an exception and should be done ONLY after research efforts to discover her name have failed.

7. If the given name of an individual is unknown, leave the space blank. Do not list explanations, such as "died young," "boy,"

Non-Family Names to the Temple

George says, "Early one morning, some thirty years ago, I boarded an airplane in Calgary, Canada. I was tired and wanted to sleep. A Marine officer came and, although there were many seats available, he sat right next to me. He was a tall, handsome, and very personable fellow. He told me that he was on a speaking tour to the young people who were part of the Navigator organization, a group whose theme is a picture of a young man steering a ship with Christ standing right behind him.

"He was fascinated when I informed him that I was a Latter-day Saint. As the plane took off he said, 'Tell me what your Church can do for me in addition to what I already believe.'

"I felt the importance of his question. As the plane made its way toward Billings, Montana, I told him of the temple and of eternal marriage. As I spoke and he listened, the Spirit of the Lord was with us. He was deeply touched. In that short time, I felt a great love for him and could tell that he felt the same toward me.

"His destination was Billings. In the last few minutes we had together, I asked him for his address so that I could write to him and tell him more. He told me that he was headed to Vietnam the next week but that he would write to me with his new address. We said good-bye. Tears filled his eyes and mine. The time with him had been a sacred experience for both of us.

"Several weeks later I did receive a letter. But it was not the letter I expected. I opened it and read, 'Our son was killed in Vietnam. When he died, he had your name and address on a paper in his shirt pocket.'

"The family wanted to know how I knew him. I wrote them a long letter telling of our experience together. A week or two later they sent a letter saying that they did not favor the LDS Church and that they would hear no more of the matter. Nevertheless, later I had a friend who lived in their state go see them and inquire if I could take their son's name to the temple. They adamantly said that I could not.

"I long to go to the temple for this young man, but without his parents' permission, I cannot."

"girl," "infant," "twin," "unmarried," "no name," "unknown," "wife," etc. The only exception is noted in #6 above.

8. Do not put nicknames in parentheses or quotation marks. Use the word *or*. For example, *Robert or Bob* instead of *Robert (Bob)* and instead of *Robert "Bob."*

9. Do not estimate dates and locations when the information can be found with reasonable effort.

10. Submit only as many names as you and your family and friends can do in a reasonable amount of time. When the work for one batch of names is completed then submit another batch.

11. Do not resubmit the names of ancestors for whom ordinances have already been done in order to get the ordinance dates. Check the Ordinance Index on FamilySearch or check the records of members of your extended family instead.

12. Check with members of your extended family before submitting names. They may have already performed the ordinance work for these ancestors. The dates of their work would not appear on the Ordinance Index until it is updated.

13. Proofread names, dates, and places carefully before submitting them. Errors result in duplication of ordinances.

14. Coordinate the performance of ordinance work among living family members. Some LDS family members may have a special desire to serve as proxy for a certain ancestor. Non-LDS family members may prefer that the ordinance work not be performed at all. Respect their wishes.

Remember, keep a careful record of the dates you perform ordinance work for your ancestors. Many duplications come when members submit the same name more than once because they failed to enter the dates the ordinance work was performed.

Want to Know More?

- Read "Using TempleReady," in *Family History SourceGuide* on CD-ROM, available at LDS distribution centers, the Family History Library, and Family History Centers.

- Meet with your ward family history consultant or the trained volunteer at your Family History Center and have them teach you how to use TempleReady.

Try This

❏ 1. Visit with someone who has Family File cards about how they maintain control of the cards.

❏ 2. If you need help completing the temple ordinances on your Family Files cards, invite family and friends who have temple recommends to your home. Let them know you will be telling them briefly about the ancestors on your Family File cards and asking for their help in performing the ordinance work. This can be a casual gathering with refreshments or it can be more spiritual and include your testimony of family history work. Don't pressure people. Let them know this is simply an invitation.

❏ 3. Gather a few friends or family members together to go to the temple to perform the ordinance work for your ancestors. Many members do not often participate in baptisms, initiatory work, or sealings. This is a sacred opportunity for them.

TempleReady is a tool that helps Latter-day Saints provide temple ordinances to ensure a family will be together for eternity.

The Last Chapter

George's Story: He Sure Was Prominent to Me

Several years ago I was showing the Family History Library in Salt Lake City to a friend who was visiting from out of town. I thought I was really impressing her as I told her about the library's collection of tens of thousands of microfilms and the many other tools available to help family historians find their ancestors. But at the end of the tour I was surprised when she said, "It sure is impressive, but I just can't figure out why you go to all this bother to look into the past."

Her comment caught me so off guard that before I could gather my wits about me to reply, she added, "I would sooner live in the present and look to the future than to focus on the past."

I tried to tell her why I was interested in the past, but nothing I said seemed to reach her.

I guess we all ask ourselves, "What is the value in all this looking back? What has some ancestor whom I don't even know got to do with me anyway?" The answer for us all is that we are who we are in part because of who our ancestors were. "But," you say, "my life as a child was filled with heartache and emotional pain. How am I supposed to be grateful when looking back is like a nightmare for me?"

Of course, I don't have any easy answers to assuage such feelings. But I do know that with help from the right people and through prayer, hope can again find its way into broken hearts. With hope comes healing. And part of the healing will be forgiveness and understanding. Then will come the joy of looking back.

Even as I write I experience a deep feeling of love for my ancestors. I'd love to meet my grandparents, whom I never knew. And then I'd want to meet my great-grandparents, and on and on. I guess I'm getting carried away with this, but I can't help it. The spirit of family history work fills me with appreciation and gratitude, and with those feelings in your heart or in mine, we want to shout, "I'm glad I'm me. I'm glad that my mom is my mom and that my dad is my dad. I'm glad that my grandparents are my grandparents and that my ancestors are my ancestors!"

My favorite ancestor is my grandfather William Durrant. I never knew him, and until I tried to find out about him, I had no specific feelings for him at all. As part of my search, I learned that my grandfather had worked at the sugar factory and on farms and had run a threshing machine. Those who knew him remembered that he was an excellent gardener and that he knew a lot about plants, shrubs, and trees.

When I found his obituary it didn't say much, but one line struck deep into my heart: "William was neither prominent in the church or in the community." I was a little upset about this statement, and I thought, "Well, maybe he wasn't prominent to whoever wrote the obituary, but he sure was prominent to me."

I became determined to learn more about him. I continued my research and found a newspaper article about the death of one of his children, a young boy named Stewart. The family lived near the railroad tracks, and seven-year-old Stewart had been near the tracks as a train passed by. The boy fell under the train, and his legs were cut off. Grandfather was one of the first ones at the scene. He held his little son in his arms as the boy died. I was close to tears, but not for Stewart as much as for my grandfather.

My uncle Jim told me: "As a small child I remember there was a dirt road in front of our house. Much of the time this road was muddy. Each Sunday we children would all get ready to go to church. Father wouldn't go, but he would lead us all to the side of the muddy road. Then, one at a time, he would put us up on his shoulders and carry us piggyback across the mud to the dry path on the other side. I can remember him carrying me on his back as well as if it were yesterday. He did this every time the road was muddy, and when we returned from church he was always there to carry us back."

One day as I was thinking about my grandfather, I had a very strange feeling. I could feel him very near to me. In my heart I heard his voice telling me, "My dear grandson, I hope there is something to make you proud of me because I am deeply proud of you."

I include this account of my feelings about William Durrant because he was typical of my people. They were not a prominent bunch. There were no presidents, or governors, or mayors. And somehow that makes them more dear to me than if they had been the subject of the television show *Lifestyles of the Rich and Famous*. Oh, I wouldn't have been upset if one or two of them had been in the "Who's Who of American Fork," but there is no way I could love them more than I do.

Maybe your people were prominent, and maybe they were horse thieves. Either way, I think when you find them and come to know them, you'll want everyone to listen to your stories of them, too.

Well, there is my answer to the lady who did not want to look back. I wish she could have seen in my heart how important family history is to me. She couldn't, but I believe you get the idea.

Try This

❏ 1. Reread Chapter 1 and get started. You'll be glad you did.

❏ 2. Search for personal stories of an ancestor for whom you know only their name, dates, and places.

❏ 3. Prayerfully seek to forgive an ancestor or family member.

PART FOUR:
Ten Tens

These ten lists of ten serve as quick references to a multitude of resources. Each list is by no means complete; neither are the items listed in any particular order. These lists simply serve as a starting point as you venture into new territory. Hopefully, you will add to these lists as you learn from your own experiences.

In This Part

- You'll discover important books, magazines, Web sites, and CDs.

- You'll learn of family history conferences.

- You'll learn of possible expenses associated with family history.

- You'll even find a place where you can write down the important things you have learned as you have done your family history.

References

10 Reference Books

1. Loretto Dennis Szucs and Sandra Hargreaves Luebking, *The Source: A Guidebook of American Genealogy,* revised ed., Ancestry, Inc., 1997. (P.O. Box 476, Salt Lake City, UT 84110-0476)

2. Val D. Greenwood, *The Researcher's Guide to American Genealogy,* 3rd ed., Baltimore, MD: Genealogical Publishing, Co., 1999.

3. *The Handybook for Genealogists,* 8th ed., Logan, UT: Everton Publishers, Inc., 1991. (P.O. Box 368, Logan, UT 84321)

4. Alice Eicholz, Ph.D., *Ancestry's Red Book,* revised ed., Salt Lake City, UT: Ancestry, Inc., 1992. (P.O. Box 476, Salt Lake City, UT 84110-0476)

5. Elizabeth Petty Bentley, *The Genealogist's Address Book,* 3rd ed., Baltimore, MD: Genealogical Publishing, Co., 1995.

6. Cyndi Howells, *Cyndi's List: A Comprehensive List of 40,000 Genealogy Sites on the Internet,* Baltimore, MD: Genealogical Publishing Co., 1999.

7. Cyndi Howells, *Netting Your Ancestors: Genealogical Research on the Internet,* Baltimore, MD: Genealogical Publishing, Co., 1997.

8. E. Kay Kirkham, *The Handwriting of American Records for a Period of 300 Years,* Logan, UT: Everton Publishers, Inc., 1981.

9. Jay Androit, comp., *Township Atlas of the United States* (1977–91), Documents Index, Inc. (Box 195, McLean, VA 22101)

10. James Swan, *The Librarian's Guide to Genealogical Research,* Fort Atkinson, WI: Highsmith Press LLC, 1998.

10 Magazines and Newspapers

1. *Everton's Genealogical Helper,* Logan, UT: Everton Publishers Inc., published bi-monthly. (P.O. Box 368, Logan, UT 84323-0368)

2. *Genealogical Computing,* Salt Lake City, UT: Ancestry, Inc., published quarterly. (P.O. Box 476, Salt Lake City, UT 84110-0476)

3. *National Genealogical Society Quarterly* (NGSQ), Arlington, VA: National Genealogical Society, published quarterly. (4527 Seventeenth Street North, Arlington, VA 22207-2399)

4. *The New England Historical and Genealogical Register* (NEHGR), Boston, MA: New England Historic Genealogical Society, published quarterly. (101 Newbury St., Boston, MA 02116)

5. *Genealogical Journal,* Salt Lake City, UT: Utah Genealogical Association, published quarterly. (P.O. Box 1144, Salt Lake City, UT 84110)

6. *Heritage Quest,* Bountiful, UT: AGLL, Inc., published quarterly. (P. O. Box 329, Bountiful, UT 84010-7018)

7. *The American Genealogist* (TAG), Demorest, GA: privately published, published quarterly. (P.O. Box 398, Demorest, GA 30535–0398)

8. *The New York Genealogical and Biographical Record* (NYGBR), New York, NY: New York Genealogical and Biographical Society, published quarterly. (122 East 58th St., New York, NY 10022-1939)

9. *Reunions Magazine,* Milwaukee, WI: Reunions Magazine, published quarterly. (P.O. Box 11727, Milwaukee, WI 53211-0727)

10. For forms and charts:
    American Genealogical Lending Library (AGLL), P.O. Box 329, Bountiful, UT 84011
    Ancestry, Inc., P.O. Box 476, Salt Lake City, UT 84110-0476
    Everton Publishers, Inc., P.O. Box 368, Logan, UT 84323-0368
    Hearthstone Bookshop, 5735-A Telegraph Rd., Alexandria, VA 22303

10 LDS CDs You Can Use at Home

Early Church Membership Records, compiled by Susan Easton Black, is part of *LDS Family History Suite* published by Infobases. All other CDs are available through the distribution centers of The Church of Jesus Christ of Latter-day Saints or by calling 1-800-537-5971 in the United States. In other countries, dial your international prefix plus 801-240-1126.

1. *Family History SourceGuide* (1 CD)

2. Vital Records Index for North America (7 CDs)

3. Early Church Membership Records (compiled by Susan Easton Black)

4. 1881 British Census (25 CDs)

5. Vital Records Index for the British Isles (5 CDs)

6. 1851 British Census (Devon, Norfolk, and Warwick Counties) (1 CD)

7. Vital Records Index for Australia: 1788–1905 (4 CDs)

Remember, there are only seven now, but others are in production. Add them to this list as they are released.

8.

9.

10.

10 Web Sites

1. **www.familysearch.org** (Access to Ancestral File, International Genealogical Index, and the card catalog for the Family History Library in Salt Lake City, Utah. Links to surname sites.)

2. **www.cyndislist.com** (Links to more than 59,000 sites and growing daily.)

3. **www.usgenweb.com** (Links to county and state.)

4. **www.worldgenweb.org** (Links to other countries.)

5. **www.ancestry.com** (Links to lots of sites, including Social Security Death Index.)

6. **www.everton.com** (Online shopping for family history supplies, including books and *The Genealogical Helper* magazine.)

7. **www.rootsweb.com** (Oldest genealogy site and surname list.)

8. **www.familytreemaker.com** (Search 147 million names.)

9. **www.nara.gov** (National Archives and Records Administration site.)

10. **www.genealogy.com** (Links to other sites.)

10 More Web Sites

1. **www.lcweb.loc.gov** (Library of Congress)

2. **www.gendex.com/gendex/** (Searches more than 1,800 online genealogical databases.)

3. **www.genealogysitefinder.com** (Identifies over 76,000 online genealogical sites.)

4. **www.archives.ca/** (National Archives of Canada)

5. **www.pro.gov.uk/** (Public Record Office for the United Kingdom)

6. **www.iigs.org/** (International Internet Genealogical Society)

7. **www.mayo-ireland.ie/general/roots.htm** (Irish Family History Foundation)

8. **www.mtjeff.com/~bodenst/page3.html** (Adoptee and Genealogy Page)

9. **www.ouareau.com/adoptee/index.html** (Adoption information)

10. **home.earthlink.net/~howardorjeff/instruct.htm** (Genealogy Instruction for Beginners, Teenagers, and Kids.)

10 References for Ethnic Genealogy

1. Donna Beasley et al., *Family Pride: The Complete Guide to Tracing African American Genealogy,* n.p., MacMillan General Reference, 1997.

2. Paula K. Byers, editor, *Native American Genealogical Sourcebook,* New York: Gale Research Inc., 1995. (Part of a series of Genealogical Sourcebooks, including Asian-American, Hispanic-American, and African-American.)

3. John Phillip Calletta, *Finding Italian Roots: The Complete Guide for Americans,* Baltimore, MD: Genealogical Publishing, Co., 1993.

4. Olga K. Miller, *Genealogical Research for Czech and Slovak Americans,* Detroit, MI: Gale Research, 1978.

5. Lovoll Odd, *The Promise of America: A History of the Norwegian-American People,* Minneapolis, MN: University of Minnesota Press, 1999.

6. Lyman D. Platt, *Hispanic Surnames and Family History,* Baltimore, MD: Genealogical Publishing, Co., 1996.

7. George Ryskamp, *Finding Your Hispanic Roots,* Baltimore, MD: Genealogical Publishing, Co., 1997.

8. Colleen She, *A Student's Guide to Chinese American Genealogy,* Phoenix, AZ: Oryx Press, 1996. (Part of a series of student guides, including Italian-American, Japanese-American, Mexican-American, Native-American, African-American, British-American, German-American, Irish-American, Jewish-American, Polish-American, and Scandinavian-American.)

9. Jessie Carney Smith, editor, *Ethnic Genealogy: A Research Guide,* Westport, CT: Greenwood Publishing Group, 1983.

10. Loretto Dennis Szucs, *They Became Americans: Finding Naturalization Records and Ethnic Origins,* Salt Lake City, UT: Ancestry, Inc., 1998.

10 Web Sites for Ethnic Research

1. **www.nara.gov/publications/microfilm/amerindians/indians. html** (Catalog of microfilm publications for American Indians.)

2. **www.nara.gov/publications/microfilm/blackstudies/blackstd. html** (Catalog of microfilm publications for Black studies.)

3. **www.indians.org/tribes/** (Tribes officially recognized by the U.S. government.)

4. **www.afrigeneas.com** (African ancestry.)

5. **user.aol.com/mrosado007/index.htm** (Hispanic research.)

6. **www.rootsweb.com/~easeurgw/** (Links to helps for Eastern Europe and the former Soviet Union.)

7. **www.southamerican.org** (Links to helps for South America— under development.)

8. **www.familytreemaker.com/00000383.html** (Russian research.)

9. **www.familytreemaker.com/00000369.html** (Filipino research.)

10. **www.familytreemaker.com/00000376.html** (Japanese research.)

10 Reference Tools

Library reference tools that will help with family history research.

1. Atlases (bound collections of maps)

2. Gazetteers (geographical dictionaries)

3. Indexes (alphabetized lists that describe where to go to find more information)

4. Inventories (catalogs of the holdings of an institution)

5. Paleography guides (studies of early writing)

6. City directories

7. Language dictionaries

8. Textbooks

9. Letter writing guides

10. Your librarian

10 Conferences and Institutes

The three biggest nationwide conferences are:

1. National Genealogical Society, 4527 17th Street North, Arlington, VA 22207-2399. ("American Genealogy: A Basic Course," Independent Study)

2. Association of Professional Genealogists, P.O. Box 40393, Denver, CO 80204-0393.

3. Utah Genealogical Association, P.O. Box 1144, Salt Lake City, UT 84110.

Other conferences include:

4. Brigham Young University Conferences and Workshops, 136 Harman Building, Provo, UT 84602. (Independent Study)

5. Federation of Genealogical Societies, P.O. Box 830220, Richardson, TX 75083-0220.

Institutes include:

6. Genealogical Institute of Mid-America, Continuing Education, University of Illinois, Springfield, IL 62794-9243.

7. Institute of Genealogical Studies, P.O. Box 25556, Dallas, TX 75225-5556.

8. Institute of Genealogy and Historical Research, Samford University Library, Birmingham, AL 35229-7008.

9. National Institute on Genealogical Research, P.O. Box 14274, Washington, DC 20044-4274.

10. Salt Lake Institute of Genealogy, Utah Genealogical Association, P.O. Box 1144, Salt Lake City, UT 84110.

10 Possible Expenses

1. Forms, books, magazine subscriptions, and CDs.

2. Office supplies: pencils, pens, paper clips, stapler, 3-hole punch, paper, manila folders, and so on.

3. Computer and family history software, and Internet service provider.

4. Copying or preserving old family photographs.

5. Long distance phone calls.

6. Photocopying, postage, and parking.

7. Copies of documents from government sources: birth, marriage, and death certificates, military records, and so on.

8. Classes or workshops.

9. Membership dues to family history organizations.

10. Travel expenses, if you visit a home town, attend a family history conference, or visit family members who live elsewhere.

PART FIVE:
Appendixes

Some information, such as that on documentation, the Internet, and old photographs, is so important that it has application in many areas of family history work. These topics are covered in the Appendixes so they can be cross-referenced to different chapters in this book.

Reference information—such as relationship charts and the addresses of Latter-day Saint temples, libraries, historical societies, and the National Archives—is also in the Appendixes for easy accessibility.

In This Part

- You'll learn how to use a relationship chart.

- You'll learn how to document your sources of information.

- You'll learn how the Internet can open up a new world of family history information to you.

- You'll learn how to preserve and share old family photographs.

- You'll find a list of addresses for libraries and historical societies in every state, and for the National Archives and its branches.

Relationship Charts

Complete Relationship Chart

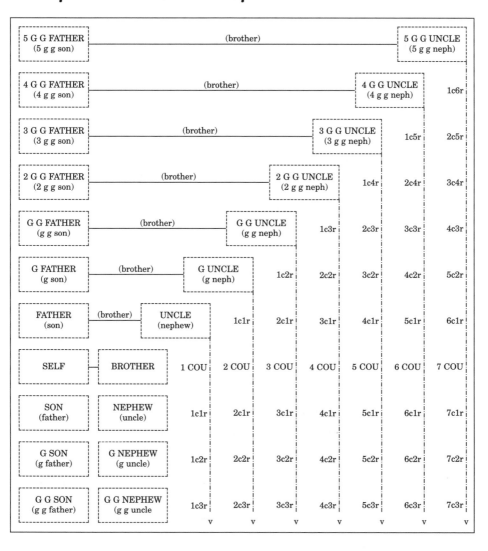

5 G G FATHER (5 g g son)		(brother)						5 G G UNCLE (5 g g neph)	
4 G G FATHER (4 g g son)		(brother)				4 G G UNCLE (4 g g neph)		1c6r	
3 G G FATHER (3 g g son)		(brother)			3 G G UNCLE (3 g g neph)		1c5r	2c5r	
2 G G FATHER (2 g g son)		(brother)		2 G G UNCLE (2 g g neph)		1c4r	2c4r	3c4r	
G G FATHER (g g son)		(brother)	G G UNCLE (g g neph)		1c3r	2c3r	3c3r	4c3r	
G FATHER (g son)	(brother)	G UNCLE (g neph)		1c2r	2c2r	3c2r	4c2r	5c2r	
FATHER (son)	(brother)	UNCLE (nephew)	1c1r	2c1r	3c1r	4c1r	5c1r	6c1r	
SELF	BROTHER	1 COU	2 COU	3 COU	4 COU	5 COU	6 COU	7 COU	
SON (father)	NEPHEW (uncle)	1c1r	2c1r	3c1r	4c1r	5c1r	6c1r	7c1r	
G SON (g father)	G NEPHEW (g uncle)	1c2r	2c2r	3c2r	4c2r	5c2r	6c2r	7c2r	
G G SON (g g father)	G G NEPHEW (g g uncle	1c3r	2c3r	3c3r	4c3r	5c3r	6c3r	7c3r	

Key to Using the Relationship Chart

1. To determine the relationship of the brothers (or sisters) of direct ancestors, follow the horizontal line from the direct ancestor.

Examples:

  a. The brother of your 5 gg father is your 5 gg uncle. Your relationship to him is shown in parentheses immediately below the uncle relationship—in this case 5 gg nephew.
  b. The sister of your 5 gg father is your 5 gg aunt.

2. To determine your relationship to the children of the brothers (and sisters) of your direct ancestors, follow the vertical line down from the uncle (or aunt) relationship.

Examples:

  a. The son of your 4 gg uncle is your 1c5r (1st cousin, 5 times removed).
  b. The grandson of your gg uncle is your 2c1r (2nd cousin, once removed).

Cousin Relationships

Common Ancestors	William and Elizabeth		
Children of Common Ancestors	John	brothers	Chris
Grandchildren	Dennis	1st cousins	Robert
Great-Grandchildren	Lisa	2nd cousins	Keith
2nd Great-Grandchildren	Ashley	3rd cousins	Tracy
3rd Great-Grandchildren	Stephen	4th cousins	Edward
4th Great-Grandchildren	George	5th cousins	Rebecca

To determine your relationship to another cousin, create a work chart like the one above. Place the names of the common ancestors at the top of the page. Then list your pedigree in descending order on the left side and your cousin's pedigree in descending order on the right side.

As long as you and your cousin are the same number of generations removed from the common ancestors, your relationship is straight cousins—first cousins, second cousins, and so on. In the above chart, for example, Lisa and Keith are both on the second cousins line and are therefore simply second cousins.

When you and your cousin are not on the same line, then you are cousins "once removed," or "twice removed." This refers to the number of generations you are removed from the common ancestors. For example, let's take second cousins Lisa and Keith. Keith has a son named Tracy. What is Tracy's relationship to Lisa?

Lisa is on the second-cousins line and Tracy is on the third cousins line. **Always start with the person closest to the common ancestor.** So, start with Lisa. Come across the chart on the second-cousins line, and then down one more generation to Tracy. They are one generation apart from each other; hence, Lisa and Tracy are second cousins once removed (2c1r).

Let's take another example. What is the relationship between Tracy and Dennis? Since you start with the person closest to the common ancestor, and Dennis is on the first-cousins line while Tracy is on the third-cousins line, you'll start with Dennis. Come across the chart on the first-cousins line, and then down two more generations to Tracy. They are two generations apart; therefore, Tracy and Dennis are first cousins twice removed (1c2r).

Keith and Ashley are second cousins once removed (2c1r).

Ashley and Rebecca are third cousins twice removed (3c2r).

Most family history computer software programs have the ability to calculate the relationship between any two people in the same database.

Sisters Anne and Gretchen Hopman of Hammond, Indiana

Maps

Learning to identify place names and geographical jurisdictions is an important skill for anyone doing family history research. Maps, atlases, and gazetteers are important tools for any genealogist.

Kinds of Maps

Topographical	Shows cities, counties, states, mountain ranges, rivers, and so on. Indicates elevation.
Historical	Can be topographical, but also shows the location and size of towns as they were in the past. Often shows the migration routes, former county boundaries, land grant bounds, colonial roads, and so on.

Useful Maps

Anyone doing research in the United States should have a current copy of the Rand McNally *Road Atlas*. Paperback and inexpensive, this atlas allows you to locate easily the state, county, and town or township of each of your surname lines.

Two excellent books designed to clearly identify county lines within each state of the United States are:

1. *The Handybook for Genealogists,* 8th ed., Logan, UT: Everton Publishers, Inc., 1991.

2. Alice Eicholz, Ph.D., *Ancestry's Red Book,* Salt Lake City, UT: Ancestry, Inc., 1992.

How to Read Maps

All maps are drawn to scale, such as 1:24,000. This means that the map reproduces a real feature at 1/24,000th its actual size. The scale is printed in the corner of the map. In topographical maps, elevations are identified by actual numbers as well as by a change in color (e.g., green indicates high elevation and brown indicates low elevation).

Atlases and gazetteers usually have an index that will identify the page and quadrangle where the town and county are located.

Where to Find Maps

- Most libraries will have maps, atlases, and gazetteers.

- Family history libraries and Family History Centers will usually have copies of Everton's *Handybook* and *Ancestry's Red Book*, which will provide state and county information. They will also have books clearly identifying townships. Plat books and county histories are a wonderful source of old maps.

- At home, map programs available on CD-ROM can be a big help.

- The Internet is also a source for maps. Start with **www.lib. utexas.edu/Libs/PCL/Map_collection/Map_collection.html**.

- The National Archives has an estimated two million maps. The *Guide to Genealogical Research in the National Archives* (Washington, DC: National Archives Trust Fund, 1982, 255–62) can help. The cartographic department of the National Archives can make copies of their maps for you. Check the Internet at **www.nara.gov**.

- The Library of Congress has a vast collection of maps in its Geography and Map Division. Copies are available. Check the Internet at **www.lcweb.loc.gov**.

Letting Maps Help You with Your Family History

Locate for each surname:

❏ 1. The ancestor's home state map with counties clearly identified. Shade in the county.

❏ 2. County map with townships or cities clearly identified. Shade in the township or city.

❏ 3. Township or city map with roads or streets clearly identified. Mark the location of your ancestor's residence.

❏ 4. Create multiple 8½″ x 11″ copies of a United States map. Using one surname for each map, mark the migration of your ancestors over the generations.

❏ 5. Make plenty of copies of all of your maps.
   a. Keep one set of maps for each surname in a separate folder of a unique color so it is easy to find.
   b. Keep state, county, or township maps in folders with census, cemetery, or surname family records.

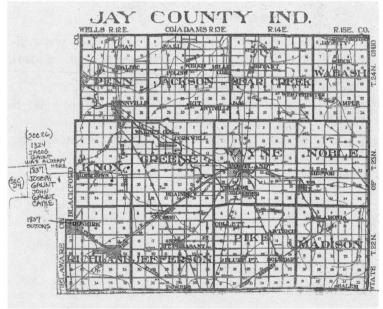

American mid-west counties are divided into townships with thirty-six sections.

Documentation

The two types of documentation are for source notes and for bibliographies.

?   **Source Notes** are (1) intended to give specific citations to source volumes and page numbers for major items of information cited in the bibliography and (2) may also be used to explain circumstances regarding an item of information.

?   **Bibliographies** are general lists of sources consulted and are usually provided at the end of the work.

Citation Formats for Source Note Entries and for Some Bibliographic Entries

Type of Record	Elements for Source Notes	Example
Books, Pamphlets, and Monographs	(1) author, (2) title, (3) publication facts (place of publication: name of publisher, year), (4) page numbers.	Source Note: Richard S. Lackey, *Cite Your Sources* (New Orleans: Polyanthos, 1980), 31. Bibliographic: Lackey, Richard S. *Cite Your Sources.* New Orleans: Polyanthos, 1980.
Periodicals	(1) title of the article, (2) name of periodical, (3) volume, (4) month/season and year, (5) page numbers.	Source Note: "William Henry of Henry's Knob," *The South Carolina Magazine of Ancestral Research,* IV (Winter 1976), 24. Bibliographic: "William Henry of Henry's Knob." *The South Carolina Magazine of Ancestral Research,* IV (Winter 1976).

(continued)

Type of Record	Elements for Source Notes	Example
Newspapers	(1) name of newspaper (place of publication is optional), (2) date of issue, (3) page numbers, section, column numbers, (4) location is optional.	Source Note: *Clarion Ledger* (Jackson, Hinds Co., MS), 1 Nov. 1898, p. 2, col. 2, MS. Dept. of Archives and History, Jackson.
Unpublished Documents	(1) descriptive title of the document, (2) significant dates or numbers, (3) specific location of the document, (4) form used and repository.	Source Note: "Account Book of Rosehill Plantation, Hinds County, Mississippi," 1840–1846, original owned by John Doe, 5157 South River Street, Clinton, MS. Photocopy examined at Clinton Public Library, Clinton, MS.
Census Records	(1) specific descriptive title, (2) civil division, (3) page numbers or other specific designation, (4) location and form of record.	Source Note: John Doe household, 1850 U.S. census, Newton Co., MS, population schedule, Knox township, Riverport post office, page 403, dwelling 304, family 28, National Archives micropublication M-408, roll 315. Bibliographic: Mississippi. Newton County. 1850 U. S. census, population schedule. Micropublication M-408, roll 315. Washington: National Archives.
Tax Lists	(1) specific descriptive title, (2) civil division, (3) page number or other specific designation, (4) location and form or record.	Source Note: 1807 Tax List (Real and Personal Property), Scott Co., MS, p. 1, line 5, Record Series G (State Auditor's Records), Vol. 84, MS. Dept. of Archives and History, Jackson.
Family Bible Records	(1) name and principal residences of original owner, (2) publication information, including title, city, publisher, and date of publication,	Source Note: Family Bible Record of Alexander Gordon of Clarke Co., MS. *The Holy Bible, Containing the Old and New Testaments, Translated out of the Original Tongues and*

(continued)

Type of Record	Elements for Source Notes	Example
	(3) present owner's name and address (or agency or library), (4) form used and location.	*With the Former Translations Diligently Compared and Revised* (New York: D. & G. Brace, 1811), owner (1977) Mrs. Frank York, 410 Naples Rd., Jackson, MS 39206. Original record was hand copied, appeared authentic, and the family record, dim with age, unaltered. In possession of the writer.
Letters	(1) description of the letter, (2) date, (3) specific location of the letter, (4) form used and repository.	Source Note: John Doe to author, 16 April 1971. Original in possession of the writer.
Civil Vital Records	(1) descriptive title, (2) significant dates and numbers, (3) specific location of the document, (4) form used and repository.	Source Note: Jacob Gaunt, death certificate no. 555 (1918), Indiana State Board of Health, Indianapolis. Bibliographic: Indiana. Indianapolis. State Board of Health. Death Registrations. Jacob Gaunt certificate.
Courthouse Records	(1) descriptive title of the record, (2) significant dates, (3) specific location of the records, (4) form used and repository.	Source Note: "Deed of Sale from Jacob Blount to Henry Warren," 18 Jan. 1775 (recorded March 1775), Craven County, NC, Deed Bk. 22, pp. 12–13, NC State Library, County Core Collection microfilm No. 84–21.
Church and Cemetery Records	(1) descriptive title, (2) significant dates, (3) specific location, (4) form used and repository.	Source Note (Church): "Baptism Record for John Doe," born 14 June 1815, baptized 15 June 1815, St. Mary's Catholic Church Misc. Bk. II, p. 182, Gulf City, AL. Photocopy sent to author by Richard Roe, 180 River St., Gulf City, AL.

(continued)

Type of Record	Elements for Source Notes	Example
		Source Note (Cemetery): Headstone inscription for Nathan Smith, Lot No. 17, Smith Cemetery, Concord, MA. (1 mile west of city limits on state route no. 82). Author's visit 1 July 1997.
State and Federal Land Records	(1) title for the particular record, (2) type of record from which the entry was taken, (3) statement with reference to the government agency or land office, (4) specific location of the record, (5) form used and repository.	Source Note: "John McRae ledger account," Credit Entry, U.S. Tract Book, St. Stephens (AL), Vol. 14 (W.N.L.), 5-10-5, 3751, Augusta (MS) Land Office, Vol. 4, No. 3947, R.G. 49, Washington National Records Center, Suitland, MD.
Military Records	(1) title for a particular record, (2) file title and number, (3) statement with reference to the government and the service, (4) specific location of the file, (5) form used and repository.	Source Note: "Confederate Service Record for Joshua I. Dyess," Muster Roll, July 1862, Co. C, 36 Reg't Miss. Vols., Service in Army of the Conf. States of America, Misc. Conf. Rolls, Box 16, MS Dept. Archives and History, Jackson.
Oral Interviews	(1) title of notes or tapes, (2) date of interview, (3) interviewer, (4) present owner's name and address, (5) form used and location, (6) evaluation information is optional.	Source Note: "Oral interview with John Doe," 13 September 1968, by Richard Roe, recording owned by author, Gulf City, MS. John Doe was living in Mobile, AL, on 10 June 1920 and was about 16 years old.
Electronic Web Site		Source Note: Information regarding the schedule of The Library of Virginia, Richmond, online **http://www.lva.lib. va.us/**. Information downloaded 27 August 1999.

(continued)

Type of Record	Elements for Source Notes	Example
		Bibliographic: Virginia. The Library of Virginia, Richmond. Online **http://www.lva.lib. va.us/**. Information downloaded 27 August 1999.

Want to Know More?

- Elizabeth Shown Mills, *Evidence! Citation and Analysis for the Family Historian,* Baltimore, MD: Genealogical Publishing, Co., 1997.

- *The Chicago Manual of Style,* 14th ed., Chicago, IL: University of Chicago Press, 1994.

- *Citing Records in the National Archives of the United States,* General Information Leaflet No. 17, Washington, DC: Government Printing Office [revised periodically]

- Sarah Bryd Askew Library, William Paterson University of New Jersey, Guide for Citing Electronic Information [Online]. **www.wpunj.edu/library** (click Publications link).

- See also Chapter 2 and Chapter 4 of this book.

Remember that behind every source is a real-life story, such as the marriage of Sarah Ethel Kerr and John Gneiting of Payson, Utah.

The Internet

Somehow it seems right that the word *line* is used to describe both the use of the Internet and a branch of your family tree, because the Internet is among the newest helps available to those searching out their roots.

Getting Online to Find Your Line

The Internet, or World Wide Web, is a system of computer networks joined together by high-speed data lines. Vast amounts of data, including family history data, reside there. The Internet can be accessed by computer through an Internet service provider (ISP) and a Web browser.

If you do not have a computer, or if you are not currently connected to the Internet, be aware that libraries and universities usually have a computer with Internet access available for use.

The Church and the Internet

The Church of Jesus Christ of Latter-day Saints launched **www.familysearch.org** on 24 May 1999. It quickly became a top-rated Internet genealogy service, with 60 million hits the first day and 100 million hits the second day. This incredible tool allows people everywhere to use FamilySearch™ from their home, library, or school.

FamilySearch online offers the following resources.

Ch. 8

- Ancestral File: A collection of millions of names from individuals, families, and genealogical organizations throughout the world is organized into pedigrees and family groups. For deceased individuals, Ancestral File shows the names of individuals; their family relationships and pedigrees; and the dates and places of their births, marriages, and deaths. For living individuals, Ancestral File shows the name of the individual, their spouse, their parents, and their children, but the word LIVING appears where the dates and places would be. No LDS ordinance information is listed for living individuals.

- International Genealogical Index (IGI): The IGI is an index of some 330 million names of deceased persons for whom temple ordinances have been completed since 1970. This index has been divided into two parts: (1) the International Genealogical Index, which contains valuable genealogical information such as dates and places of birth, christening, and marriage and names of parents, spouses, and children (it also lists sources for this information); and (2) the Ordinance Index, which lists the dates of temple ordinances performed for these deceased persons. Only the first part is on the Internet. You must search the Ordinance Index at your local Family History Center.

> ⭐ **At the present time, only the North America, British Isles, and Finland records are on the Internet. The rest of the regions are scheduled to be added in about one year.**

- Family History Library Catalog (FHLC): The FHLC describes the records for books, microfilms, and microfiche in the Family History Library in Salt Lake City. It includes the call number and a summary of contents. Records can be searched by surname and locality. The catalog will guide you to family histories; birth, marriage, and death records; census records; church registers; and many other records that may contain information about your ancestors. Most of the microfilms listed here can be ordered through your local Family History Center.

- Pedigree Resource File: This quickly growing site also allows you to publish your own family history here without charge.

- Window-based Personal Ancestral File 4.0.3 (PAF): Check "Order Family History Resources" at **www.familysearch.org** to download this family history computer software program for free. Allow about 20 minutes. In early 2000, this program will also be available on CD-ROM for $5.00 at The Church of Jesus Christ of Latter-day Saints' distribution centers worldwide.

- Links to more than 70,000 Collaboration Lists: These lists can connect people together who are researching the same surname. Check **www.familysearch.org/Share/**.

- An index to thousands of other Web sites worldwide.

You Still Need a Family History Center

Even though FamilySearch on the Internet is a valuable tool, you will still enjoy the services provided through your Family History Center. A trained volunteer is available at all times to help you. In addition, TempleReady, the Ordinance Index, and the ability to order films and read them are only available at a Family History Center or the Family History Library.

What Other Family History Is on the Internet?

1. *Compiled Family Histories.* About 90 percent of the material on the Internet has been compiled by others using a variety of sources. Its accuracy is only as valid as the ability of the person compiling it and the sources they used. Nevertheless, compiled materials are essential because they provide a framework of existing research. Just remember to verify the facts using primary sources (original records) or two independent sources.

Important sites for family histories are **www.familytreemaker. com/ifftop.html** and **www.ancestry.com**. Also check **www.genealogy library.com**, **www.genserv.com**, **www.rootsweb.com**, and **www. gendex.com**.

2. *How-to Sites.* Some Web sites provide information to help you find out how to begin your family history research and how to use certain records. Check the *Family History SourceGuide* (**www.family search.org/sg/**), Online University (**www.genealogy.com/university. html**), and the Learning Center (**www.ancestry.com/learn/learning/ main.htm**).

3. *Indexes.* Around the world there are many groups indexing census, cemetery, and other records. These indexes appear on the Internet as they are produced.

Some states have put indexes of their vital records on the Internet. You can look up births, marriages, and deaths. Once you find what you need, you can order a copy of the certificate by e-mail. Kentucky in the United States and British Columbia in Canada are among the first to offer this service.

The best way to locate these indexes is to use a comprehensive Web site, such as **www.cyndislist.com**, which lists more than 59,000 sites divided into more than 120 categories. Another important site is **www. genealogy.com/links/index.htm**, which lists more than 76,000 sites.

4. *Actual Records.* This category is small but growing. Currently there are not many sites that offer actual records. However, one that does is the Bureau of Land Management. It has placed the original land records of thirteen states on the Internet. These records show the transfer of land from the government to the people, all original land purchases, and homesteads. Enter your ancestor's name and location and the date the land was transferred in the site at **www.glorecords.blm.gov**.

> **Some people place "hearsay" and other incomplete ancestral research onto the Internet. So when you copy this information into your files, consider it a starting point rather than a finished product.**

5. *Chat Rooms and Queries.* Some genealogical chat rooms can be found through **www.talkcity.com**, **chat.genforum.com**, or **www.genealogy.about.com/hobbies/geneal ogy/mpchat.htm** to name a few. Not all chat rooms are moderated, so browse around and find one that you like. For queries check **www. usgenweb.org**, **www.genforum.com**, and **query.genealogytoolbox. com/**. Remember, attaching a GEDCOM file to an e-mail is an easy way to transfer family history data.

6. *Research Coordination Sites.* If you are looking for a particular ancestor in a certain locality, you can register your name at several Internet sites. This will put you in contact with others who share your interest. Perhaps you can coordinate your efforts. The largest of these Web sites is the Roots Surname List, with more than three-quarters of a million surnames listed by nearly 100,000 researchers. Check **rsl.**

> **If the volume of information on the Internet is intimidating to you, create a list of favorites to serve as your core sites. Eventually, you will feel comfortable with the expanding nature of the Internet.**

Ten Tens, Appendix B

rootsweb.com/cgi-bin/rslsql.cgi.

7. ***Reference Tools.*** One of the important facets of the Internet is the availability of maps, gazetteers, directories, and indexes that can be easily located. In addition, many libraries have their card catalogs listed on the Internet.

Creating Your Own Web Page

Not only can the Internet provide family histories, it can provide a simple and inexpensive way to publish your own work. Creating your own Web page is becoming easier.

Most of the family history computer software programs on the market have the ability to convert your family history information into HTML (HyperText Mark-up Language), the programming language of the Internet. This language is translated into graphical pages by your Web browser.

Most of the family history computer software programs can also help you design a Web page. Windows-based Personal Ancestral File 4.0 (PAF) is among the programs that is capable of designing a Web page.

Before you create your own family history site, explore other family history Web pages. Study the similarities and differences and decide which details you want to include on your Web page. Make sure to include an e-mail link. Remember to include information about deceased ancestors only. It is essential to protect the privacy of living people.

Once you have created a basic Web page, you may want to enhance it with photographs, sound, or video. This is worth the extra effort and your family history computer software can help.

How to Make a Query

Keep your query concise and include the answers to five basic facts: Who, What, When, Where, and How.

- **Who?** List full name, surname in all caps.

- **What?** List exactly what you want to know.

- **When?** List important dates, such as birth date or death date.

- **Where?** List important places, such as birthplace or death place.

- **How?** List e-mail or home address and phone number so others can contact you.

To see an example of a program that converts a GEDCOM file into a Web page, check **help.surnameweb.org/knight/**.

Want to Know More?

- Matthew and April Leigh Helm, *Genealogy Online for Dummies,* Foster City, CA: IDG Books Worldwide, Inc., 1998.

- Cyndi Howells, *Cyndi's List: A Comprehensive List of 40,000 Genealogy Sites on the Internet,* Baltimore, MD: Genealogical Publishing, Co., 1999.

- Cyndi Howells, *Netting Your Ancestors: Genealogical Research on the Internet,* Baltimore, MD: Genealogical Publishing, Co., 1997.

Try This

❏ 1. Log onto **www.familysearch.org** and look for one of your ancestors in Ancestral File.

❏ 2. Look for the name of a deceased grandparent in the Social Security Death Index on FamilySearch.

❏ 3. Log onto **www.cyndislist.com** and explore.

Old Photographs

Nothing really draws you into the past faster and with more power than an old photograph. Jimmy Parker remembers seeing the faces of his ancestors: "When I was in my early teens, I sat next to Grandmother on the davenport and together we looked at her large collection of family photos. I felt like I was in heaven as she told me the names of the people in each photo. It all seemed so mysterious to me. She told me how I was related to each one. I can still hear her voice, 'This one is my father. He is your great-grandfather. And here he is standing by the wagon with his wife, your great-grandmother, and me. I was only four or five there. It was so long ago and yet it seems like yesterday.'

"I think it was those sessions with my grandmother that caused me to have such deep feelings about my ancestors. Later when I was introduced to The Church of Jesus Christ of Latter-day Saints, I was taught the doctrine of baptism for the dead and that families could all be together in heaven. That doctrine tasted very sweet to me. I believe that hearing of the eternal destiny of families, more than anything else, led to my baptism into the Church."

Finding Family Photos

Most family photos are hidden away in drawers, closets, and scrapbooks of older family members. What a shame! These treasures should be found, preserved, copied, and made available to all family members.

Ask parents, grandparents, aunts and uncles, brothers and sisters, and other family members if they have any family photos. If so, offer to make copies of them for other family members and to have the originals preserved and returned.

Local museums or libraries may also have old photos of previous residents on display. Some local county historical societies may have photos of prominent 19th-century citizens who may also be a part of your family.

Preserving
Old Photos

Light, moisture, oil, and acid from paper are the enemies of all photographs. Following are some suggestions on how to preserve your old photographs:

1. Take your rarest, oldest photographs to a professional to have them preserved and duplicated. A professional can enhance old photographs, remove scratches, or take one face from a group photograph and enlarge it into a single photograph. Have plenty of copies made for family members. Keep the negatives in an envelope in a separate place in case of fire or other natural disaster. (See Chapter 16 for a way to make passable copies of photos when visiting family members who do not want to part with their photographs.)

   Ch. 16

2. Keep your original old photos in a dark, dry place. Store them year-round at about 65 to 70 degrees Fahrenheit with less than 50 percent humidity.

3. Store photographs in steel file cabinets or in acid-free storage boxes. If you mount photographs in a photo album, use acid-free paper and a safe adhesive.

4. Display copies of your most precious old photographs, not the originals. Light will damage them. Avoid exposing your photographs to prolonged direct sunlight and fluorescent lights, but don't be afraid to look at them or show them to others. If viewing especially rare or fragile originals, please ask guests to wear latex or cloth gloves to protect the photos from normal oils on human skin.

5. Since color photos fade more quickly than black and white, rephotograph your most prized color pictures on black-and-white film.

6. Always preserve your important photographs (and documents) electronically by scanning them into your computer or by having a photo CD made. Once photographs are stored electronically, it is easy to use them in a variety of ways with your family history computer software program.

Types of Old Photographs

Old photographs generally fall into one of the following categories. These are listed in chronological order:

Type of Photograph	Years	Description
Daguerreo-type	Typically taken between 1839 and 1860.	A type of photograph taken on silver-plated copper and requiring a long exposure. They are often found encased in a leather case. When you tilt a daguerreotype, the image appears to change from a positive to a negative.
Glass Plate Negatives	Typically produced between 1848 and 1930.	This glass has been coated with light-sensitive silver bromide and immersed in gelatin.
Stereographic Cards	Typically produced between 1850 and 1925.	These photographs on curved cardstock appeared to be three-dimensional when viewed with a stereographic viewer.
Ambrotypes	Typically taken between 1858 and 1866.	A type of photograph made on thin glass with a black backing. They required a shorter exposure time than a daguerreotype.
Cartes-de-visite	Produced between 1858 and 1891.	These photographic prints are mounted on cardstock and then bound together into an album.
Albumen Prints	Typically produced between 1858 and 1910.	These are the prints used in cartes-de-visite and cabinet

(continued)

Type of Photograph	Years	Description
		cards. They are images printed on thin paper coated with albumen and silver nitrate and then mounted on cardboard.
Tintype	Typically taken between 1858 and 1910.	A type of photograph made on a metal sheet with the image coated with varnish. Often found in a paper cover.
Cabinet Cards	Produced between 1865 and 1906.	These are larger versions of cartes-de-visite.
Platinum Prints	Typically produced between 1880 and 1930.	These prints, which appear to be embedded in the paper, are often highlighted with chalk. They have a matte surface.

Printing Your Own

It used to be that the only way to get copies of old family photos was to have it done professionally. That is still a fine option; however, now that computer software, scanners, and color printers are affordable, more and more genealogists are making copies of old photographs at home.

Once you scan in your old photographs, you can adjust the size, color, and detail. Print photos on photographic paper. A picture pedigree chart or a single family photo suitable for framing makes a wonderful and priceless gift for yourself and family members.

Want to Know More?

- See **www.daguerre.org** for daguerreotype photo information.

- See **www.kodak.com/country/US/en/corp/albums/archiving/archivingMain.shtml** for tips on how to preserve your photos.

- See **www.maine.com/photos** for tips on how to preserve your black-and-white photos and documents.

- Ask a professional photographer where acid-free supplies can be found in your city.

Latter-day Saint Temples

Temples in Operation as of December 31, 1999

The mailing address is listed first. If only one address is listed, then the mailing and street address are the same.

- Anchorage Alaska Temple (ANCHO)
  P. O. Box 112069
  Anchorage, AK 99511-2069
      13111 Brayton Drive
      Anchorage, AK 99511
  Telephone: (907) 348-7890

- Apia Samoa Temple (APIA)
  P.O. Box 1621
  Apia, Samoa
  Telephone: 011-685-21018

- Atlanta Georgia Temple (ATLAN)
  6450 Barfield Road
  Atlanta, GA 30328
  Telephone: (707) 393-3698

- Bern Switzerland Temple (SWISS)
  Tempelstrasse 4 - Postfach
  CH–3052 Zollikofen
  Switzerland
  Telephone: 011-41-31-911-0912

- Billings Montana Temple (BILLI)
  3100 Rim Point Drive
  Billings, MT 59106
  Telephone: (406) 655-0607

Jordan River Utah Temple

- Bismarck North Dakota Temple (BISMA)
  2930 Cody Drive
  Bismarck, ND 58501
  Telephone: (701) 258-9590

- Bogotá D.C. Colombia Temple (BOGOT)
  c/o Apartado Aereo 91831
  Bogotá, Colombia
  Telephone: 011-571-625-8000

- Boise Idaho Temple (BOISE)
  1211 South Cole Road
  Boise, ID 83709-1781
  Telephone: (208) 322-4422

- Bountiful Utah Temple (BOUNT)
  640 South Bountiful Boulevard
  Bountiful, UT 84010
  Telephone: (801) 296-2100

- Buenos Aires Argentina Temple (BAIRE)
  Autopista Richieri y Puente 13
  1778 Ciudad Evita
  Buenos Aires, Argentina
  Telephone: 011-54-11-4487-1520

Doors on Vernal Utah Temple

- Cardston Alberta Temple (ALBER)
  P.O. Box 25
  Babb, MT 59411
      348-3rd St. West
      Cardston, Alberta T0K 0K0
      Canada
  Telephone: (403) 653-3552

- Chicago Illinois Temple (CHICA)
  4151 West Lake Avenue
  Glenview, IL 60025
  Telephone: (847) 299-6500

- Colonia Juárez Chihuahua México Temple (COLJU)
  P. O. Box 1820
  Santa Teresa, NM 88008
      Calle Chihuahua y Diaz
      Apartado Postal Num. 2
      Colonia Juárez, Chihuahua 31857
      Mexico
  Telephone: 011-52-169-5-0144

- Columbia South Carolina Temple (COLSC)
  2905 Trotter Road
  Columbia, SC 29061
  Telephone: (803) 647-9472

- Columbus Ohio Temple (COLUM)
  P. O. Box 597
  Hilliard, OH 43026
      3870 Gateway Boulevard
      Columbus, OH 43228
  Telephone: (614) 351-5001

Salt Lake Temple

- Dallas Texas Temple (DALLA)
  6363 Willow Lake
  Dallas, TX 75230
  Telephone: (972) 991-1273

- Denver Colorado Temple (DENVE)
  P. O. Box 3969
  Littleton, CO 80161
      2001 East Phillips Circle
      Littleton, CO 80122
  Telephone: (303) 730-0220

- Detroit Michigan Temple (DETRO)
  P. O. Box 494
  Westland, MI 48303
      425 North Woodward
      Bloomfield Hills, MI 48304
  Telephone: (248) 593-0690

- Edmonton Alberta Temple (EDMON)
  7 1203 Carter Crest Road
  Edmonton Alberta T6R 2R1
  Canada
  >   14325-53rd Ave. NW
  >   Edmonton, Alberta T6H 5G6
  >   Canada
  Telephone: (780) 434-7436

- Frankfurt Germany Temple (FRANK)
  Talstrasse 10
  D-61381 Friedrichsdorf/TS
  Germany
  Telephone: 011-49-6172-5900-0

Seagull Monument on Temple Square in Salt Lake City, Utah

- Freiberg Germany Temple (FREIB)
  Hainichener Strasse 64
  D–09599 Freiberg
  Germany
  Telephone: 011-49-3731-35960

- Guatemala City Guatemala Temple (GUATE)
  24 Avenida 2-20, Zona 15
  Vista Hermosa 1
  Guatemala City, Guatemala
  Telephone: 011-502-369-8981

- Guayaquil Ecuador Temple (GUAYA)
  Avenida Rodrigo Chavez Gonzalez
  Calle 6
  Principado de las Lomas
  Urdesa Norte
  Guayaquil, Ecuador
  Telephone: 011-593-4889-388

- Halifax Nova Scotia Temple (HALIF)
  P. O Box 21034
  Cole Harbour, R.P.O.
  Dartmouth, Nova Scotia B2W 6B2
  Canada
    44 Cumberland Drive
    Dartmouth, Nova Scotia B2V 2C7
    Canada
  Telephone: (902) 434-6920

- Hamilton New Zealand Temple (NZEAL)
  Private Bag 3003
  Hamilton, New Zealand
  Telephone: 011-64-7-846-2750

*Angel Moroni statue on
temple spire*

- Hong Kong China Temple (HKONG)
  2 Cornwall Street
  Kowloon Tong
  Kowloon, Hong Kong, China
  Telephone: 011-852-2339-8100

- Idaho Falls Idaho Temple (IFALL)
  1000 Memorial Drive
  Idaho Falls, ID 83402
  Telephone: (208) 522-7669

- Johannesburg South Africa Temple (JOHAN)
  7 Jubilee Road—Parktown
  Johannesburg 2193
  South Africa
  Telephone: 011-27-11-642-4952

- Jordan River Utah Temple (JRIVE)
  10200 South 1300 West
  South Jordan, UT 84095
  Telephone: (801) 254-3003

- Laie Hawaii Temple (HAWAI)
  P.O. Box 988
  Laie, HI 96762-0988
    55-600 Naniloa Loop
    Laie, HI 96762
  Telephone: (808) 293-2427

- Las Vegas Nevada Temple (LVEGA)
  827 Temple View Drive
  Las Vegas, NV 89110
  Telephone: (702) 452-5011

- Lima Peru Temple (LIMA)
  Av. Javier Prado Este y
  Av. Los Ingenieros s/n
  Urb. Santa Patricia
  La Moline, Lima
  Peru
  Telephone: 011-51-13-48-0418

- Logan Utah Temple (LOGAN)
  175 North 300 East
  Logan, UT 84321
  Telephone: (435) 752-3611

- London England Temple (LONDO)
  Newchapel, Nr. Lingfield
  Surrey RH7 SHW
  England
  Telephone: 011-441-342-832759

- Los Angeles California Temple (LANGE)
  10777 Santa Monica Boulevard
  Los Angeles, CA 90025
  Telephone: (310) 474-5569

- Madrid Spain Temple (MADRI)
  Calle Del Templo No. 2
  E–28030 Madrid
  Spain
  Telephone: 011-3491-307-7607

- Manila Philippines Temple (MANIL)
  13 Temple Drive
  Green Meadows Subdivision
  1110 Quezon City Metro Manila
  Philippines
  Telephone: 011-63-2-635-0954

Manti Utah Temple

- Manti Utah Temple (MANTI)
  Temple Hill
  P. O. Box 280
  Manti, UT 84642-0280
      Temple Hill
      Manti, UT 84642
  Telephone: (435) 835-2291

- Mesa Arizona Temple (ARIZO)
  101 South LeSueur
  Mesa, AZ 85204
  Telephone: (480) 833-1211

- México City D.F.
      México Temple (MEXIC)
  Avenida 510 #90
  Col San Juan de Aragon
  México DF 07950
  Telephone: 011-525-747-4860/61

- Monticello Utah Temple (MONTI)
  P. O. Box 520
  Monticello, UT 84535
      347 North 200 West
      Monticello, UT 84535
  Telephone: (435) 587-3500

Monticello Utah Temple

- Mount Timpanogos Utah Temple (MTIMP)
  742 North 900 East
  American Fork, UT 84003
  Telephone: (801) 763-4540

- Nuku'alofa Tonga Temple (NUKUA)
  P.O. Box 40
  Nuku'alofa, Tonga
      Loto Rd Tongatapu
      Nuku'alofa, Tonga
  Telephone: 011-676-29-255

- Oakland California Temple (OAKLA)
  4700 Lincoln Avenue
  Oakland, CA 94602
  Telephone: (510) 531-3200

- Ogden Utah Temple (OGDEN)
  350-22nd Street
  Ogden, UT 84401
  Telephone: (801) 621-6880

- Orlando Florida Temple (ORLAN)
  9000 Windy Ridge Road
  Windermere, FL 34786
  Telephone: (407) 876-0022

*Angel Moroni statue on
Vernal Utah Temple*

- Papeete Tahiti Temple (PAPEE)
  B.P. 5682
  Pirae, Tahiti, French Polynesia
      Allee Pierre Loti, Titioro
      Tahiti, French Polynesia
  Telephone: 011-689-50-3939

- Portland Oregon Temple (PORTL)
  13600 SW Kruse Oaks Boulevard
  Lake Oswego, OR 97035
  Telephone: (503) 639-7066

- Preston England Temple (PREST)
  Temple Way, Hartwood Green
  Chorley, Lancashire PR6 7EQ
  England
  Telephone: 011-441-257-226100

- Provo Utah Temple (PROVO)
  2200 Temple Hill Drive
  Provo, UT 84604
  Telephone: (801) 375-5775

- Raleigh North Carolina Temple (RALEI)
  P. O. Box 985
  Apex, NC 27502
      574 Bryan Drive
      Apex, NC 27502
  Telephone: (919) 362-4135

- Recife Brazil Temple (RECIF)
  Rua Dr. Jose De Goes
  #262 Parnamirim
  Recife PE 52060-380
  Brazil
  Telephone: 011-55-81-441-4173

- Regina Saskatchewan Temple (REGIN)
  111 Wascana Gate North
  Regina, Saskatchewan S4V 2J6
  Canada
  Telephone: (306) 545-8194

- St. George Utah Temple (SGEOR)
  250 East 400 South
  St. George, UT 84770
  Telephone: (435) 673-3533

- St. Louis Missouri Temple (SLOUI)
  12555 North Outer Forty Drive
  Town & Country, MO 63141
  Telephone: (314) 514-1122

San Diego California Temple Spires

- Salt Lake Temple (SLAKE)
  50 West North Temple Street
  Salt Lake City, UT 84150
  Telephone: (801) 240-2640

- San Diego California Temple (SDIEG)
  7474 Charmant Drive
  San Diego, CA 92122
  Telephone: (619) 622-0991

- Santiago Chile Temple (SANTI)
  Pocuro #1940 Providencia
  Santiago, Chile
  Telephone: 011-56-2-223-9976

- São Paulo Brazil Temple (SPAUL)
  Av. Prof Francisco Morato
  São Paulo 05512-300
  Brazil
  Telephone: 011-55-11-3721-9622

- Seattle Washington Temple (SEATT)
  2808 148th Avenue SE
  Bellevue, WA 98007
  Telephone: (425) 643-5144

- Seoul South Korea Temple (SEOUL)
  500-23 Chang Chun-dong
  Seodaemun-Ku
  Seoul 120-180 Korea
  Telephone: 011-82-2-334-9100

- Spokane Washington Temple (SPOKA)
  P. O. Box 141420
  Spokane, WA 99214-1420
      13608 East Belle Terre
      Spokane, WA 99214-1420
  Telephone: (509) 926-2824

Seattle Washington Temple

- Stockholm Sweden Temple (STOCK)
  Box 153
  S-13723 Vasterhaninge
  Sweden
      Tempelvagen 4
      Vasterhaninge, Sweden
  Telephone: 011-46-8500-65500

- Sydney Australia Temple (SYDNE)
  756 Pennant Hill Road
  (Pennant Hill Road and Moseley Street)
  Carlingford, NSW 2118
  Australia
  Telephone: 011-61-2-9841-5471

- Taipei Taiwan Temple (TAIPE)
  256 Ai Kuo East Road
  Taipei, Taiwan
  Republic of China
  Telephone: 011-886-2-2351-0218

- Tokyo Japan Temple (TOKYO)
  5-8-10 Minami-Azabu
  Minato-Ku
  Tokyo, Japan 106
  Telephone: 011-813-3-442-8171

- Toronto Ontario Temple (TORON)
  10060 Bramalea Road
  Brampton, Ontario L6R 1A1
  Canada
  Telephone: (905) 799-1122

- Vernal Utah Temple (VERNA)
  170 South 400 West
  Vernal, UT 84078
  Telephone: (435) 789-3220

Vernal Utah Temple

- Washington D.C. Temple (WASHI)
  9900 Stoneybrook Drive
  Kensington, MD 20895
  Telephone: (301) 588-0650

Announced or Under Construction

- Accra Ghana Temple (ACCRA)
- Adelaide Australia Temple (ADELA)
- Albuquerque New Mexico Temple (ALBUQ)
- Baton Rouge Louisiana Temple (BROUG)
- Birmingham Alabama Temple (BIRMI)
- Boston Massachusetts Temple (BOSTO)
- Brisbane Australia Temple (BRISB)
- Campinas Brazil Temple (CAMPI)
- Caracas D. F. Venezuela Temple (CARAC)
- Ciudad Juárez México Temple (CIUJU)
- Cochabamba Bolivia Temple (COCHA)
- Copenhagen Denmark Temple (COPEN)
- Fresno California Temple (FRESN)
- Fukuoka Japan Temple (FUKUO)

- Guadalajara México Temple (GUADA)
- The Hague Netherlands Temple (HAGUE)
- Harrison New York Temple (NYORK)
- Hermosillo Sonora México Temple (HERMO)
- Houston Texas Temple (HOUST)
- Kiev Ukraine Temple (KIEV)
- Kona Hawaii Temple (KONA)
- Louisville Kentucky Temple (LOUIS)
- Medford Oregon Temple (MEDFO)
- Melbourne Australia Temple (MELBO)
- Memphis Tennessee Temple (MEMPH)
- Mérida Yucatán México Temple (MERID)
- Monterrey México Temple (MONTE)
- Montevideo Uruguay Temple (MNTVD)
- Montreal Quebec Temple (MONTR)
- Nashville Tennessee Temple (NASHV)
- Nauvoo Illinois Temple (NAUV2)
- Oaxaca México Temple (OAXAC)
- Oklahoma City Oklahoma Temple (OKLAH)
- Palmyra New York Temple (PALMY)
- Perth Australia Temple (PERTH)
- Porto Alegre Brazil Temple (PALEG)
- Reno Nevada Temple (RENO)
- St. Paul Minnesota Temple (SPMIN)
- San José Costa Rica Temple (SJOSE)
- Santo Domingo Dominican Republic Temple (SDOMI)
- Suva Fiji Temple (SUVA)
- Tampico México Temple (TAMPI)
- Tuxtla Gutiérrez México Temple (TGUTI)
- Veracruz México Temple (VERAC)
- Villahermosa Tabasco México Temple (VILLA)
- Winter Quarters Temple (WINTE)

No Longer in Use

- Nauvoo Temple (NAUVO)—Destroyed 1848
- President's Office (POFFI)
- Endowment House (EHOUS)

Libraries

There's More Than One Kind of Library!

Public Libraries

Public libraries can be small or large and are a place where the books can be checked out by residents. Reference books, which may be fragile or irreplaceable and include genealogical material, are not allowed out of the library.

Private Libraries

Many private libraries make their collections accessible to the general public. Some excellent collections, however, are restricted. Often librarians can assist you by mail.

Genealogical and Historical Society Libraries

Genealogical and historical society libraries may be public or private. If it is a private library, restrictions may apply. In some cases, members have open stack privileges, while nonmembers do not. There can be a delay from the time you request the record to when it is brought to you from the stacks. Most libraries with closed stacks have some of their commonly requested books available on shelves.

Lending Libraries

Genealogical libraries usually do not allow patrons to borrow the books, but there are exceptions. For example, the Sutro Library in San Francisco, California, and the Library of Virginia in Richmond both have interlibrary loan.

The New England Historic Genealogical Society (101 Newbury Street, Boston, MA 02116-3087) maintains a lending library, as does the

National Genealogical Society Library (4527 Seventeenth Street North, Arlington, VA 22207-2399). Both loan to members only. If you are interested in borrowing books by mail, examine the list of lending libraries in Elizabeth Petty Bentley, *The Genealogist's Address Book,* 3rd ed., Baltimore, MD: Genealogical Publishing, Co., 1995, 515–16.

University and College Libraries

Some of these libraries have rich genealogical holdings. Many universities and colleges will allow nonstudents to check out books for a limited time.

Family History Library

The Family History Library is located at 35 North West Temple Street, Salt Lake City, UT 84150. Write here for a listing of branch libraries, called Family History Centers. You can also find a listing at **www.lds.org** or by calling (801) 240-2331.

The Magnificent Allen County Collection

The public county library at Ft. Wayne, Indiana, has one of the largest collections of genealogy material in the United States and is considered one of the finest in the country. They have thousands of books. For their large collection of periodicals, they developed the PERSI index. Check it out at **www.acpl.lib.in.us**.

Religious and Ethnic Libraries

Some churches and ethnic groups maintain libraries and archives but have limited hours. Some have their early minutes and registers available on microfilm. The Baptist Church in Virginia and the Lutheran Church of Pennsylvania are among those who have libraries. Check with your reference librarian or check Elizabeth Petty Bentley's *The Genealogist's Address Book,* 457–77.

Lineage Society Libraries

The Daughters of the American Revolution Library (1776 D Street NW, Washington, DC 20006-5392) is the best known and most extensive library in this category. Besides their book holdings, they have considerable material, such as family Bible records and other items, that has been submitted in support of applications or copied by members of their chapters throughout the country. (See Elizabeth Petty Bentley, *The Genealogist's Address Book,* 479–88; and Szucs and Luebking, *The Source: A Guidebook of American Genealogy,* revised ed., Salt Lake City, UT: Ancestry, Inc., 692–707.)

The Library of Congress

In addition to the genealogy department, the Library of Congress has rare books, newspaper finding aids, photographs, and maps. See James C. Neagles, *The Library of Congress: A Guide to Genealogical and Historical Research,* Salt Lake City, UT: Ancestry, Inc., 1990.

Major Libraries and Repositories for Genealogical Records

Alabama

- Alabama Department of Archives
  624 Washington Ave.
  Montgomery, AL 36130

- Birmingham Public Library
  2100 Park Place
  Birmingham, AL 35203

- Samford University Library
  800 Lakeshore Dr.
  Birmingham, AL 35229

Alaska

- Alaska State Archives and Library
  141 Willoughby Ave.
  Juneau, AK 99801-1720

Arizona

- Arizona State Archives
  1700 W. Washington St.
  Phoenix, AZ 85007

- Arizona Historical Society
  949 E. Second St.
  Tuscon, AZ 85719

Arkansas

- Arkansas History
  Commission
  One Capitol Mall
  Little Rock, AR 72201

California

- California State
  Archives
  201 N. Sunrise Ave.
  Sacramento, CA 95561

- California State Library
  914 Capitol Mall
  Sacramento, CA 95814

- California State Library
  Sutro Branch
  480 Winston Dr.
  San Francisco, CA
  94132

Colorado

- Colorado State Archives
  1313 Sherman St.,
  I-B20
  Denver, CO 80203

- Denver Public Library
  Social Sciences and
  Genealogy
  1357 Broadway
  Denver, CO 80203

Connecticut

- Connecticut State
  Library
  231 Capitol Ave.
  Hartford, CT 06106

- Connecticut Historical
  Society
  1 Elizabeth Ave.
  Hartford, CT 06105

Delaware

- Delaware Bureau of
  Archives
  Hall of Records
  Dover, DE 19901

- The Historical Society
  of Delaware
  505 Market St.
  Wilmington, DE 19801

District of Columbia

- Library of Congress
  Humanities and
  Social Sciences
  Division
  Thomas Jefferson
  Building, Room
  UG42
  Washington, DC
  20540-4660

- Daughters of the
  American
  Revolution Library
  1776 D St. NW
  Washington, DC
  20006-5392

- District of Columbia
  Archives
  1300 Naylor Court NW
  Washington, DC
  20001-4255

- Martin Luther King Jr.
  Memorial Library
  Washingtonian Division
  901 G St. NW
  Washington, DC 20001

Florida

- Florida State Archives
  and Libraries
  R.A. Gray Building
  500 South Bronough St.
  Tallahassee, FL
  32399-0250

- P.K. Yonge Library of
  Florida History
  University of Florida
  Gainesville, FL 32611

Georgia

- Georgia Department of
  Archives
  330 Capitol Ave. SE
  Atlanta, GA 30334

- Georgia Historical
  Society
  501 Whittaker St.
  Savannah, GA 31498

Hawaii

- Hawaii State Archives
  Lolani Palace Grounds
  Honolulu, HI 96813

- Hawaiian Historical
  Society
  560 Kawaiahoa St.
  Honolulu, HI 96813

- Hawaii State Library
  1390 Miller St.,
  Box 2360
  Honolulu, HI 96804

Idaho

- Idaho Library and
  Archives
  450 North Fourth St.
  Boise, ID 83702

Illinois

- Illinois State Archives
  Archives Building
  Spring and Edwards
  Springfield, IL 62756

- Illinois State Library
  Second and Capitol
  Streets
  Springfield, IL 62756

- Illinois State Historical
  Library
  Old State Capitol
  Springfield, IL 62701

- Newberry Library
  60 West Walton St.
  Chicago, IL 60610

Indiana

- Indiana State Library
  140 North Senate Ave.
  Indianapolis, IN 46204

- Indiana State Archives
  Commission on Public
  Records
  140 North Senate Ave.
  Indianapolis, IN 46204

- Indiana Historical
  Society
  315 West Ohio St.
  Indianapolis, IN 46202

- Allen County Public
  Library
  Historical Genealogy
  Department
  900 Webster St.
  Fort Wayne, IN 46802

Iowa

- State Historical Society
  of Iowa
  Library and Archives
  600 East Locust
  Des Moines, IA 50319

- Library and Archives
  Bureau
  Centennial Building
  402 Iowa Avenue
  Iowa City, IA
  52240-1806

Kansas

- Kansas State Historical
  Society
  Archives Division
  6425 SW Sixth Ave.
  Topeka, KS 66615-1099

Kentucky

- Kentucky Department
  for Archives
  300 Coffee Tree Rd.
  P.O. Box 537
  Frankfort, KY
  40602-0537

- Kentucky Historical
  Society
  300 West Broadway
  P.O. Box 1792
  Frankfort, KY 40602

- Filson Club Library
  1310 S. Third St.
  Louisville, KY 40205

Louisiana

- Louisiana Division of
  Archives
  3851 Essen Lane
  P.O. Box 94125
  Baton Rouge, LA 70804

- Louisiana State Library
  760 Third St.
  P.O. Box 131
  Baton Rouge, LA 70821

Maine

- Maine State Archives
  Capitol House Station
  84
  Augusta, ME
  04333-8598

- Maine State Library
  State House Station 64
  Augusta, ME 04333

- Maine Historical
  Society Library
  485 Congress St.
  Portland, ME 04101

Maryland

- Maryland State
  Archives
  350 Rowe Blvd.
  Annapolis, MD 21401

- Maryland Historical
  Society
  201 West Monument St.
  Baltimore, MD 21201

Massachusetts

- New England Historic
  Genealogical Society
  101 Newbury St.
  Boston, MA 02116-3087

- American Antiquarian
  Society
  185 Salisbury St.
  Worcester, MA 01609

- Massachusetts State
  Archives at
  Columbia Point
  220 Morrissey Blvd.
  Boston, MA 02125-3384

Michigan

- State Library of
  Michigan
  717 West Allegan St.
  Lansing, MI 48909

- Burton Historical
  Collection
  Detroit Public Library
  5201 Woodward Ave.
  Detroit, MI 48202

Minnesota

- Minnesota Historical
  Society and
  Archives
  345 West Kellogg Blvd.
  St. Paul, MN
  55102-1906

Mississippi

- Mississippi Department
  of Archives
  100 South State St.
  P.O. Box 571
  Jackson, MS 39205

Missouri

- The State Historical
  Society of Missouri
  1020 Lowry St.
  Columbia, MO 65201

- Missouri State Archives
  600 West Main
  P.O. Box 778
  Jefferson City, MO
  65101

Montana

- Montana Historical
  Society and
  Archives
  225 North Roberts
  P.O. Box 201201
  Helena, MT 59601-1201

Nebraska

- Nebraska State
  Historical Society
  1500 "R" St.
  P.O. Box 82554
  Lincoln, NE 68501

Nevada

- Nevada State Library
  and Archives
  Division of Archives and
  Records
  100 North Stewart St.
  Carson City, NV
  89701-4285

New Hampshire

- New Hampshire
  Archives
  71 South Fruit St.
  Concord, NH 03301

- New Hampshire
  Historical Society
  30 Park St.
  Concord, NH 03301

- New Hampshire State
  Library
  20 Park St.
  Concord, NH 03301

New Jersey

- New Jersey State
  Archives
  State Library Building
  185 West State St.,
  CN-307
  Trenton, NJ 08625-0307

- New Jersey State
  Library
  State Library Building
  185 West State St.,
  CN-520
  Trenton, NJ 08625-0520

- New Jersey Historical
  Society
  230 Broadway
  Newark, NJ 07104

New Mexico

- New Mexico Commission
    of Records
  404 Montezuma Ave.
  Santa Fe, NM 87501

- Special Collections
  Albuquerque Public
    Library System
  423 Central Ave. NE
  Albuquerque, NM
    87102

New York

- New York State
    Archives
  The State Education
    Department
  Cultural Education
    Center, 11-D40
  Empire State Plaza
  Albany, NY 12230

- New York State Library
  Cultural Education
    Center, 7th Floor
  Empire State Plaza
  Albany, NY 12230

- New York Genealogical
    and Biography
    Society
  122 East 58th St.
  New York, NY
    10022-1939

- The New York Public
    Library
  5th Avenue and 42nd
    Street
  New York, NY 10018

North Carolina

- North Carolina Division
    of Archives
  109 East Jones St.
  Raleigh, NC 27611

- North Carolina State
    Library
  109 East Jones St.
  Raleigh, NC 27611

North Dakota

- State Historical Society
    of North Dakota
  Heritage Center
  612 East Boulevard Ave.
  Bismarck, ND 58505

- North Dakota State
    Library
  Liberty Memorial
    Building
  604 East Boulevard Ave.
  Bismarck, ND
    58505-0800

Ohio

- Ohio Historical Society
  1982 Velma Ave.
  Columbus, OH 43211

- State Library of Ohio
  Genealogy Division
  65 South Front St.
  Columbus, OH 43215

- Western Reserve
    Historical Society
  10825 East Blvd.
  Cleveland, OH 44106

Oklahoma

- Oklahoma Historical
    Society
  2100 North Lincoln Blvd.
  Oklahoma City, OK
    73105-3298

- Oklahoma Department
    of Libraries
  200 NE 18th St.
  Oklahoma City, OK
    73105

- Oklahoma City Public
    Library
  131 Northwest Third St.
  Oklahoma City, OK
    73102

Oregon

- Oregon State Archives
  800 Summer St. NE
  Salem, OR 97310

- Oregon State Library
  Summer and Courts
    Streets
  Salem, OR 97310

- Oregon Historical
    Society Library
  1230 SW Park Ave.
  Portland, OR 97205

- Genealogical Forum of
    Oregon, Inc.
  1410 SW Morrison,
    Suite 812
  Portland, OR 97205

Pennsylvania

- Pennsylvania State
    Archives
  3rd and Forster Streets
  P.O. Box 1026
  Harrisburg, PA
    17108-1026

- State Library of
    Pennsylvania
  Commonwealth Avenue
    and Walnut Street,
    Room 102
  P.O. Box 1601
  Harrisburg, PA
    17105-1601

- The Historical Society
    of Pennsylvania
    Library
  1300 Locust St.
  Philadelphia, PA 19107

Rhode Island

- Rhode Island State
    Archives
  337 Westminster St.
  Providence, RI 02903

- Rhode Island Historical
    Society
  121 Hope St.
  Providence, RI 02903

South Carolina

- South Carolina
     Department of
     Archives
  1430 Senate St.
  P.O. Box 11669
  Columbia, SC
     29211-1669

- South Carolinian
     Library
  University of South
     Carolina
  Columbia, SC 29208

South Dakota

- South Dakota State
     Historical Society
  Cultural Heritage
     Center
  900 Governors Dr.
  Pierre, SD 57501

Tennessee

- Tennessee State Library
     and Archives
  403 Seventh Ave. North
  Nashville, TN
     37243-0312

- Lawson McGhee Library
  East Tennessee
     Historical Center
  314 West Clinch Ave.
  Knoxville, TN
     37802-2203

Texas

- Texas State Library
  State Archives and
     Library Building
  P.O. Box 12927
  Austin, TX 78711-2927

- Dallas Public Library
  1515 Young St.
  Dallas, TX 75201

- Clayton Library
  5300 Caroline
  Houston, TX 77004

Utah

- Family History Library
  35 North West Temple St.
  Salt Lake City, UT
     84150

- Utah State Archives
  Archives Building,
     State Capitol
  Salt Lake City, UT
     84114

Vermont

- Vermont Historical
     Society Library
  109 State St.
  Montpelier, VT
     05609-0901

- Vermont State Archives
  State Office Building
  109 State St.
  Montpelier, VT
  05609-1101

Virginia

- The Library of Virginia
  800 East Broad St.
  Richmond, VA
  23219-1905

- Virginia Historical
  Society
  428 North Blvd.
  P.O. Box 7311
  Richmond, VA 23221

- Jones Memorial Library
  434 Rivermont Ave.
  Lynchburg, VA 24504

- National Genealogical
  Society Library
  4527 17th Street, North
  Arlington, VA
  22207-2399

Washington

- Washington State
  Archives
  1120 Washington St. NE
  P.O. Box 40238
  Olympia, WA 98504

- Washington State
  Library
  415 15th Ave. SW
  P.O. Box 42460
  Olympia, WA 98504

West Virginia

- Archives Library
  Division of Culture and
  History
  1900 Kanawha Blvd.
  East
  Charleston, WV 25305

- West Virginia and
  Regional History
  Collection
  West Virginia University
  Library
  Colson Hall
  Morgantown, WV 26506

Wisconsin

- State Historical Society
  of Wisconsin
  816 State St.
  Madison, WO
  53706-1488

Wyoming

- Wyoming State
  Archives
  Barrett Building
  Cheyenne, WY 82002

The National Archives

The National Archives houses a full set of microfilmed copies of the U.S. Census (1790–1920) except for the 1890 records, which were destroyed by fire. They also have the largest repository of military records before 1900, including service and pension records. They house naturalization records. Land records for public domain land for the western states are here, including maps in the cartographic department. Other records useful to genealogists include records for African-Americans and Native Americans.

The National Archives Web site is **www.nara.gov**.

- The main National Archives (NARA) is located in Washington DC at:
  700 Pennsylvania Ave. NW
  Washington, DC 20408-0001
  (201) 501-5400

- Another main branch of the National Archives is located at:
  8601 Adelphi Rd.
  College Park, MD 20740-6001
  (301) 713-6800

Where Else Can I Look?

Regional branches of the National Archives are located in the following U.S. cities:

- National Archives—New England Region
  380 Trapelo Rd.
  Waltham, MA 02154-6399
  (617) 647-8100

- National Archives—Pittsfield Region
  100 Dan Fox Dr.
  Pittsfield, MA 01201-8230
  (413) 445-6885

- National Archives—Northeast Region
  201 Varick St., 12th Floor
  New York, NY 10014-4811
  (212) 337-1300

- National Archives—Mid-Atlantic Region
  900 Market St.
  Philadelphia, PA 19107-4292
  (215) 597-3000

- National Archives—Southeast Region
  1557 St. Joseph Ave.
  East Point, GA 30344-2593
  (404) 763-7477

- National Archives—Great Lakes Region
  7358 South Pulaski Rd.
  Chicago, IL 60629-5898
  (773) 581-7816

- National Archives—Central Plains Region
  2312 East Bannister Rd.
  Kansas City, MO 64131-3060
  (816) 926-6272

- National Archives—Southwest Region
  501 West Felix St., P.O. Box 6216
  Fort Worth, TX 76115-0216
  (817) 334-5525

- National Archives—Rocky Mountain Region
  Building 48
  Denver Federal Center, P.O. Box 25307
  Denver, CO 80225-0307
  (303) 236-0817

- National Archives—Pacific Southwest Region
  24000 Avila Rd., P.O. Box 6719
  Laguna Niguel, CA 92607-6719
  (714) 643-4241

- National Archives—Pacific Sierra Region
  1000 Commodore Dr.
  San Bruno, CA 94066-2350
  (415) 876-9009

- National Archives—Pacific Northwest Region
  6125 Sand Point Way NE
  Seattle, WA 98115-7999
  (206) 526-6507

- National Archives—Alaska Region
  634 West Third Ave., Room 012
  Anchorage, AK 99501-2145
  (907) 271-2441

Catalogs and Books Available on the Internet at www.nara.gov:

- *American Indians: A Select Catalog of National Archives Microfilm Publications,* Washington, DC: National Archives Trust Fund Board, G.S.A., 1984.

- *Black Studies: A Select Catalog of National Archives Microfilm Publications,* Washington, DC: National Archives Trust Fund Board, G.S.A., 1996. [Updated]

- *Immigrant and Passenger Arrivals: A Select Catalog of National Archives Microfilm Publications,* Washington, DC: National Archives Trust Fund Board, G.S.A., 1983.

- *Genealogical and Biographical Research: A Select Catalog of National Archives Microfilm Publications,* Washington, DC: National Archives Trust Fund Board, G.S.A., 1983.

- *Military Service Records: A Select Catalog of National Archives Microfilm Publications,* Washington, DC: National Archives Trust Fund Board, G.S.A., 1984.

- *National Archives Microfilm Resources for Research: A Comprehensive Catalog,* Washington, DC: National Archives and Records Administration, 1996. [Tapes]

- Robert B. Matchette et al., *Guide to Federal Records in the National Archives of the United States,* 3 vols., Washington, DC: National Archives and Records Administration, 1995.

- Loretto Dennis Szucs and Sandra Hargreaves Luebking, *The Archives: A Guide to the Field Branches of the National Archives,* Salt Lake City, UT: Ancestry, Inc., 1988.

- Loretto Dennis Szucs and Sandra Hargreaves Luebking, *The Source: A Guidebook of American Genealogy,* revised ed., Salt Lake City, UT: Ancestry, Inc., 1997.

Julie's Search

Julie Mink Durrant is George's daughter-in-law. A mother of six, she became interested in family history several years ago. Her enthusiasm and experience is typical of many beginning researchers. She will tell her story.

Setting a Research Goal

I knew that my third great-grandfather was John Mink and his wife was Amy Hackler. John was born in North Carolina about 1820. My research goal was to find John's father.

Ancestral File

The first thing I did was to look on Ancestral File where I found John Mink listed as the son of William Mink with fourteen brothers and sisters. I checked F9 for the names of the submitters and wrote to the man who had submitted the information. When I asked him for his sources, he just laughed and said he had no sources. It was just a paper someone else had given him, and he submitted it. I put the information in my research file.

Searching Censuses

The next thing I did was to look at the state census index for North Carolina. I started with the first census index of 1790 and worked my way up through 1880. I looked for the surname Mink, and I found that in 1820 there was only one Mink living in the state of North Carolina. His name was William Mink and he was living in Ashe County. This record even told me the numerical listing for the William Mink family on the actual microfilm.

Since I was in the Family History Library, I just went to the drawer of films where the 1820 Ashe County, North Carolina, census was located, got the film, took it to a microfilm reader, and looked until I came to the page number listed in the index. If you are at a local Family History Center, you will have to order the film from Salt Lake City. This is what I found:

1820 Ashe County, North Carolina, Census
William Mink
5 males under age 10
1 male age 16–26
1 female under 10
1 female age 26–45

1830 Ashe County, North Carolina, Census
2 males age 0–5
3 males age 10–15
2 males age 15–20
1 male age 40
1 female age 5–10
1 female age 15–20
1 female age 30–40

1850 Ashe County, North Carolina, Census #899
Rufus Mink 39 b. NC
Kapsanna 39 b. NC
Mary 12 b. NC
James 9 b. NC
Sarah 7 b. NC
William 5 b. NC
S.O. 3 b. NC
Pheby 6 months b. NC

1850 Ashe County, North Carolina, Census #900
    (This is my third great-grandfather.)
John Mink 34 farmer b. VA
Amy 40 b. VA
Hiram 14 b. VA
Wm. 12 b. VA
Jacob 9 b. VA
Calvin 7 b. VA
James 5 b. VA
Wiley 4 b. VA
Crefina 60 female b. VA

1850 Ashe County, North Carolina, Census #628
Calem Mink 37 b. NC
Pheby 36 b. VA
Jane 14 b. NC
Riley 11 b. NC
Mahaley 8 b. NC
Melvel 5 b. NC
Casanna 3 b. NC

Evaluation of Research So Far

This was very good information for me. It looked like William Mink was the only possible choice as the father for John. He was the only Mink living in North Carolina at the time of my ancestor's birth. The problem was that in the 1850 census it said that my third great-grandfather John was born in Virginia, not in North Carolina. Also, where was everyone in 1840?

More Census Research

Because the 1850 census said my ancestor John was born in Virginia, I decided to check the index for Virginia. I found that in 1840 there were four men with the surname Mink living in Grayson County, Virginia: William Mink, Calvin Mink, Rufus Mink, and John Mink. When I looked on the microfilm this is what I found:

1840 Grayson County Virginia Census #318
William Mink
1 male 50–60
1 male 20–30
1 male 15–20
2 males 10–15
1 male 5–10
1 female 40–50
1 female 20–30
1 female 15–20
1 female 5–10

1840 Grayson County, Virginia, Census #310
Calvin Mink
1 male under 5
1 male 20–30
1 female 5–10
1 female 20–30

1840 Grayson County, Virginia, Census #311
Rufus Mink
1 male 20–30
1 female under 5
2 females 5–10
1 female 20–30

1840 Grayson County, Virginia, Census #312
John Mink
2 males under 5
1 male 20–30
1 female 20–30

1860 Grayson County, Virginia, Census #164
Amy Mink 44 VA (my ancestor John's wife living alone)
Hyram 22 VA
Jacob 20 VA
Madison 16 VA
James C. 15 VA
Wiley 14 VA
Louisa 9 VA

More Evaluation

So what did it all mean? In 1820, William Mink had five sons under 10. In 1830 (ten years later), those five sons had become two sons ages 15–20 and three sons ages 10–15. In 1840, there were three men with the surname Mink living in Grayson County near William Mink (they were counted as families 310, 311, 312 and 318 so they were living very close). Two of the original five sons were still living at home as shown by the one male age 20–30 and one male age 15–20.

In the 1850 census John Mink was 34, so he was born about 1816. In 1840, he was listed in the census as a male between the ages of 20 and 30. That fits. In the 1830 census, William Mink had three boys between the ages of 10 and 15. That fits. In the 1820 census, John would have been four and William Mink had five boys under ten. That fits.

I still needed more proof. And I still had the unanswered question: why was John's birthplace listed as Virginia while his brothers Rufus and Calvin (Calem) are listed as being born in North Carolina? I needed more information.

The man who submitted the information to Ancestral File seemed to be right about the fact that William was the father of John, but I hadn't found fifteen children. When I followed each child through the census, I found only eight sons and three daughters. Could some of the missing children have been born and died during the 10 years between censuses?

Using the SourceGuide

The next thing I did was to get research guides for North Carolina and Virginia on *Family History SourceGuide*. These four- to five-page guides identified the various records available in each state. Addresses where vital records and church records could be found as well as the addresses of public libraries were also listed.

Land Records and Military Records

I started with the books for North Carolina. In my searching, I came across a land registration book wherein land owners registered their land. Here I found that William Mink had registered his land from 1812 to 1817. Entry #2594, 7 August 1813, says: "William Mink enters 150 acres in Ashe County on East fork of Long Branch of Little Helton Creek, border begins at mouth of two branches below where Wm. Camel lived and runs various courses; includes the vacant land."

Another book suggested by the *SourceGuide* contained the muster rolls of the soldiers of the War of 1812. Here I found William Mink. Could the 150 acres in Ashe County, North Carolina, be bounty land given to him because of his service in the War of 1812?

In the Ashe County Deed Book S, page 225, I found that Amy Mink (John's wife) sold her land on 28 December 1854 to Johnson Perkins. The description of the land was as follows: "Amy Mink to Johnson Perkins 50 acres for $250.00, for land lying on Wolf trap branch, a branch of Little Helton." That sounded to me a lot like part of the land William Mink registered in 1813.

More Evaluation

John and Amy Mink are listed in the 1850 census together, but in the 1860 census Amy was living alone with her children. One more girl named Loviza (born 1851) was also living with Amy's family. Amy sold the land in 1854. Did John die between 1851 and 1854, when Amy sold the land? If Amy sold a piece of land with a similar description to the one William held, then could William have given his son John the rest of his land? If the answer was yes, then it supported the idea that John was William's son.

Still, why did the census report that John was born in Virginia when his brothers were born in North Carolina? If the family owned land prior to 1854 when Amy sold it, why weren't they living on it in the 1840 census?

Maps and Gazetteers

It was time to pull out the maps and gazetteers (geographical dictionaries). I looked at the map and discovered that Grayson County, Virginia, and Ashe County, North Carolina, are right next to each other. In addition, William's land was on a mountain ridge right on the border, so it was difficult to know where one state ended and the other one began. Could the census taker from Grayson County, Virginia, have wandered a little too far in 1840? It seems possible, especially in 1840 when the boundaries weren't as firmly established as they are today. This could also be the reason why it says that John was born in Virginia.

Telephone Directories and Correspondence

I went to the computerized phone directory and found many listings for Minks. I sent a letter and a descendancy chart to each one and asked if they were related to my Mink family. I received lots of information from those letters. One man called me and said, "My father just died and he has been collecting Mink obituaries from the newspaper for years, and I was wondering what to do with them. Would you mind if I sent them to you?" It was wonderful, but no one had information as far back as William.

Searching Vital Records at the Library

My next step was to search the vital records of Grayson County, Virginia, and Ashe County, North Carolina. I began going to the Family History Library in Salt Lake City to do my searching. I simply copied everything I found on the Minks. Then, back home, I sorted all the information into families. There were some more answers and some more questions.

Expression of Joy

And so the search continues. I still have not proved that William is the father of John, but it seems likely. Nevertheless, I find excitement and joy in gathering ancestors from the limbs of my family tree that have rarely been touched by others. It's exciting and fulfilling to find my ancestors and learn to love each one of them as part of my family.

I felt nervous when I first started this adventure. I didn't think that I would ever be able to find the records I needed, but to my surprise every time I looked for my ancestors, small miracles occurred. I believe that my ancestors are very interested in helping me find out who they are. I believe your ancestors are, too.

Glossary, Abbreviations, and Acronyms

abstract: A brief summary of document contents.

abt.: About

administration: An estate for which there is no will.

admr.: Administrator, administratrix

ae., aet.: Aged

affidavit: Written declaration made under oath before a notary public or other authorized official.

aft.: After

age of majority: Legal age of adulthood. Varies from area to area.

Ahnentafel: A well-known method of numbering family histories that has a mathematical relationship between parents and children.

a.k.a.: Also known as

ancestor: A person from whom you are descended.

Ancestral File: A database created and maintained by The Church of Jesus Christ of Latter-day Saints with millions of names available in family group sheets and pedigree charts. Part of the FamilySearch™ collection, available on CD-ROM at Family History Centers, the Family History Library, and on the Internet at **www.familysearch.org**.

ante: Before, prior to

archive: A physical location where historical documents and records are stored.

ascendancy chart: Starts with an individual and moves back through the generations of all of his or her ancestors.

assn.: Association

b.: Born

banns: Announcement, usually in church, of an intended marriage.

baptismal certificate: A certificate issued by a church at or near the time of baptism. Can be used to approximate birth in the absence of a birth certificate.

bef.: Before

betw.: Between

bibliography: A list of books or other materials that were used in a certain research project. Also a list of books or other materials that are available on a specific topic.

biographical sketch: A brief written account of a person's life.

biography: A more detailed written account of a person's life.

birth certificate: A legal record stating when and where a person was born. Includes the names of the parents.

bk.: Book

bounty land: Federal land given to a person in exchange for military duty or some other civic service.

b.p., b.pl.: Birthplace

bp.: Baptized

bro.: Brother

bur.: Buried

ca.: Circa (about)

Canon Code: A code that explains the bloodline relationship in legal terms by identifying how many degrees of separation (or steps) are between two people related by blood. Canon law counts only the number of steps from the nearest common ancestor of both relatives.

CD-ROM: Compact Disk-Read Only Memory. A CD-ROM stores large amounts of information (including multimedia) that can be retrieved by a computer using its compact disk drive.

cem.: Cemetery

census: The governmental counting of a population.

census index: A listing of the people who are included in particular census records, with references indicating where they can be found in the actual census records.

cert.: Certificate or certified

ch.: Church or children

chr.: Christened

cite: To name the source of information and thus provide reference to the original source.

civil records: Government documents containing information on the civic duties of ancestors, proceedings of municipal governments, or any other records of your ancestors' interaction with the government. Often found in local and state archives or courthouses.

civil registration: Primary record of a vital event in life: birth, death, or marriage. Usually kept by local governments. Also called vital records in the United States.

co.: County or company

collateral relative: Someone with whom you share a common ancestor, but not a direct line.

Compiled Military Service Records: A packet of information gleaned from a variety of sources that recreate lost military records from 1800 and 1814.

copyright: The exclusive right of a creator to reproduce, prepare derivative works, distribute, perform, display, sell, lend, or rent his or her creations.

county clerk: The clerk of the county court that records or maintains records of transactions in that county. Sometimes called the county recorder.

county seat: Town or city that is the administrative center for a county.

d.: Died

DAR: Daughters of the American Revolution

database: A computer software program that allows information to be entered into rows and columns. The information can then be sorted and resorted in a variety of ways—for example: alphabetically, by date, by event, and so on.

dau.: Daughter

d.b.: Deed book

death certificate: A legal record stating when and where a person died.

declaration of intent: A sworn statement by a person who intends to become a naturalized citizen of the United States.

deed: A document that records the transfer of ownership of a piece of property or land.

descendant: A person who descended from a particular ancestor.

descendancy chart: A list of all of the descendants of one couple, including all of their children with their spouses, all of the grandchildren with their spouses, and so on down.

decd.: Deceased

deft.: Defendant

dept.: Department

desc.: Descendant

digital camera: A camera that captures images to memory instead of to film and then downloads the images to your computer.

directory: A collection of information about individuals who live in a particular town, city, county, or district.

dist.: District

div.: Divorce or division

d-m-y: Day, month, year

do.: Ditto (the same)

d/o: Daughter of

doc.: Document

DOS: Original operating system for IBM and IBM-compatible personal computers. Replaced in 1995 by Windows 95.

download: Transfer information electronically to your computer from another computer using a disk or the Internet.

e-mail: Short for electronic mail—messages that are sent from one person to another electronically over the Internet or other computer network.

emigrant: A person who moves away from one country or region to settle in another country or region.

enumeration district: The area assigned to a particular enumerator or collector of the census.

enumerator: A person who collected details on individuals during a census.

est. or estate: The assets and liabilities of a person who dies.

exec. or executor: Person appointed by the testator to handle an estate after the testator's death.

f. or fem.: Female

fa.: Father

family association: A group organized to research a particular family or surname.

family group record (previously called **family group sheet**): A form on which is recorded biographical information about a husband, wife, and their children.

family history (also known as **genealogy**): The written account of a family's experiences over time.

family traditions: Stories handed down from generation to generation, usually by word of mouth.

Family History Center: Local branches of the Family History Library of The Church of Jesus Christ of Latter-day Saints in Salt Lake City, Utah. Currently more than 3,400 in number.

Family History Library: The Church of Jesus Christ of Latter-day Saints' main library in Salt Lake City, Utah. Has the world's largest collection of genealogical holdings, including printed sources and microfilmed records. Used by genealogical researchers worldwide.

Family History Library Catalog: A listing of records (books, films, microfiche, CDs, cassette tapes, videos, and microfilms) available at the Family History Library in Salt Lake City, Utah. Part of the FamilySearch™ collection, available on CD-ROM at Family History Centers, the Family History Library, and on the Internet at **www. familysearch.org**.

Family Record Extraction Program: The goal of the Family Record Extraction Program, sponsored by The Church of Jesus Christ of Latter-day Saints, is to extract enough information from records to compile computer indexes. The work is done by members of the Church on their own computers at home. The Scottish Church Records on FamilySearch™ and the Vital Records Index for North America are examples of these indexes.

FamilySearch™: A collection of information compiled by The Church of Jesus Christ of Latter-day Saints. It includes the Ancestral File, International Genealogical Index, Military Index, Social Security Death Index, Family History Library Catalog, and Scottish Church Records.

ff.: And following pages

FHC: Family History Center

FHL: Family History Library

fn.: Footnote

f/o: Father of

forum: An electronic meeting place on the Internet where messages can be exchanged.

FHLC: Family History Library Catalog

FREP: Family Record Extraction Program

GAR: Grand Army of the Republic (Civil War)

gazetteer: Geographical dictionary that provides information about places.

gdn.: Guardian

GEDCOM: Genealogical Data Communications

genealogy (also known as **family history**): The study of a person's ancestors, descendants, and family origins.

GEnealogical Data COMmunications (GEDCOM): The standard file format for exporting and importing information between genealogical databases.

genealogical society: An organized group that attempts to preserve documents and history for the area in which the society is located. Often a genealogical society has a second purpose, which is to help its members research their ancestors.

given name: First (and middle) name given to a child at birth or baptism. Also called a Christian name.

GJ: Genealogical Journal

grantee: Buyer of property

grantor: Seller of property

grdau.: Granddaughter

grdsn.: Grandson

g.s.: Gravestone

h. or hus.: Husband

historical society: An organized group that preserves documents and history for the area in which the society is located.

h/o: Husband of

home page: A multimedia document viewable on the Internet.

HTML: HyperText Mark-up Language used on the Internet.

IGI: International Genealogical Index

Immigrant: A person who moves into or settles in a country or region.

Immigration record: A record of the entry of a person into a specific country where they were not natively born or naturalized.

Indentured servant: One who entered into a contract binding himself or herself into the service of another for a specified term, usually in exchange for passage from one country to another.

Index: An alphabetized list that refers to the more detailed, non-alphabetized information in another document.

Ind. Ter.: Indian Territory

Inf., inf.: Infantry; infant

Infant: Person who has not reached the age of majority.

int.: Intestate or interred

Interlibrary loan: A system in which one library loans a book to another library to lend to a specific person who requested it.

International Genealogical Index: A list of births and marriages of deceased individuals reflected in records collected by The Church of Jesus Christ of Latter-day Saints. Part of the FamilySearch™ collection, available on CD-ROM at Family History Centers, the Family History Library, and on the Internet at **www.familysearch.org**.

inv.: Inventory or invalid

ISP: Internet Service Provider

Internet: A system of computer networks joined together by high-speed data lines. A repository for vast amounts of data, including family history data, that is accessed by computer through an Internet Service Provider and Web browser.

intestate: A person who died without leaving a valid will.

J.P.: Justice of the Peace

kinship report: A list of family members and how they are related to one particular ancestor.

land grant: Permission to purchase land or a gift of land in exchange for military duty or civic service.

land record: A document recording the sale or exchange of land. Most land records are maintained at the local level where the property is located.

LC: Library of Congress

LDS: The Church of Jesus Christ of Latter-day Saints

lic.: License

lineage society: Organization whose members are directly descended from an ancestor who participated in a specific event, such as the Revolutionary War or the voyage of the *Mayflower*.

m.: Male, married, month, or mother

maiden name: A woman's surname prior to marriage. Sometimes identified with the letters "nee" on records and documents.

marriage banns: A proclamation in front of a church congregation of the intent to marry.

marriage bond: A financial contract guaranteeing a marriage was going to take place. Usually posted by the groom and another person (typically the father or brother of the bride).

marriage certificate: A legal document certifying the union of a man and a woman. Includes the names of the bride and groom, the date and place of marriage, and usually who performed the marriage.

marriage license: A document from a civil or ecclesiastical authority granting permission to marry.

mat.: Maternal

maternal: Relating to the mother's side of the family.

M.G.: Minister of the Gospel

microfiche: A rectangular piece of film that contains minute reproductions of documents, records, books, and so on. Must be read on a microfiche reader or with other magnifying equipment.

microfilm: A roll of film that contains reproductions of documents, records, books, and so on. Must be read on a microfilm reader.

Military Index: A list of those killed in the Korean and Vietnam Wars. Part of the FamilySearch™ collection, available on CD-ROM at Family History Centers, the Family History Library, and on the Internet at **www.familysearch.org**.

m/o: Mother of

Modified Register System (also known as **NGSQ System**): A widely used numbering system used in descending genealogies. The *National Genealogical Society Quarterly* modified the Register System.

mortality schedule: Special federal census schedules that list those who died within a certain time period—usually June 1 of the previous year to May 31 of the current year. Taken in 1850, 1860, 1870, and 1880. Also taken with a special 1885 federal census.

mortgage: Pledge to repay money borrowed to buy a home or other real property.

ms., mss.: Manuscript; manuscripts

muster record: Military pay record. Proves a person was present with a military unit at a particular time and place.

naturalization: The process of becoming a citizen of a particular country when not born in that country.

naturalization record: The legal document proving a person is a naturalized citizen.

NARA: National Archives and Records Administration

n.d.: No date

nee: Relating to birth, as in birth name

n.f.r.: No further records found

n.p.: No place

NEHGR: New England Historical and Genealogical Register

NEHGS: New England Historic Genealogical Society

NGS: National Genealogical Society

NGSQ: National Genealogical Society Quarterly

nr.: Near

Oath of Allegiance: As part of the process of naturalization to become an American citizen, you must swear an Oath of Allegiance wherein you renounce allegiance to any foreign government.

obit.: Obituary

obituary: An account of one's life and death that usually appears in a newspaper at the time of death.

online: Refers to computer connection to the Internet. Made possible through the use of an Internet Service Provider and Web browser.

orphan: An infant whose parents are both deceased. In early times, a child was considered an orphan if his or her father had died but the mother was still living.

p.a.: Power of attorney

PAF: Personal Ancestral File

parent county: Original county from which a second county was formed.

passenger list: Names of passengers who traveled from one country to another on a particular ship.

pat.: Paternity or parent

paternal: Relating to the father's side of the family.

patronymics: A system of surnames that change each generation. The new surname is derived from a combination of the father's given name and "sen" for son or "datter" for daughter. For example, Niels Jensen's son, Peder, becomes Peder Nielson. Peder's son, Hans, becomes Hans Pederson, and so forth. Patronymics were typically used in the Scandinavian countries, and also in Wales, where "ap Owen" (son of Owen) would become Bowen. Other countries used patronymics, too.

pedigree chart: A chart that tracks your direct ancestors only. Lists only one name from each generation and links that name to his or her parents. Then the name of the father is linked to his parents, and the name of the mother is linked to her parents. This pattern repeats for every generation.

pension record: Shows the amount of money paid to the soldier or to the widow or orphans of a man who served in the military during a particular war and became disabled or had financial need.

Personal Ancestral File (also known as **PAF**): A family history software program.

plat map: A map identifying the boundaries of the individual lots within a tract of land.

plt. or pltf.: Plaintiff

poss.: Possible or possibly; possession

PR: Probate record; public record

primary source: A document, oral account, photograph, or any other item created at or near the time an event occurred. Information for the record was supplied by a person who witnessed the event.

prob.: Probate or probably

probate: Settlement of an estate after death.

probate records: Types of court records that deal with the settling of an estate upon one's death. Includes contested wills and their readings. Often the file contains testimonies and the ruling.

professional researcher: A trained person who will research genealogy for a fee.

progenitor: The oldest known ancestor in a particular surname line.

pub.: Published

query: A research question that you post on a particular Web site, mailing list, or news group so that other researchers can help you solve your genealogical challenges.

R.: Range (land description)

rec.: Record; received

rem.: Removed

res.: Resides, residence

Register System: A numbering system widely used in descending genealogies created by the New England Historic Genealogical Society.

Roots Surname List: A list of surnames, their associated dates, and locations accompanied by the contact information for persons researching those surnames. Available on the Internet at **www. rootsweb.com**.

RSL: Roots Surname List

s.: Son

SASE: Self-Addressed, Stamped Envelope

scanner: A device that captures digital images of photographs and documents and downloads them into your computer.

search engine: A program that searches for specific information on the Internet.

sec.: Section

secondary source: A document, oral account, or any other record that was created some time after an event took place, or information that was supplied by someone who was not an eyewitness to the event.

service record: A type of military record that tells of the military career of an individual.

Sexton: Caretaker responsible for the maintenance of a cemetery and burials there.

sic.: Thus

site: Refers to one or more World Wide Web pages on the Internet. Also called a Web site.

s/o: Son of

soc.: Society

Social Security Death Index: An index of those persons for whom Social Security death claims were filed with the United States government. Part of the FamilySearch™ collection, available on CD-ROM at Family History Centers, the Family History Library, and on the Internet at **www.familysearch.org**. Also available at **www. ancestry.com**.

Soundex: A system of indexing the U.S. federal censuses that places names that have a similar pronunciation but different spelling into groups. The Soundex code for any particular name is made up of one letter followed by three numbers.

source: Any person, book, record, document, periodical, and so on that provides information for your research.

sponsors: People vouching for the suitability of the applicant to be admitted to a lineage society. Also people who sponsor a child at baptism.

SSDI: Social Security Death Index

surname: A last name or family name.

survey: Detailed drawing and legal description of the boundaries of a parcel of land.

T.: Township (land description)

tax record: A record of any taxes paid, including property, inheritance, and church taxes. Most taxes were collected at the local level, but the records have now been turned over to government archives.

Temple work: Ordinances an individual performs in an LDS temple as proxy for deceased ancestors.

TempleReady: A software program created by The Church of Jesus Christ of Latter-day Saints that determines if temple ordinances have been performed previously for an individual and prepares a disk of names to take to the temple.

testator: Person making a will.

topographical map: Detailed, precise description of a place or region with graphic representations of the surface features.

tr: Town record

tract book: A book describing the lots within a township or other geographic area.

transcript or **transcribed record:** A copy of the content of a record that has been copied word for word.

twp.: Township

unm.: Unmarried

unpub.: Unpublished

vital record: Primary record of a vital event in life—birth, death, or marriage. Originals are usually kept by local county governments. Often called civil registrations outside the United States.

V.R.: Vital records

V.S.: Vital statistics

vs.: Versus (against)

w.: Wife

warrt. or **Warrant:** A certificate to receive land after a petition for a land grant has been approved.

Web site: Refers to one or more World Wide Web pages on the Internet. Also called a site.

wid.: Widow or widower

will: A legal document that explains how a person wishes his or her estate to be distributed upon death.

Windows®: The operating system that replaced DOS on IBM and IBM-compatible personal computers. Versions Windows 95, Windows 97, and Windows 2000 are available.

witness: One who claims that he or she saw an event.

w/o: Wife of or without

World Wide Web: A system for viewing and using multimedia documents on the Internet.

World Wide Web browser: Software that enables you to view documents on the Internet.

World Wide Web page: A multimedia document that is created and viewable on the Internet with the use of a World Wide Web browser. Also called a home page.

yr.: Year

Forms

Pedigree Chart

CHART NO. _____

(No. 1 on this chart is the same as no. _____ on chart no. _____.)

16
B: cont._____
D:

17
B: cont._____
D:

8
Ch:
P:
M:
P:
D:
P:

18
B: cont._____
D:

4
B:
P:
M:
P:
D:
P:

9
B:
P:
D:
P:

19
B: cont._____
D:

2
B:
P:
M:
P:
D:
P:

20
B: cont._____
D:

21
B: cont._____
D:

10
B:
P:
M:
P:
D:
P:

5
B:
P:
D:
P:

22
B: cont._____
D:

11
B:
P:
D:
P:

23
B: cont._____
D:

1
B:
P:
M:
P:
D:
P:

24
B: cont._____
D:

25
B: cont._____
D:

12
B:
P:
M:
P:
D:
P:

6
B:
P:
M:
P:
D:
P:

26
B: cont._____
D:

13
B:
P:
D:
P:

27
B: cont._____
D:

3
B:
P:
D:
P:

28
B: cont._____
D:

29
B: cont._____
D:

14
B:
P:
M:
P:
D:
P:

7
B:
P:
D:
P:

30
B: cont._____
D:

15
B:
P:
D:
P:

31
B: cont._____
D:

Prepared by:
Date:

Family Group Record

HUSBAND:		OCCUPATION:		SOURCES:	
BD		BP			
MD		MP			
DD		DP			
BRD		BRP			
FATHER:		MOTHER:			
OTHER MARRIAGES:					
RELIGION:		MILITARY:		SS	
B		E		SP	
WIFE:					
BD		BP			
DD		DP			
BRD		BRP			
FATHER:		MOTHER (MAIDEN NAME):			
OTHER MARRIAGES:					
B		E		SP	

SEX	CHILDREN—NAME		DAY—MONTH—YEAR		CITY—COUNTY—STATE		SOURCES
1			BD		BP		
			MD		MP		
	SPOUSE:		DD		DP		
	SS		BRD		BRP		
	B		E		SP		
2			BD		BP		
			MD		MP		
	SPOUSE:		DD		DP		
	SS		BRD		BRP		
	B		E		SP		
3			BD		BP		
			MD		MP		
	SPOUSE:		DD		DP		
	SS		BRD		BRP		
	B		E		SP		
4			BD		BP		
			MD		MP		
	SPOUSE:		DD		DP		
	SS		BRD		BRP		
	B		E		SP		
5			BD		BP		
			MD		MP		
	SPOUSE:		DD		DP		
	SS		BRD		BRP		
	B		E		SP		
6			BD		BP		
			MD		MP		
	SPOUSE:		DD		DP		
	SS		BRD		BRP		
	B		E		SP		

PREPARED BY:	DATE:	OTHER MARRIAGES OF CHILDREN:
ADDRESS:	E-MAIL:	
TELEPHONE:		

BD=BIRTH DATE	MD=MARRIAGE DATE	DD=DEATH DATE	BRD=BURIAL DATE	B=BAPTIZED	SP=SEALED TO PARENTS
BP=BIRTH PLACE	MP=MARRIAGE PLACE	DP=DEATH PLACE	BRP=BURIAL PLACE	E=ENDOWED	SS=SEALED TO SPOUSE

Research Log

Goal:		For (Name):
		Researcher:

Date	Call Number / Repository	Source	Results

Correspondence Log

Date Sent	TO: (Name and Address)	QUESTION	Reply Date	ANSWER

U.S. Census Chronology

_____
SURNAME

Census	Family Information
1790	
1800	
1810	
1820	
1830	
1840	
1850	
1860	
1870	
1880	
1890	
1900	
1910	
1920	

1790 Census United States

State	County		Town/Township	
Microfilm number				

Name of Head of Household	Free White Males 16+	Free White Males under 16	Free White Females	Slaves	Page Number

1800—1810 Census United States

State		County		City		Call number

Page	Head of family	Free white males				Free white females					All others	Slaves	Remarks
		Under 10	10—16	16—26	26—45	45 and over	Under 10	10—16	16—26	26—45	45 and over			

Form 0388   12/79   36C   92b   Printed in USA

1820 Census United States

Page	Head of family	Free white males						Free white females						Foreigners not naturalized	Agriculture	Commerce	Manufactures	Free colored	Slaves	Remarks
		Under 10	10–16	16–26	26–45	45 and over		Under 10	10–16	16–26	26–45	45 and over								

State _____ County _____ City _____ Call number _____

Form 0389 7/79 Printed in USA

1830—1840 Census United States

State		County	City	Call number	

Page	Head of family	Free white males	Free white females	Slaves	Free colored	Foreigners not naturalized
		Under 5 / 5-10 / 10-15 / 15-20 / 20-30 / 30-40 / 40-50 / 50-60 / 60-70 / 70-80 / 80-90 / 90-100 / Over 100	Under 5 / 5-10 / 10-15 / 15-20 / 20-30 / 30-40 / 40-50 / 50-60 / 60-70 / 70-80 / 80-90 / 90-100 / Over 100			

30430   9/90   Printed in USA

1850 Census United States

State ___ County ___ Town/Township ___ Call number ___

Page	Dwelling number	Family number	Names	Age	Sex	Color	Occupation, etc.	Value Real estate	Birthplace	Married within year	School within year	Cannot read or write	Enumeration date	Remarks

Form 0391   12/78   6M   92e   Printed in USA

1860 Census United States

State	County	Town/Township	Post office	Call number

Page	Dwelling number	Family number	Names	Age	Sex	Color	Occupation, etc.	Value Real estate	Value Personal property	Birthplace	Married in year	School in year	Can t read or write	Enumeration date	Remarks

Form 0392   2/80   6M   921   Printed in USA

1870 Census United States

Page	Dwelling number	Family number	Names	Age	Sex	Color	Occupation, etc.	Value Real estate	Value Personal Property	Birthplace	Father foreign born	Mother foreign born	Month born in census year	Month married in census year	School in census year	Can't read or write	Eligible to vote	Date of enumeration

State   County   Town/Township   Post office   Call number

Form 0393 9/78 6M 92g Printed in USA

1880 Census United States

State	County	Town/Township		Town/Township	
		Date		Sheet number	
			Enumeration district number	Page number	

Page	Dwelling number	Family number	Names	Color	Sex	Age prior to June 1	Month of birth in census year	Relationship to head of house	Single	Married	Widowed	Divorced	Married in census year	Occupation	Other information	Can't read or write	Place of birth	Place of birth of father	Place of birth of mother	Enumeration date

30434 9/89 Printed in USA

1900 Census United States

State _____ County _____ Town/Township _____

Microfilm roll number _____ Date _____ Enumeration district number _____ Supervisor's district number _____ Sheet number _____ Page number _____

Location				Name of each person whose place of abode on June 1, 1900, was in this family	Relation to head of family	Personal description									Nativity			Citizenship			Occupation		Education				Home owned or rented	Home owned free or mortgage	Farm or house
Street	House number	Dwelling number	Family number			Color	Sex	Month of birth	Year of birth	Age	Marital status	Number of years married	Mother of how many children	No. of these children living	Place of birth	Place of birth of father	Place of birth of mother	Year of immigration to US	Number of years in US	Naturalization	Occupation	No. of months not employed	Attended sch. (months)	Can read	Can write	Can speak English			

Form 0395   10/78   6M   921   Printed in USA

1910 Census United States

State		County		Town/Township		
Microfilm roll number		Date	Supervisor's district number	Enumeration district number	Sheet number	Page number

Location					Name of each person whose place of abode on April 15, 1910, was in this family	Relation to head of family	Personal description							Nativity			Citizenship			Occupation				Education		Property				Veteran of Civil War	Blind or deaf-mute
Street	House number	Dwelling number	Family number				Sex	Race	Age	Marital status	Number of years married	Mother of how many children	No. of these children living	Place of birth	Place of birth of father	Place of birth of mother	Year of immigration to US	Naturalized or alien	Language spoken	Occupation	Nature of trade	Employer, worker, or own account	No. of months not employed	Can read and write	Attending school	Owned or rented	Owned free or mortgage	Farm or house			

1920 Census United States

State		County		Town/Township/City and ward			
Microfilm roll number		Enumeration date		Supervisor s district number	Enumeration district number	Sheet number	Page number

Place of abode				Name	Relation to head of family	Tenure		Personal description				Citizenship			Education		Nativity and mother tongue											Occupation
Street	House number	Dwelling number	Family visit number	Name of each person whose place of abode on January 1, 1920, was in this family		Home owned or rented	Owned free or mortgaged	Sex	Color or race	Age	Marital status	Year of Immigration to US	Naturalized or alien	Year of naturalization	Attending school	Can read and write	Person			Father			Mother			Can speak English	
																	Place of birth	Mother tongue		Place of birth	Mother tongue		Place of birth	Mother tongue			

34555 5/92 Printed in USA

Index